HIDDEN ORDER

Previous Works by David Friedman

Price Theory

The Machinery of Freedom

HIDDEN ORDER

The ECONOMICS of EVERYDAY LIFE

DAVID FRIEDMAN

HarperBusiness
A Division of HarperCollins*Publishers*

HarperCollins books may be purchased for educational, business, or sales promotional use. For information please write: Special Markets Department, HarperCollins Publishers, Inc., 10 East 53rd Street, New York, NY 10022.

FIRST EDITION

Designed by Nancy Singer

Library of Congress Cataloging-in-Publication Data

Friedman, David.
    Hidden order: the economics of everyday life / by David Friedman.
        p.   cm.
    Includes index.
    ISBN 0-88730-750-7
    1. Economics. 2. Consumer behavior.   I. Title.
    HB171.F767   1996
    330—dc20   96-11703

---

96 97 98 99 00 ❖/RRD 10 9 8 7 6 5 4 3 2 1

This book is dedicated to:
My parents, for early lessons in rationality,
Julius Margolis and James Buchanan, for
getting me into this business,
and my co-conspirators living and dead,
the colleagues from whom I have learned:

Adam Smith
David Ricardo
Alfred Marshall
Harold Hotelling
George Stigler
Ronald Coase
Thomas Schelling
Gordon Tullock
Gary Becker
Robert Frank
John Von Neumann
Jack Hirschleifer
Earl Thompson
Howard Demsetz
Yew-Kwang Ng
Lawrence Iannaccone
Harold Margolis
Stephen Landsberg
Robin Hanson

. . .

CONTENTS

Introduction   xi

Section I: Economics for Pleasure and Profit   1

1   Rush-Hour Blues and Rational Babies   3

2   Actions Speak Louder Than Words   14

Section II: Price=Value=Cost: Solving a Simple Economy   23

3   Thinking on Paper: The Geometry of Choice   25

4   What Would You Give to Get Off a Desert Island?   41

5   Bricks Without Clay: Production in a One-Input World   54

6   Ptolemaic Trade Theory   65

7   Putting It Together: Price Theory in a Simple Economy   78

8   The Big Picture   100

     Halftime: What We Have Done So Far   106

Section III: In Search of the Real World   109

9   Bosses, Workers, and Other Complications   111

10   Monopoly for Fun and Profit   130

11   Hard Problems: Game Theory, Strategic Behavior, and Oligopoly   147

12   Time . . .   167

13   . . . And Chance   180

14   Who Gets How Much Why?   195

Section IV: Standing in for Moral Philosophy: The Economist as Judge   215

15   Summing People Up   217

16   What Is Efficient?   227

17   How to Gum Up the Works   245

18   Why We Are Not All Happy, Wealthy,
     Wise, and Married   260

Section V: Applications: Conventional and Un   279

19   Law and Sausage: The Political Marketplace   281

20   Rational Criminals and Intentional Accidents   298

21   The Economics of Love and Marriage   317

     Final Words   333

     Index   335

FOREWORD

To know David Friedman is to fully grasp the meaning of "infectious enthusiasm." There is no such thing as a casual encounter with this man. Pass him on the street and he'll stop to explain what's wrong with our tort system, or why farmers have more political clout than grocers, or how to design a Doomsday Machine, or Friedman's Law for how to find the men's room. Take him to lunch and you'll learn why there are so many religious broadcasters, the principles of medieval Icelandic criminal justice, and how to keep your home safe from burglars.

Now, people who teem with ideas are a dime a dozen. Usually, we call them crackpots. But *disciplined thinkers* who teem with ideas are rare and precious. And a disciplined thinker who can express his ideas with clarity and wit is a national treasure. Meet David Friedman.

The discipline at the core of David's thought is that of economic theory. Everything he says is a rigorous application of the fundamental principles of economics. Indeed, his thinking is so thoroughly intertwined with economics that one book can serve simultaneously as an introduction to mainstream economic theory and an introduction to the extraordinary mind of David Friedman. This is that book.

And it's high time for it. My local chain bookstore carries over two dozen popularizations of physics, but only one popularization of economics. As it happens, that book is called *The Armchair Economist*, and I wrote it. Writing that book taught me this: To make economics both clear and entertaining, one ought to quote liberally from the writings and conversations of David Friedman. David's name appears in my book more than any other economist's.

Now readers have an opportunity to experience David Friedman firsthand. Don't let me delay you any longer. Go for it. Prepare to be exhilarated.

Steve Landsburg

INTRODUCTION

I once had a colleague whose very popular performances included undressing in the middle of his lecture. In advertising, this approach is known as vampire video. You create an arresting ad featuring a lady of striking beauty. Half an hour afterwards, the audience remembers the lady and the punchline, but is vague about what she was selling and who makes it.

Economics itself is both more interesting and more entertaining than naked professors. Convincing you of that is the project of this book. You will see some very odd things in these pages, including discussions of war, love, marriage, virtue, and vice. All of it is economics. One of the oddest things—Gary Becker's Rotten Kid theorem, which tells us when a rational child will or will not find it in his interest to kick his sister—is part of a major piece of theoretical work by one of the world's leading economists. The discussion of the economics of virtue and vice is in part original with me, in part lifted from a book by Robert Frank—a man who can fill a room at the national economics meetings, where they run fifty sessions at a time.

This is economics as many economists—I am tempted to say all good economists—see it: a blend of theory, intuition, real world puzzles, and ingenious, if sometimes bizarre, solutions. Not a way of predicting the GNP, but a powerful engine for understanding behavior—principally human behavior, but with applications to genes, computers, and animals as well. We start with a single assumption—rationality—and with it set out to conquer the world.

David Friedman
School of Law
Santa Clara University
DDFr@Best.com
http://www.best.com/~ddfr

ECONOMICS FOR PLEASURE AND PROFIT

1

RUSH-HOUR BLUES AND RATIONAL BABIES

To most people, economics is a dull science full of statistics and jargon, mainly concerned with money and designed to answer a narrow (but important) set of questions. To economists, economics is a powerful tool for understanding why armies run away, voters are ignorant, and divorce rates rise, as well as solving practical problems such as how not to get mugged. Its theme is not money but reason—the implications, especially the nonobvious implications, of the fact that humans act rationally. Or to put it more formally:

> Economics is that way of understanding behavior that starts from the assumption that individuals have objectives and tend to choose the correct way to achieve them.

"Economic rationality" summons up an image of a cold-blooded calculator—perhaps Mr. Spock. But economics is not just for Vulcans; the assumption describes our actions, not our thoughts. If you had to understand something intellectually in order to do it, none of us would be able to walk—as became clear when people started trying to program robot walkers. We learn not through logic alone but by a complicated process of feel, feedback, and intuition.

There are lots of ways to behave rationally without reasoning your way to it. Whether or not you have logically deduced that in order to live you must eat, if you don't eat you won't be around long to have your behavior analyzed by economists. So evolution is one source of rational behavior. Trial and error is another. I have never run a map of Santa Clara County through my computer, but I think I know the shortest way home from my office.

For a familiar example of rational behavior without reasoning, consider the situation of an infant—with only one tool available for achieving his objectives. When he is hungry or wet, he makes loud and unpleasant noises—giving any adults in the vicinity an incentive to deal with the problem. I doubt that babies think through the logic of their situation—but they take the action most likely to achieve their ends.

Babies are rational. So are cats. If you insist on reading the newspaper when you should be petting your cat, the cat solves the problem by lying down on the paper. I don't know if that tactic is the product of calculation or trial and error—but it works.

In order to get very far with economics, one must assume not only that people have objectives but that their objectives are reasonably simple. Without that assumption, economics becomes an empty theory; any behavior, however peculiar, can be explained by assuming that the behavior itself was the objective. (Why did I stand on my head on the table while holding a burning $1,000 bill between my toes? I *wanted* to stand on my head on the table while holding a burning $1,000 bill between my toes.)

WHY ECONOMICS MIGHT WORK

Economics is based on the assumptions that people have reasonably simple objectives and choose the correct means to achieve them. Both assumptions are false—but useful.

Suppose someone is rational only half the time. Since there is generally one right way of doing things and many wrong ways, the rational behavior can be predicted but the irrational cannot. If we assume he is rational, we predict his behavior correctly about half the time—far from perfect, but a lot better than nothing. If I could do that well at the racetrack I would be a very rich man.

One summer, a colleague asked me why I had not bought a parking permit. I replied that not having a convenient place to park made me more likely to ride my bike. He accused me of inconsistency: As a believer in rationality, I should be able to make the correct choice between sloth and exercise without first rigging the game. My response was that rationality is an assumption I make about other people. I know myself well enough to allow for the consequences of my own irrationality. But for the vast mass of my fellow humans, about whom I know very little, rationality is the best predictive assumption available.

One reason to assume rationality is that it predicts behavior better than any alternative assumption. Another is that, when predicting a market or a mob, what matters is not the behavior of a single individual but the summed behavior of many. If irrational behavior is random, its effects may average out.

A third reason is that we are often dealing not with a random set of people but with people selected for the particular role they are playing. If firms picked CEOs at random, Bill Gates would still be a programmer and Microsoft would have done a much worse job than it did of maximizing its profits. But people who do not want to maximize profits or do not know how are unlikely to get the job. If they do get it, perhaps through the accident of inheritance, they are unlikely to keep it. If they do keep it, their companies are likely to go on a downhill slide. So the people who run companies can safely be assumed to know what they are doing—generally and on average. And since businesses that lose money eventually shut down, the assumption of rational profit maximization turns out to be a pretty good way of predicting and explaining the behavior of firms.

A similar argument applies to the stock market. Investors who consistently bet wrong soon have little left to bet with. Investors who consistently bet right have an increasing amount of their own money to risk—and often other people's money as well. So well-informed investors have an influence on the market out of proportion to their numbers.

SOME SIMPLE EXAMPLES OF ECONOMIC THINKING

You are designing a park: a pattern of sidewalks in a sea of grass. One of the objectives of many people is to get where they are going with as little effort as possible—and a straight line is the shortest distance between two points. You would be well advised to take precautions accordingly: fences, diagonal walkways, tough ground cover, or green concrete instead of grass.

A less effective approach is to put up signs pointing out the effect on the grass of taking shortcuts across it—the people in the park already know that. Rationality is an assumption about individual behavior, not group behavior. Even if I am very fond of green grass, my decision to cut across provides me more benefit (time saved) than cost (slight damage to the grass). My shortcut also imposes a cost on everyone else, which may make the total costs of my action greater than the total benefits, but it is cost and benefit to me that determine my action.

A second simple example of economic thinking is Friedman's Law for Finding Men's Washrooms—"Men's rooms are adjacent, in one of the three dimensions, to ladies' rooms." One of the builder's objectives is to minimize construction costs; it costs more to build two small plumbing stacks (the set of pipes needed for a washroom) than one big one. So it is cheaper to put washrooms used by different people close to each other in order to get them on the same stack. The law does not hold for buildings constructed on government contracts at cost plus 10 percent.

As a third example, consider someone making two decisions—what car to buy and what politician to vote for. He can improve either decision by investing time and effort in studying the alternatives. In the case of the car, his decision determines with certainty which car he gets. In the case of the politician, his decision changes by one ten-millionth the probability that one candidate will win. If the candidate would be elected without his vote, he is wasting his time; if the candidate would lose even with his vote, he is also wasting his time. He will rationally choose to invest much more time in the decision of which car to buy—the payoff to him is enormously greater. We expect voting to be characterized by *rational ignorance*—it is rational to be ignorant when information costs more than it is worth.

On the other hand, if you or your company will receive almost all of the benefit from some proposed law, you may be willing to invest lots of money and effort seeing to it that the law passes. If the cost of the law is diffused among many people, no one of them will find it in his interest to discover what is being done to him and oppose it. That is one reason why special interests are so successful in benefiting themselves at the cost of the rest of us—even though we outvote them a thousand to one. We will return to that subject in chapter 19, where we explore the economics of politics.

In the course of this example, I have subtly changed my definition of rationality. Before, it meant making the right decision about *what to do*—voting for the right politician, for example. Now it means making the right decision about *how to decide what to do*—collecting information on whom to vote for only if the information is worth more than the cost of collecting it. For many purposes, the first definition is sufficient. The second becomes necessary where an essential part of the problem is the cost of getting and using information.

A final example is the problem of winning a battle. In modern warfare, many soldiers don't shoot and many who do shoot don't aim. This is not irrational behavior—on the contrary. In many situations, the soldier correctly believes that nothing he can do will have much effect on who wins the battle; if he shoots, especially if he takes time to aim, he is more likely to get shot himself.

The general and the soldier have two objectives in common. Both want their army to win. Both also want the soldier to survive the battle. But the relative importance of the soldier's life is much greater for the soldier than for the general. Hence the soldier rationally does not do what the general rationally wants him to do.

Studies of U.S. soldiers in World War II revealed that the soldier most likely to shoot was the member of a squad who was carrying the Browning Automatic Rifle. He was in a situation analogous to that of the special interest; since his weapon was much more powerful than an ordinary rifle (an automatic rifle, like a machine gun, keeps firing as long as you keep the trigger pulled), his actions were much more likely to determine who won—and hence whether he got killed—than the actions of an ordinary rifleman.

The problem is not limited to modern war. It is a thousand years ago. You are one of a line of men on foot with spears, being charged by a mass of men on horseback, also with spears. If you all stand, you will probably break their charge and only a few of you will die; if you run, most of you will be ridden down and killed. Obviously you should stand.

Obvious—and wrong. You only control you, not the whole line. If the rest of them stand and you run, you run almost no risk of being killed—at least by the enemy. If all of them run, your only chance is to start running first. So whatever the rest are going to do, you are better off running. Everyone figures that out, everyone runs, and most of you die. Welcome to the dark side of rationality.

Group loyalty, patriotism, esprit de corps, belief in a god who rewards heroes and punishes cowards are all ways of trying to solve this problem. Another approach is to march your army over a bridge, line up on the far side of the river, and burn the bridge. You then point out to your soldiers that there is no longer anywhere to run to. Since your troops do not run and the enemy troops (hopefully) do, you win the battle. This is a high-risk strategy.

High school history books, in their chapter on the American Revolution, tell how the foolish British dressed their troops in bright scarlet uniforms and marched them around in neat geometric formations, providing easy targets for the heroic Americans. My own guess is that the British knew what they were doing. It was the same British army, a few decades later, that defeated the greatest general of the age at Waterloo.

Neat geometric formations make it hard for a soldier to fall unobtrusively to the rear. Bright uniforms with lots of shiny buttons make it hard for soldiers to hide after their army has been defeated. The mistake in high school history texts is not realizing that those policies were designed by British generals to control their own soldiers.

The conflict of interest between the soldier as an individual and soldiers as a group is nicely illustrated by the account of the battle of Clontarf that appears in *Njal Saga*. Clontarf was an eleventh-century battle between an Irish army on one side and a mixed Irish-Viking army on the other side. The Viking leader was Sigurd, the Jarl of the Orkney Islands. Sigurd had a battle flag, a raven banner, of which it was said that as long as the flag flew, his army would always go forward, but whoever carried the flag would die.

Sigurd's army was advancing; two men had been killed carrying the banner. The jarl told a third man to take the banner; the third man refused. After trying unsuccessfully to find someone else to do it, Sigurd remarked, "It is fitting the beggar should bear the bag," cut the banner off the staff, tied it around his own waist, and led the army forward. He was killed and his army defeated. If one or two more men had been willing to carry the banner, Sigurd's army might have won the battle—but the banner carriers would not have survived to benefit from the victory.

And you thought economics was about stocks and bonds and the unemployment rate.

PUZZLE

You are a hero with a broken sword (Conan, Boromir, or your favorite Dungeons and Dragons character) being chased by a troop of bad guys (bandits, orcs, . . .). Fortunately you are on a horse and they are not. Unfortunately your horse is tired and they will eventually run you down. Fortunately you have a bow. Unfortunately you have only ten arrows. Fortunately, being a hero, you never miss. Unfortunately there are forty bad guys. The bad guys are strung out in a line behind you, with the fastest in front. They are close enough to count your arrows.

Problem. Use economics to get away.

Applied Economics: A Low-Tech Fix for the Silent Student Problem

Halfway through my lecture I pause to ask my students if everyone has followed me so far. Nobody replies. I keep going—and discover my mistake when I grade the final.

This problem, familiar to every teacher, is another example of the conflict between individual and group rationality. The students as a group would learn more if they had the courage to give the honest answer—that they are totally lost, and if I keep going I will be wasting both my time and theirs. But each individual student is afraid to make himself look stupid by admitting that he is totally lost, exposing his ignorance both to me and to his fellow students.

I have a simple solution to this problem, although I have not yet persuaded any university to put it into practice. On the floor in front of each seat is a button, which a student can easily and unobtrusively push with his foot. At the back of the classroom is a large sign, showing how many buttons are currently being pushed. When I notice the eyes of my audience beginning to glaze, I pause and ask everyone who has followed me so far to push his button. The number two appears on the screen. I go back and start over.

Not So Simple Examples: Why and When Everything Is Equal

You are at the far end of a row of checkout counters with your arms full of groceries. Should you stagger from line to line looking for the shortest or just get in the nearest?

The first and simplest answer is that all the lines will be about the same length, so it is not worth the trouble of searching for a shorter one. Why?

Shoppers in a position to see two different lines will go to whichever seems shorter. By doing so, they increase its length; the process continues until both lines are the same length. The same thing happens to every pair of adjacent lines, so all lines will be about the same length. It is not worth a costly search for the shortest.

This assumes that everyone can easily tell which line is shorter. But the relevant length is not in space but in time; you would rather be behind ten customers with only a few items each than eight with full carts. Estimating which line gets you out of the store faster requires a certain amount of mental effort. If the system worked so well that all lines were exactly the same length (in time), it would never be worth the effort, so there would be nothing keeping lines the same length. On average, the time length of lines will differ by just enough to repay the effort of figuring out which line is shorter. If it differed by more than that, everyone would look for the shortest line, making all lines the same length. If it differed by less than that, nobody would.

Suppose customers are not all the same; a few know that the checker on line 3 is twice as fast as the others. The experts go to line 3. Line 3 is now longer than the other lines—but still faster. Nonexperts avoid line 3 until it shrinks back to the same length as the others. The experts (and some lucky nonexperts in line 3) get out twice as fast as everyone else.

Word spreads; the number of experts increases. Eventually there are enough of them to fill the line. As the number increases further, line 3 begins to lengthen. When there are enough experts to make line 3 twice as long as the other lines, the gain from being an expert disappears and the line stops growing.

Another hidden assumption in my example is that shoppers want to get out as quickly as possible. Suppose the grocery store (Westwood Singles Market) is actually the local social center; people come to stand in long lines gossiping with and about their friends and trying to make new ones. Since they do not want to get out as fast as possible, they do not try to go to the shortest line, so the whole argument breaks down.

Rush-Hour Blues

When traffic gets heavy, your lane is always the slow one. You switch. A few minutes later, the battered blue pickup that was just behind you in the lane you left is in front of you.

To understand why it is so difficult to follow a successful strategy of lane changing, consider that other people are also looking for a faster lane—and cars moving into a fast lane slow it down, just as people moving into a short line in the supermarket lengthen it. In equilibrium, all lanes are equally slow.

A more elaborate analysis would allow for the costs in frayed nerves and dented fenders of continual lane changes. On average, if everyone is rational, there must be a small gain in speed from changing lanes—if there were not, nobody would do it and the mechanism described above would not work. The payoff must equal the cost for the *marginal* lane changer—the one to whom changing lanes is just barely worth the trouble. If the payoff were less than that, he would not be a lane changer; if it were more, someone else would be.

Even More Important Applications

Doctors make a lot of money. Becoming a doctor takes many years of hard work as medical student and intern. These two facts are not unrelated. Wages in different professions are controlled by the same sort of process that equalizes lines and lanes. In picking your profession, it is not enough to ask which pays most; the fact that one profession is better paid is evidence that it is less desirable in other ways—riskier, or more unpleasant, or more expensive to get into. If that were not the case, everyone would be in that profession—making the wages very low indeed. The right question to ask is which profession you are particularly suited for in comparison to other people making similar choices. This is like deciding whether to follow a lane-switching strategy by how old your car is, or whether to look for a shorter line by how many groceries you are carrying.

The stock market version of equally long lines and equally fast lanes is the *efficient markets hypothesis*: Stock prices reflect all public information about companies (if buying is obviously a good deal, who would sell?), so you might as well save the cost of hiring an investment analyst and pick stocks by throwing darts at the *Wall Street Journal*.

You now know both why the hypothesis is true and why it is false. If it were entirely true, investors would ignore information about firms—and there would be nothing to keep the market efficient. Actual stock prices must deviate from what the stocks should be worth by just enough to make it worth somebody's time to figure out what they should be worth and trade accordingly.

The person who ought to change lanes on the highway is someone driving a dented car. The person who ought to keep the market efficient is someone with inside information, or someone with lots of expertise trading on a large scale. If that is not you, get out the darts.

The logical structure of these examples—economic equilibrium—will appear again and again throughout this book. Once you clearly understand when and why supermarket lines are all the same length and lanes in the expressway equally fast, and why and under what circumstances they are not, you will have added to your mental tool kit one of the most useful concepts in economics. If it is all obvious the first time you read it (or even the second), then in your choice of careers you should give serious consideration to becoming an economist.

Rationality Without Mind: A Biological Digression

The inventors of the theory of evolution based their work in part on the ideas of the classical economists. That was not merely a historical accident; while economics and evolutionary biology are concerned with different things, the logical structure of the two fields is very similar. The economist expects people to figure out how to achieve their objectives but is not much concerned with how they do so. The evolutionary biologist expects genes—the fundamental units of heredity that control the construction of our bodies—to construct animals whose structure and behavior maximize their reproductive success, but is not much concerned with the detailed biochemical mechanisms by which the genes control the organism. Similar patterns appear in both fields; the conflict between individual interest and group interest echoes the conflict between the interest of the gene and the interest of the species.

My favorite example is Sir R. A. Fisher's explanation of observed sex ratios. In many species, including ours, male and female offspring are produced in roughly equal numbers. There is no obvious reason why this is in the interest of the species; one male suffices to fertilize many females. Yet the sex ratio remains about even, even in species such as some deer in which only a small fraction of the males succeed in reproducing. Why?

Imagine, contrary to fact, that two-thirds of the members of each generation are female. Since there are twice as many mothers as fathers but each child has one of each, the average male must be having twice as many children as the average female. It follows that a couple that has a son will, on average, have twice as many grandchildren as a couple that has a daughter. Since couples who produce sons have more descendants, more of the population is descended from them and has their genes—including the gene for having sons. Genes for producing male offspring increase in the population. The process continues until the numbers of male and female offspring are equal. If we start with a ratio either higher or lower than that, the situation must swing back toward an even sex ratio.

I have omitted a number of possible details, such as differing costs of producing or rearing male and female offspring, that might complicate the argument. Yet even this simple version of the analysis is strikingly successful in explaining one of the observed regularities of the world around us by the rational behavior of microscopic entities. Genes cannot think—yet in this case and many others, they behave as if they had carefully calculated how to maximize their own survival in future generations.

TO THINK ABOUT

In a conversation with a dean, I commented that I was rather absentminded—I had missed two or three faculty meetings that year—and wished he would remind me when I was supposed to be somewhere. He replied that he had already solved that problem, so far as the (luncheon) meetings he was responsible for. He made sure I would not forget them by always arranging to have a scrumptious chocolate dessert. His method worked. Does it follow that I choose whether to forget to go to meetings?

For Further Reading

For a good introduction to the economics of genes I recommend Richard Dawkins's *The Selfish Gene* (New York: Oxford University Press, 1976).

A more extensive discussion of the economics of warfare can be found in my essay, "The Economics of War," in J. E. Pournelle (ed.), *Blood and Iron* (New York: Tom Doherty Associates, 1984).

For a very different application of economic analysis to warfare, read Donald W. Engels's *Alexander the Great and the Logistics of the Macedonian Army* (Berkeley: University of California Press, 1978). The author analyzes Alexander's campaigns—omitting all of the battles—as solutions to the problem of keeping a large army alive. Hunger and thirst are just as deadly as spears and arrows.

2

ACTIONS SPEAK LOUDER
THAN WORDS

PART 1: CHOICE AND VALUE

Economists are often accused of believing that everything—health, happiness, life itself—can be measured in money. What we actually believe is even odder. We believe that everything can be measured in anything. My life is much more valuable than an ice cream cone, just as a mountain is much taller than a grain of sand, but life and ice cream, like mountain and sand grain, are measured on the same scale.

This seems plausible if we are considering different consumption goods: cars, bicycles, microwave ovens. But how can a human life, embodied in access to a kidney dialysis machine or the chance to have an essential heart operation, be weighed on the same scale as the pleasure of eating a candy bar or watching a television program?

The answer is that value, at least as economists use the term, is observed in choice. If we look at how real people behave with regard to their own lives, we find that they make trade-offs between life and quite minor values. Many smoke even though they believe that smoking reduces life expectancy. I am willing to accept a (very slightly) increased chance of a heart attack in exchange for a chocolate sundae.

While I routinely trade away tiny bits of life, I am much less likely to trade away my entire life, even for a very large amount of money. There is a good reason for that: Once I am dead, I cannot spend the money. This is evidence not that life is infinitely valuable but that money is of no use to a corpse.

Even if you neither smoke nor overeat, you still routinely give up life for other values. Whenever you cross the street you are (slightly) increasing your chance of being run over. Every time you spend money on books or movies that could have gone for a medical checkup or additional safety equipment on your car, every time you eat anything a nutritionist would not have recommended, you are choosing to give up, in a probabilistic sense, a little life in exchange for something else.

One possible response is that people should, and wise people do, first buy enough medical care and then devote the rest of their resources to other and infinitely less valuable goals. The economist replies that since additional expenditures on medical care may produce benefits well past the point at which they consume your entire income, the concept of "enough" as some absolute amount determined by medical science is meaningless. How much is enough depends on what it is worth and what it costs. You are buying too much medical care if you could have a better life by spending less on doctors and more on other things. You are buying just enough safety when the pleasure you get from running across the street to talk to a friend just balances the cost to you of the resulting risk of getting run over.

The noneconomist (perhaps I mean the anti-economist) might reply that even if we don't have enough of everything now, we could and should. With enough movies and enough ice cream and enough of everything else, you no longer need to choose less medical care or nutrition in order to get more of something else (although combining good nutrition with enough ice cream could be a problem for some of us). If, by a proper application of the marvels of modern technology, we greatly increase the nation's total output, and if at the same time we eliminate expenditures on things not worth having, why shouldn't we be able to provide every American with everything he should want? In order to consume still more, we would each have to drive three cars and eat six meals a day.

This argument confuses value with quantity. I have no use for four cars, but I would like a car four times as fast and four times as safe as the one I now have—and I expect it would cost more than four times as much. My desire for pounds of food is already satiated and my desire for number of cars could be satiated with a moderate increase in my income, but my desire for quality of food or quality of car would remain even at a much higher income, and my desire for more of *something* would remain as long as I remained alive and conscious under any circumstances I can imagine.

Most of us believe in our hearts that all we need—all any reasonable person needs—is a little more than we have. That belief is wrong, but it is the result of rational behavior. Whether you are an Indian peasant living on $500 a year or an American attorney living on $200,000 a year, the consumption decisions you make, the goods you consider buying, are those appropriate to your income. Heaven would be a place where you had all the things you have considered buying and decided not to. Most of us could do that at twice our current income, with a reasonable amount left over.

There are no needs, only wants. Nothing, including life, is infinitely valuable. We can never have enough of everything, and so must accept trade-offs among the different things we value—including life, love, and the most trivial pleasures.

Value

In talking about value, I have implicitly introduced an important definition—that value is value to us, revealed not by words but by actions. Economists call this the *principle of revealed preference*.

Some might reject this principle because they believe that value should be based on some external criterion—not what we do want but what we should want. Others might claim that they really value health and life but just cannot resist one more cigarette. But economics exists to explain and predict behavior. A smoker's claim that he puts infinite value on his own life is less useful for predicting his future behavior than is the information revealed every time he lights a cigarette.

If using the word *value* to refer equally to a crust of bread in the hands of a starving man and a syringe of heroin in the hands of an addict makes you uncomfortable, substitute *economic value* instead. But remember that the addition of "economic" does not mean "having monetary value," "being material," "capable of producing profit for someone," or anything similar. Economic value is simply value to individuals as judged by them and revealed in their actions.

Revealed preference is part of our definition of value, but it has immediate practical uses as well. Suppose you want to know whether a new colleague has come to stay or regards his present position as a stepping stone to something better elsewhere. You could ask him—but he might be reluctant to tell you the truth. Instead, ask if he has bought or is renting. Action reveals preference.

Economics Joke #1: Two economists walked past a Porsche showroom. One of them pointed at a shiny car in the window and said, "I want that."
"Obviously not," the other replied.

Choice or Necessity?

Economists insist that virtually all human behavior is chosen. To many noneconomists, this seems unrealistic. One cannot choose what one cannot afford. What role does choice play in the lives of people who have barely enough to survive?

The answer is that choice plays a very important role in their lives—more important than in ours. Choosing between life and death is more important than between chocolate and vanilla.

Poor people, it is said, do not really choose not to go to doctors— they simply cannot afford to. Therefore, a benevolent government should provide the poor with the medical services they need—even if, as is typically the case in poor countries, the people who receive the medical services are also the people whose taxes pay for them.

Try translating this into the language of choice. Poor people choose not to go to doctors because to do so they would have to give up things still more important to them—food, perhaps, or heat. It sounds heartless to say that someone in that situation chooses not to buy medical care, but at least it reminds us that forcing him to buy medical care means forcing him to starve or freeze. We do not usually make people better off by reducing their alternatives.

The same clash between the economic view of action as choice and the noneconomic view of action compelled by circumstance reappears on a larger scale in discussions of how flexible the economy as a whole is. When oil prices shot up in the early 1970s, many argued that Americans would continue to use as much gasoline as before at virtually any price. After all, how many suburbanites are willing to walk two miles to the grocery store?

There are many ways to save gasoline. Carpooling and driving more slowly are obvious ones. Buying lighter cars is less obvious. Workers moving closer to their jobs or factories locating nearer to their workers are still less obvious. Another way of "saving gas" is to use less heating oil, allowing us to refine a larger fraction of raw petroleum into gasoline. Insulation, smaller houses, and moving south are all ways of saving gasoline. Warnings by noneconomists consistently, and in many cases enormously, overestimated the increase in price necessary to bring down consumption.

The fundamental mistake is in taking the patterns we observe around us as facts of nature. They are not; they are the result of rational individuals adjusting to a particular set of constraints—including, in this case, cheap gasoline. Change the constraints and, given a little time to adjust, the patterns change.

PART 2: PRICE THEORY

You live in the middle of a very highly organized system with nobody in charge. Items you use daily, even very simple objects such as a pen or pencil, are produced by the coordinated activity of millions of people. Someone had to cut down the tree to make the pencil. Someone had to season the wood and cut it to shape. Someone had to make the tools to cut down the trees and the tools to make the tools and the fuel for the tools and the refineries to make the fuel. No living person knows how to make a pencil.

An American economist who had visited China told me about a conversation with an official in the ministry of materials supply. The official was planning to visit the United States in order to see how things were done there. He wanted, naturally enough, to meet and speak with his opposite number—whomever was in charge of seeing that U.S. producers got the materials they needed in order to produce. He had difficulty understanding the answer—that no such person exists.

Economics is both a way of thinking and a body of worked-out ideas applying that way of thinking to the world. The central core of those ideas is *price theory*—the explanation of how prices coordinate economic activity. One reason to understand that theory is to make sense out of the impossible world on which your life depends, millions of people coordinating their efforts with nobody in charge. A second reason is that the failure to understand price theory is at the heart of most popular economic errors. Consider the following examples.

Rental Contracts. Your city passes a law requiring all landlords to give tenants six months' notice before evicting them, even if the lease provides for a shorter term. It seems obvious that such a law, by making the terms of the contract more favorable to the tenant, benefits tenants at the expense of landlords.

The reason it seems obvious is an unstated assumption—that the law does not affect the rent the tenant pays. If you are paying the same rent and have a more favorable lease, you are better off. But although the law says nothing about rents, it will surely affect them, since it changes both the operating costs of landlords (it is now harder to get rid of bad tenants) and the attractiveness of the lease to tenants. With both supply and demand conditions for rental housing changed, you can hardly expect the market rent to remain the same—any more than you would expect the market price of cars to be unaffected by a law that forced the manufacturers to include a CD player in every car. Once we take the effect on price into account, as we will in chapter 7, there is no longer any reason to expect the law to benefit tenants and some reason to think it may hurt them.

Improved Lightbulbs. A company with a monopoly on lightbulbs invents a new bulb that lasts ten times as long as the old. If the new bulb is introduced, the company can sell only one-tenth as many bulbs as before. Does it follow that the company will be better off suppressing the invention? Many people believe that it does—and stories of such suppressed inventions are widely believed.

The mistake is the assumption that the company will sell the new bulb at the same price as the old. Consumers willing to buy the old lightbulbs for $1 each should be willing to buy the new ones for about $10 each, since they need buy only a tenth as many each year. If the company sells a tenth as many bulbs at ten times the price, its revenue is the same as before. Unless the new bulb costs at least ten times as much to produce as the old, costs are less than before and profits higher.

Reselling Textbooks. Once, in the middle of a conversation with an economics editor who knew very little economics, I mentioned the resale market for textbooks. Instantly her eyes, and those of her colleagues, lit up. If there was one part of the economy they knew and hated, it was that market. Their reason was simple; every time a student bought a secondhand copy of one of their textbooks, they lost the money they would have made selling him a new copy.

I put the following question to them: Suppose an inventor walks in your door with a new product—timed ink. Print your books in timed ink and activate it when the books leave the warehouse. At the end of the school year, the pages will go blank. Students can no longer buy secondhand textbooks. Do your profits go up—or down?

Their answer was "Obviously up—we want it." Mine was "possibly down." To see why, consider a simplified version of the problem. Textbooks last two years. New textbooks sell for $30; used textbooks for $15. The cost to a student of using a textbook for a year is $15; either he buys a new one for $30 and sells it at the end of the year for $15, or he buys a used one for $15 and throws it out at the end of the year.

If the publisher switches to timed ink and keeps charging $30, he has just doubled the cost of the book to students—from $15 for a year's use to $30—which will surely decrease the number of students willing to buy it. If he wants to keep all his customers, he will have to cut his price in half, at which point revenue will be the same as before he adopted the new ink (twice as many books at half the price), cost will be higher (since he has to print twice as many books, in addition to paying the inventor to use his new ink), so profit will go down. He could, of course, keep his price at $30 and sell fewer books. But if that increases his profit, he would have done even better selling books without timed ink at $60, since that results in the same cost to the students and lower costs to him.

In this simple example, timed ink reduces profits. In more realistic cases the answer is more complicated. But the editor's instant response, which simply assumed that the price you could sell a new book for was unaffected by how long it would last, was wrong. Understanding economics is useful—even to economics editors.

Naive Price Theory

A reader unfamiliar with economics might object that when I stated the problems I said nothing about the price of apartments or lightbulbs or books changing, so he assumed it didn't. If that seems reasonable, consider the following analogy. I visit a friend whose month-old baby is sleeping in a small crib. I ask him whether he plans to buy a larger crib or a bed when the child gets older. He looks puzzled and asks me what is wrong with the crib the child is sleeping in now. I point out that when the child gets a little bigger, the crib will be too small for him. My friend replies that I had asked what he planned to do when the child got older—not bigger.

It makes little sense to assume that as a baby grows older he remains the same size. It makes no more sense to assume that the market price of a good remains the same when you change its cost of production, its value to potential purchasers, or both. In each case, "If you did not say it was going to change, it probably stays the same" ceases to make sense once you understand the causal relations involved. That is what is wrong with naive price theory.

I call this error a theory in order to point out that the alternative to correct economic theory is not doing without theory (sometimes referred to as "just using common sense"). The alternative to correct theory is incorrect theory.

PART 3: THE BIG PICTURE, OR HOW TO SOLVE A HARD PROBLEM

To understand how prices are determined, we must work through an intricately interrelated puzzle. How much of what goods a consumer buys depends on his income and on the prices of what he wants to buy. How much producers can sell and at what price will affect how much labor they choose to hire and what wage they must pay to get it. Since consumers get income mostly by selling labor, this will in turn affect the income of the consumers, bringing us full circle. It seems as though we cannot solve any one part of the problem until we have first solved the rest.

The solution is to break the problem into smaller pieces, solve each piece in a form that can be combined with whatever the solutions of the other pieces turn out to be, then reassemble. In chapters 3 and 4, we work out the consumer's side of the problem, in chapter 5 the producer's. In chapter 6, we explore the implications of trade. Chapter 7 shows how trade between consumers and producers generates market prices and quantities. Finally, in chapter 8, we close the circle, combining the results of the previous five chapters to re-create the whole interacting system.

We will be analyzing a very simple economy. Production and consumption are by and for individuals; there are no firms. The world is predictable and static; complications of change and uncertainty are assumed away. When you understand the logic of that simple economy you will understand economics the way a French five-year-old understands French. We will then be ready to fill out the picture by putting back in, one after another, the complications initially assumed away.

PRICE = VALUE = COST: SOLVING A SIMPLE ECONOMY

Why are diamonds, which most of us can get along quite well without, worth so much more than water, which is essential for life? If the answer is that it is rarity rather than usefulness that determines price, I reply that signatures of mine written in orange ink are even rarer than original autographs of Abraham Lincoln but (unfortunately) bring a much lower price.

Perhaps it is cost of production that determines price. When I was very young, I used to amuse myself by shooting stalks of grass with a BB gun. That is an expensive way of mowing the lawn, even at a nine-year-old's wage. I think it unlikely that anyone would pay a correspondingly high price to have his lawn mowed in that fashion.

This puzzle—the relation between value to the consumer, cost of production, and price—was solved a little over a hundred years ago. The answer is that price equals both cost of production and value to the user, both of which must therefore be equal to each other. How that answer is possible, and how market mechanisms produce the triple equality, is the subject of the next few chapters.

3

THINKING ON PAPER: THE GEOMETRY OF CHOICE

TRUTH IN ADVERTISING

Reading your morning paper, you come across a matching pair of grocery store ads:

CUSTOMER PROVES KROGER'S IS CHEAPER

After Mrs. Smith finished her weekly shopping at her local Kroger's, we took her to a nearby A&P. She filled her cart with the same items she bought at Kroger's and when she got to the cash register, she got a surprise. The total was $4.17 higher!

For lower prices and friendlier service, shop Kroger's.

Shop and Compare. A&P CAN'T BE BEAT.

One customer's story: "I always shop at A&P because their prices are lowest. But I wanted to make sure. So after I did my shopping at A&P, I made a list of what I bought. Then I priced the same items at Kroger's. Buying my weekly groceries would have cost me almost $4.00 more."—Julia Jones

Take the challenge yourself and see. A&P's prices can't be beat.

The stores cannot both be cheaper, so one or the other must be lying. That is obvious, but wrong; both advertisements are telling the truth.

The explanation is straightforward: Mrs. Smith and Mrs. Jones bought different things. Mrs. Smith, who decided what to buy at Kroger's, based her decisions on Kroger's prices: more than usual of whatever was particularly cheap that week, less than usual of whatever was particularly expensive. When she duplicated her purchases at A&P, she was still buying a bundle designed for Kroger's prices: lots of eggs because they were on sale at Kroger's (but not at A&P), and only half a dozen apples, even though A&P had them for two dollars a dozen. Mrs. Jones did the same thing the other way around. The experiment is biased in favor of whichever store the shopper goes into first; if the two stores are on average about equally cheap, whichever she goes into first appears cheaper.

You now know why the two advertisements might both be true, but unless your mathematical intuition is extraordinarily good you do not yet know whether the previous paragraph is a plausibility argument ("This is why it might well happen that way"), a proof ("Under the following circumstances, the first store will always appear cheaper"), or something in between. We would like to do better than that—to be able to state under exactly what circumstances we can predict the result reported in the ads.

The usual approach to getting such precise results in economics is to convert the verbal argument into formal mathematics. Doing that would require more space than I can afford, and more of a mathematical background than many of you have. We will instead employ a tactic that I frequently find useful in dealing with complicated conceptual problems. But first, a brief historical digression.

JOGGING UP EVEREST

David Ricardo was born in England in the late eighteenth century to wealthy Jewish parents; after falling in love with a Quaker and marrying her, he was disowned by his family at the age of twenty-one. In the next four years, starting with no wealth but abundant talent, he made a large fortune on the London stock exchange, leaving him free to turn his attention to more important matters—most notably economic theory. He proceeded to become the first person in the history of the world to solve the problem of general equilibrium—analyzing an economy not one piece at a time but as a single, self-consistent, interrelated system.

General equilibrium theory, as any econ graduate student can tell you, is a difficult and mathematically sophisticated field, requiring at the very least calculus at a level rarely studied before graduate school. Ricardo's single book, *The Principles of Political Economy*, contains no mathematics beyond arithmetic, and there is no evidence that he knew any advanced mathematics at all. To a modern economic theorist, reading the book and realizing what Ricardo accomplished is rather like being a member of the first Mount Everest expedition and discovering, at the top, a jogger dressed in T-shirt and tennis shoes.

Part of the explanation is that Ricardo, despite his lack of formal training, had extraordinarily good mathematical intuition, permitting him to understand the logical structure of an economy without the tools that most of us would think essential to the task. He was followed by a whole generation of economic theorists, of whom Marx is the most famous, who got into serious difficulties by trying to use Ricardo's ideas without entirely understanding them.

A second part of the explanation is a tactic that Ricardo used and that has proved very useful to economic theorists ever since: simplify. Faced with a complicated problem, assume away any feature that is not essential to what you are trying to understand. When you are finished, you are left with the simplest problem whose solution will tell you what you want to know. It is a very powerful tactic. It took more than sixty years from the time Ricardo published until another great economist, Leon Walras, succeeded in analyzing a more general version of the problem in formal mathematical terms.

We are about to apply Ricardo's tactic to the grocery store paradox. In the process, we will develop an approach to analyzing rational choice that is useful for thinking through many economic problems.

We start by constructing the simplest version of the problem that retains its essential features, analyze that, then apply the resulting insights to more realistic versions.

A GEOMETRIC INTERLUDE

The simplest version of the grocery store problem is one in which each store sells only two goods and the consumer has a fixed amount to spend. Two goods are sufficient to explain the paradox and few enough to let me diagram the problem on two-dimensional paper, which is what this book happens to be printed on.

The logic of rational choice is simple: Out of all the available alternatives, choose the one you prefer. So our analysis of choice requires a way of representing available alternatives and a way of representing preferences. Figure 3–1a shows both.

Mrs. Smith enters Kroger's with $25 in her pocket. Milk costs $1.50 a quart at Kroger's; meat (on sale) is $1 a pound. Her *budget line* shows the alternative combinations of meat and milk ("bundles") she could buy with her money. Bundle E, for example, contains ten pounds and ten quarts, adding up to $25. Bundle G contains twenty-five pounds of meat and no milk at all, also adding up to $25. If Mrs. Smith decides to buy a quart less of milk, she can use the money to buy a pound and a half of meat, so her budget line is a straight line with a slope of $-1.00/1.50 = -$ price of meat / price of milk.

We show Mrs. Smith's alternatives with a budget line, her preferences with a set of *indifference curves*. An indifference curve, such as I_3 on the figure, shows bundles all of which Mrs. Smith considers equally desirable. Bundle A on indifference curve I_3 is ten pounds of meat and fifteen quarts of milk. Bundle B, also on I_3, is fifteen pounds and ten quarts. Mrs. Smith is indifferent between them—she does not care which she has.

If one bundle has less meat than another yet is equally attractive to Mrs. Smith, it must have more milk. The argument applies to any two bundles that are on the same indifference curve, so indifference curve slopes down and to the right.

The more you have of a good the less you value having a little more (*the principle of declining marginal value*). As you move down and right along I_3, to bundles with less milk and more meat, additional milk becomes more valuable and meat less. Going from A to B, Mrs. Smith gives up five quarts of milk in exchange for an extra five pounds of meat. From B to C, the amount of milk drops by another

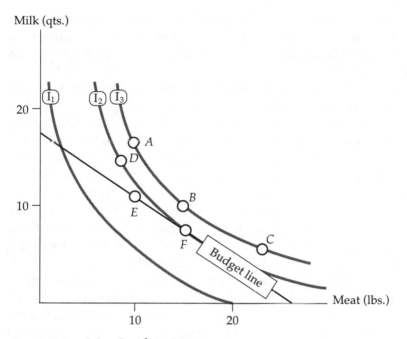

Figure 3-1a   Mrs. Smith in Krogers

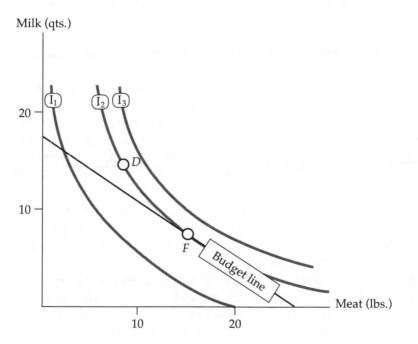

Figure 3-1b   Mrs. Smith in A&P

five quarts, but it takes an extra ten pounds of meat to make up for the loss. That is why the indifference curves all have the same general shape—with the curve getting flatter as you move right and down.

I do not actually know Mrs. Smith, nor her tastes in milk and meat. The purpose of indifference curves is not to present real information about the tastes of a real person, but to help us think clearly. The arguments we construct by using budget lines and indifference curves to think through the logic of rational choice will depend only on the general characteristics of indifference curves, not on the precise shape of the curves describing the tastes of a real person.

Every possible bundle is on some indifference curve: the curve showing all bundles equivalent to that one. If I drew all of those curves, the figure would be solid black. Curves I_1, I_2 and I_3 are three I have drawn out of an infinite number I could draw.

If Mrs. Smith shifts from Point A on I_3 to point D on I_2, she gives up both milk and meat; since both are goods, she prefers A. As you move down and left, you move to less and less desirable indifference curves. The complete set of indifference curves would provide a complete description of Mrs. Smith's preferences with regard to milk and meat, since it tells us, of any two bundles, which she prefers— the one on the higher indifference curve.

Since these are the only goods available, Mrs. Smith might as well spend all of her money; there is nothing else to buy (and never will be; in our simplified world she goes shopping only once). Her choice is simple: Out of all the bundles on her budget line, pick the one she likes best. The solution is bundle F.

How do we know that F is the preferred bundle? F is on I_2, which is the highest indifference curve that touches the budget line. Mrs. Smith would prefer a bundle on I_3, but she does not have enough money to buy one. There are lots of bundles on I_1 that she could afford to buy—but she prefers F.

We now know how to describe what happens when Mrs. Smith goes into Kroger's graphically, but so far it has not done us any good. It is only when she moves on to the A&P that our drawing begins to tell us things we did not already know.

Mrs. Smith is still Mrs. Smith, so the indifference curves representing her tastes are unchanged. At A&P, however, milk is on sale and meat is not; the prices are $1.50 a pound for meat and $1 a quart for milk. With different prices, Mrs. Smith must now choose from among a different set of alternatives; her budget line on Figure 3–1b no longer runs through the point *F*. At the A&P's prices, Mrs. Smith cannot afford the quantities of meat and milk she bought at Kroger's. Kroger's ad told the truth.

Does it follow that Kroger's is really a cheaper store, and that Mrs. Smith is better off doing her shopping there? No. She cannot duplicate what she bought at Kroger's for the same amount at A&P. But, if she were in the A&P, she would not want to.

Point *D* on Figure 3 1b is what Mrs. Smith would choose to buy at the A&P with her $25. Like point *F* on Figure 3-1a, it is, out of all the bundles she can afford, the one on the highest indifference curve. Faced with a different pattern of prices, Mrs. Smith chooses a different bundle of goods. Meat was cheap and milk expensive at Kroger's, so she bought lots of meat and little milk; at A&P the pattern is reversed.

As it happens, *D* and *F* are on the same indifference curve: I_2. The two bundles are equally attractive to Mrs. Smith. She is equally well off whichever store she shops at.

The same pair of figures can be used for A&P's customer, Mrs. Jones, if we assume that her tastes happen to be the same as Mrs. Smith's. Mrs. Jones goes into the A&P with her $25 and buys *D*, the optimal bundle on her budget line. She then goes to Kroger's, prices the same bundle, and finds that it costs about $4 more. A&P, too, was telling the truth.

We can now state our explanation of the grocery store paradox in a more precise form. From the standpoint of a particular customer with a particular amount to spend, two stores are equally cheap if the customer does not care which one she does her shopping at—is indifferent between the best bundle of goods she can get for her money at the first store and the best bundle she can get at the second. If two stores are equally cheap but have different prices, then the bundle of goods the shopper buys with her money in one store would cost her more at the other, so whichever store she goes into first will appear to be cheaper. We have sketched a proof for the case of two goods; with more effort and fancier mathematics, we could generalize it to the case of real grocery stores selling many different goods.

VALUE AND PRICE

Indifference curves help us understand more precisely what we mean by "value." The value of something is what we are just willing to give up for it. Two things have the same value if gaining one and losing the other leaves us neither better nor worse off—meaning that we are indifferent between the situations before and after the exchange. Between *A* and *B* on Figure 3–1, the value of five pounds of meat is five quarts of milk—and vice versa.

The value of goods to you depends not only on your preferences but also on how much of those goods you have. Between *A* and *B*, a pound of meat is worth a quart of milk; between *B* and *C*, it is worth half a quart. If we were being more precise, we would talk of the value not over a range (such as from *A* to *B*) but at a single point. The value of meat at point *A* is the rate at which you could exchange a little meat for a little milk without making yourself either better or worse off—the slope of the indifference curve. (Actually, the negative slope, but from here on, to make things simpler, I will ignore the minus sign.)

Just as an indifference curve helps us understand what we mean by value, so a budget line helps us understand what we mean by price. The price (or cost) of a good is the amount of something else you must give up to get it. At Kroger's, the price of a quart of milk is a pound and a half of meat—that is the rate at which a customer can convert one into the other while holding her consumption of everything else fixed. Cost is *opportunity cost*—the cost of anything, whether you buy it or produce it, is what you have to give up in order to get it. The cost of an A on a midterm for one of my students may be three parties, a night's sleep, and breaking up with his current significant other. The cost of living in my house is not only taxes, maintenance, and the like; it also includes the interest I could collect on the money I would have if I sold the house to someone else instead of living in it myself.

There is nothing special about money; the money you spend to buy something is a cost only because there are other things you would like to spend the money on instead. That is why, if you were certain that the world was going to end at midnight today, money would become almost worthless to you. Its only use would be to be spent today—so you would "spend as if there were no tomorrow."

Price (of pounds of meat measured in quarts of milk) is the slope of a budget line, the rate at which you can trade one good for the other while holding expenditure, and thus consumption of everything else, constant. Value (of pounds of meat measured in quarts of milk) is the slope of an indifference curve, the rate at which you can trade one good for the other while holding your welfare constant. The bundle you choose to consume is, as you can see from Figures

3–1a and b, the point where your budget line is just tangent to one of your indifference curves—which means that their slopes are the same. So price equals value—not everywhere, not for all possible consumption bundles, but for the particular bundle that a rational individual chooses to consume. Stay tuned.

Price Indices: A Corollary

The same paper that contained the two advertisements also contained a news story on inflation, announcing that prices rose 10 percent last year. What does that mean? Food prices rose last year, but computer prices fell. How can we average these changes together to get a single number?

The more we spend on a good, the more we are affected by a change in its price; if housing goes up 10 percent and paper clips down 10 percent, we are worse off. To make the argument more precise, we can ask how much it would cost us this year to buy everything we bought last year. If the answer is "10 percent more," it seems reasonable to say that, on average, prices have risen by 10 percent.

You now know enough economics to see why this is not quite the right answer. If I have enough money to buy the same goods that I bought last year, I could buy them and be as well off now as I was then—but I wouldn't. Prices have changed, and it is very unlikely that the bundle that was optimal then is still optimal now. If food prices went up and computer prices down, I am better off buying less steak and a better computer.

If my income increased by enough to let me buy the same goods I bought last year, I could use that money to buy those goods, but I would use it to buy a different and better bundle of goods, making me better off. So if 10 percent more income is enough to let me buy what I bought last year, then 10 percent more income would make me better off than I was last year, so some smaller increase in income would make me as well off as I was last year, so prices have increased by less than 10 percent.

The way of averaging prices I have just described (called a Laspeyres price index, after the man who invented it)—by how much income you would need in the second year to buy what you bought in the first year—overestimates the inflation rate because it ignores the benefit that the consumer gets by adjusting his pattern of purchases in the second year to the new pattern of prices. A price index calculated by asking how much income the consumer would require in the first year to buy the goods he actually bought in the second year (a Paasche price index) underestimates the inflation rate for essentially the same reason. If the first index gives us an inflation rate of 10 percent and the second a rate of 9 percent, we do not know exactly what the inflation rate actually was, but we know it was between 9 percent and 10 percent.

Paasche and Laspeyres indices are technical trivia, important to almost nobody but statisticians calculating the inflation rate and students taking econ exams. But the logic of the problem applies much more widely. Interesting and important issues hinge on understanding how rational individuals react to changes in the alternatives available to them. Examples include arguments for and against a flat tax, different ways of subsidizing education, expanding or abolishing the war on drugs. Also, and next, one of my favorite paradoxes.

HEADS I WIN, TAILS I WIN

You have just bought a house. A month later, the price of houses goes up. Are you better off (your house is worth more) or worse off (prices are higher) as a result of the price change? Most people will reply that you are better off; you own a house and houses are now more valuable.

You have just bought a house. A month later, the price of houses goes down. Are you worse off (your house is worth less) or better off (prices are lower)? Most people reply that you are worse off. The answers seem consistent. It seems obvious that if a rise in the price of housing makes you better off, then a fall must make you worse off.

It is obvious, but wrong. The correct answer is that either a rise or a fall in the price of housing makes you better off! We can see why using the same tools we used to understand how two supermarkets' inconsistent ads could both be true.

The situation is shown in Figure 3–2. The vertical axis represents housing; the horizontal axis represents expenditure on all other goods. The initial budget line shows the different combinations of housing and other goods you could have chosen at the initial price of housing. Point *A* is the optimal bundle—the amount of housing you bought.

A second budget line shows the situation after the price of housing has risen. It has a shallower slope, since more expensive housing

Amount of
housing

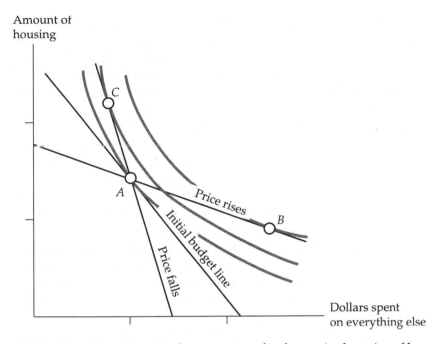

Dollars spent
on everything else

Figure 3-2   The effect on a homeowner of a change in the price of housing. The initial budget line shows the alternatives available at the original price of housing; the two other budget lines show the alternatives
available if the price rises or falls. *A* shows the homeowner's bundle of
housing and all other consumption after the house is built and before
any change in housing prices.

means that you must give up more dollars to get an extra square foot
of house. The new budget line must still go through point *A*, since
one of your alternatives is to continue living in the house you already
own. You can choose to move away from *A* along the budget line
either up (sell your house and buy a bigger one, trading dollars for
housing) or down (sell your house and buy a smaller one, trading
housing for money).

The figure shows what you choose to do; your new optimal point
is *B*. Since housing is now more expensive, you have sold your house
and bought a smaller one—the gain in income is worth more to you
than the loss in space. You are now on a higher indifference curve
than before the price change.

A third budget line shows the situation if the price of housing
goes down rather than up after you buy your house. Again you have

the choice of keeping your original house, so the line has to go through *A*—but this time with a steeper slope, since housing is now cheaper. Your new optimal point is *C*; you have adjusted to the lower price of housing by selling your house and buying a bigger one. You are again on a higher indifference curve than before the price change. The drop in the price of housing has made you better off!

By looking at the figure, you should be able to convince yourself that the result is a general one; whether housing prices go up or down after you buy your house, you are better off than if they had stayed the same. The argument can be put in words as follows:

What matters to you is what you consume—how much housing and how much of everything else. Before the price change, the bundle you had chosen—your house plus whatever you were buying with the rest of your income—was the best of those available to you; if prices had not changed, you would have continued to consume that bundle. After prices change, you can still choose to consume the same bundle, since the house already belongs to you, so you cannot be worse off as a result of the price change.

But since the optimal combination of housing and other goods depends on the price of housing, it is unlikely that the old bundle is still optimal. If it is not, that means there is now some more attractive alternative, so you are now better off; a new alternative exists that you prefer to the best alternative (the old bundle) that you had before.

The advantage of the geometrical approach to the problem is that the drawing tells us the answer. All we have to do is look at Figure 3–2. The initial budget line was tangent to its indifference curve at point *A*, so any budget line that goes through *A* with a different slope must cut the indifference curve. On one side or the other of the intersection, the new budget line is above the old indifference curve—which means that you now have opportunities you prefer to bundle *A*.

What the drawing does not tell us is *why*. When we solve the problem verbally, we may get the wrong answer (as at the beginning of this section, where I concluded that a fall in the price should make you worse off). But once we find the right answer, possibly with some help from the figure, we not only know what is true, we also know why.

WHEN A WASH ISN'T

The potato lobby convinces the government that potatoes are good for you and should therefore be subsidized. Potatoes now cost less—

which is a benefit to you, as a consumer. You buy more of them, which makes potato farmers happy. All is well with the world.

There is one problem—someone has to pay for the subsidy. Suppose, to make things simple, that everyone has the same income, the same tastes, and pays the same share of taxes. The subsidy is a dollar a pound, and you are now buying twenty pounds of potatoes a month. Since you are buying twenty pounds of potatoes a month (and so is everyone else), you are also paying $20 a month in taxes to cover the cost of the dollar-per-pound subsidy.

You are paying $20 a month in taxes; you are getting the money back when you buy twenty pounds of potatoes at a subsidized price. In accounting, a transaction that results in two terms that just cancel—a $1,000 gain balanced by a $1,000 loss—is called a wash. The tax/subsidy combination looks like a wash, since you are getting back just as much as you are paying.

Appearances are deceiving. You are paying $20 a month in taxes—and so is everyone else. You are receiving $20 a month in subsidy—and so is everyone else. The result is that you are worse off— and so is everyone else, with the possible exception of the potato farmers.

To see why, consider Figure 3–3, which shows the budget lines with and without the subsidy and associated tax. A is the optimal point with the subsidy—the point where the budget line just touches an indifference curve. It is the bundle—of potatoes and everything else—that you choose to consume, given the alternatives available to you.

Since potatoes are more expensive without the subsidy, the budget line showing your alternatives without the subsidy is steeper— you must give up more of everything else for each pound of potatoes you consume. It still runs through point A. Buying that bundle will cost you an extra $20, since potatoes are a dollar a pound more expensive without the subsidy—and that is exactly the amount you no longer have to pay in taxes.

You can still buy A if you want to—but you don't. As you can see from the figure, the most attractive bundle available to you is now B. You reduce your consumption of potatoes by ten pounds, spend the money you save on other goods, and shift up to a higher indifference curve.

The figure gives us the answer—we are better off at B than at A, so the combination of a potato subsidy and a tax to pay for it has made us worse off. But just as in the previous example, we need to convert the argument back into English before we can understand why.

All other
expenditures

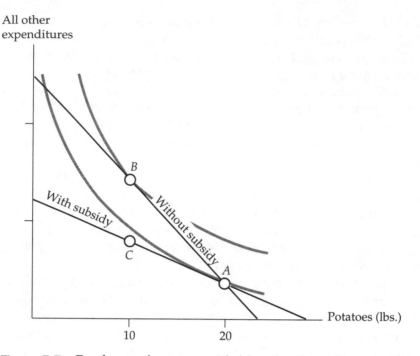

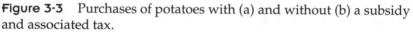

Figure 3-3   Purchases of potatoes with (a) and without (b) a subsidy and associated tax.

We start by asking why I could not get from *A* to *B* without abolishing the subsidy. For the population as a whole, tax collected equals subsidy paid, and the amount of subsidy paid depends on how many pounds of potatoes people buy. If everyone cut his consumption of potatoes in half we could cut the tax in half as well, putting all of us at *B*.

But I do not control what everybody does; I control only what I do. If only I cut my consumption, my tax remains almost the same and I am at *C*—worse off than if I remained at *A*. We would all be better off if we all cut our consumption of potatoes in half, but each individual would be worse off if he cut his consumption of potatoes in half.

Measured in money, the subsidy is a wash. Measured in human welfare, it is a net loss—because it changes individual incentives in a way that makes every consumer worse off. Economics is not about money.

Newspaper accounts of economic arguments often make it sound as though incentives are a good thing—the more incentives the better. That is a mistake. The potato subsidy gives us an incentive to eat more potatoes—and makes us worse off. What we want is not more incentives, or fewer incentives, but the right incentives.

You might find it interesting to redo the analysis of this problem, assuming that instead of subsidizing potatoes we tax them. If you do it right, you will get the same result. Measured in money, the tax is a wash—everyone gets back, in his share of the money collected, as much as he pays out in higher potato prices. Measured in human welfare the tax, like the subsidy, is a net loss.

In my discussion so far, I have considered only the consumers. What about the producers? My analysis implicitly assumed that the increased demand due to the subsidy had no effect on the price farmers get for their potatoes, with the result that the price consumers paid fell by the full amount of the subsidy. Perhaps a more complete analysis, taking account of the effect of the subsidy on the price of potatoes and the welfare of producers, would give a different answer, with the producers' gains more than making up for the consumers' losses.

The full analysis is a harder problem, but it gives the same answer. Insofar as it is possible to define and predict the net effect of the subsidy on all concerned; consumers, producers, and taxpayers; that effect is negative—on net, it makes us worse off. You will have to wait until chapter 17 to learn why.

LIVING THEORY

We started this book by talking about economics; we have now spent a chapter doing it. The first problem we solved—dueling supermarket ads—is an important part of the analysis of how to measure price changes. The last—the potato subsidy—is part of what economists mean when they talk about taxes or subsidies distorting incentives. Using arguments that depended on little more than the assumption of rational choice, we have gotten clear answers to both—as well as to a puzzle, the housing paradox, first proposed to me by a colleague at UCLA.

Textbooks in mathematics and the more mathematical sciences, including economics, usually present theory as a precise structure of formal proof. The theorist begins with axioms and assumptions, reasons step-by-step to the proof of a theorem, writes at the bottom "*Quod erat demonstrandum*," and goes home to bed. That is not the way we have been doing it in this chapter. Those of you whose picture of scientific theorizing is based on such texts may be wondering if this is the Classic Comics version.

The truth is almost exactly the opposite. Real theorists, in economics, in mathematics, or (I suspect) in anything else, very rarely build their theories in textbook fashion from the bottom up. Real theory building is less organized than that and a good deal more fun.

You start at the top, with an intuition for how some system, some structure of things or concepts, works. From there you feel your way, by intuition, trial and error, luck and logic, to what looks like the right answer. You play with that answer long enough to convince yourself that it is right, write it down before it gets away, then go home to a well-earned breakfast. At some later date, you or someone else fills in the holes, figures out exactly what assumptions went into the conclusion, dots the i's, crosses the t's, and puts the theorem, suitably embalmed, in a textbook.

4

WHAT WOULD YOU GIVE TO GET OFF A DESERT ISLAND?

Human beings choose. The world each of us lives in is an opportunity set—a collection of alternatives. Some have explicit prices—I can spend my money for meat or milk, a visit to the doctor or a visit to Hawaii. Many more have implicit prices. The price of playing in a football game is bruises and sore muscles, the price of a quarrel with your wife may be cooking your own dinner.

How much is an opportunity set worth? Think of it from Robinson Crusoe's point of view. One opportunity set is his island, with goats, a hut, a variety of interesting projects, very little company, and the risk of cannibals. The other is the world he left—England of the seventeenth century. If he could choose between them, how much would he give to get back home? What is it worth to get off a desert island?

Each of us faces his own version of that question. Taking a new job, moving to a new city, marrying or getting divorced, means a new set of alternatives to choose among. Most of the big decisions in life are choices among alternative opportunity sets.

Choosing among opportunity sets is one reason to think about how much they are worth; another is that you might some day be selling them. Consider Disneyland. What a customer buys with his admission ticket is not a thing, or an experience, but an opportunity set—the opportunity to walk through Snow White's castle, take a trip down an African river, do any of a thousand things—but not all of them.

Changes in that opportunity set, changes in what rides are available, how much they cost, how long the lines are, change its value to the customer and thus how much he is willing to pay for admission. If you are running Disneyland you will be well advised to take that into account in your decisions—in deciding, for example, whether and how much to charge for rides.

A third reason is that most of the big political issues—free trade or tariffs, raising or lowering taxes, increasing or decreasing immigration, regulation or deregulation—are arguments about the value of opportunity sets. Every time we impose a tax, we change the opportunities available to individuals by changing their income, their wealth, the prices of the goods they buy and sell. In order to compare a flat-rate income tax to a progressive income tax to a sales tax, or to decide whether using a tax to pay for some public service is better or worse than doing without both tax and service, we must somehow evaluate the gain or loss to the individuals affected by the change in their opportunities.

When someone says that the country would be a better place with fewer immigrants or more health care, what he is really claiming is that the set of alternatives available to people after the change would be more attractive than the set of alternatives available before. In deciding whether such claims are true or false, the essential tools are the ones we will be developing in this chapter.

In the previous chapter, I introduced a tactic for dealing with complicated problems: simplify. Our simplification there reduced the world to two goods. In this chapter, we carry it one step farther. We will be discovering how to measure the value to you of consuming a single good. We are still choosing—but the choice is between one good and money available to spend on all other goods.

MARGINAL VALUE

Consider oranges. How much one more is worth to you depends on how many you have. If you have only one a week, you may be willing to pay a high price to have two a week instead. If you already

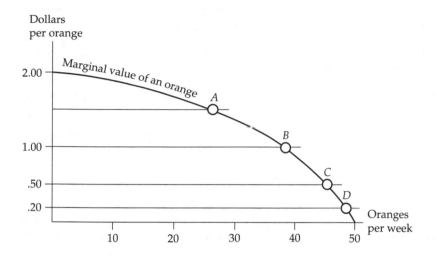

Figure 4-1   The value to you of one more orange as a function of how many oranges you are consuming.

have fifty oranges a week, you will probably not be very eager to increase it to fifty-one. With orange juice at breakfast, oranges at lunch, and orange marmalade on toast for a midnight snack, the value to you of the fifty-first orange is probably close to zero.

Figure 4–1 shows the value to you of one more orange—the *marginal value* of an orange. At a quantity of one, the marginal value of an orange is high; you would be willing to give up two dollars' worth of other goods to get a second orange. By the time quantity gets to fifty, the value of one more orange is down to zero. If you were already consuming fifty oranges a week, you would not give a penny to have one more.

Oranges have declining marginal value; the more you have, the less you value one more. This is a pattern common to many goods. If you have only a little water, you use it all for drinking. When you have more than you can drink, the excess goes for less important purposes, such as washing your hands. When, like the average American, you consume (directly or indirectly) a thousand gallons of water a day, the marginal gallon goes to water your lawn, or down the drain from the leaky faucet you have not yet bothered to fix. Water is very valuable indeed—with no water, you die. But the marginal value of the thousandth gallon is near zero.

Declining marginal value is common, but not inevitable. Consider tires for your car. The marginal value of the fourth tire is quite a lot higher than the marginal value of the first, second, and third.

MARGINAL VALUE AND DEMAND

Oranges are available for a dollar apiece; how many should you buy? Since the value to you of the first orange is more than a dollar (see Figure 4–1), you buy it. What about two instead of one? Again, the value of an additional orange is more than a dollar—you are better off buying a second orange and giving up another dollar. You keep buying additional oranges until you reach point B on the figure, where the marginal value of the last orange is exactly one dollar. If you consumed more, the additional oranges would be worth less than they cost. If you consumed fewer, you would be missing the opportunity to consume oranges worth more than they cost.

The argument applies at any price. Whether oranges cost a dollar fifty, fifty cents, or twenty cents, you buy up to the point (B, C, D on the figure) where that is the marginal value of the last orange. In equilibrium, price equals (marginal) value.

Figure 4–1 came out of my head; I have no idea whether you like oranges, how much you like oranges, or how the value of oranges to you varies with how many you are eating each week. But now we can do better than that. To draw a real version of Figure 4–1, a real graph of your marginal value for oranges, all I have to do is observe how many oranges you consume at different prices.

You are living in Florida, oranges are in season and cost twenty cents. I observe that you buy forty-eight oranges a week. I know that that is the quantity at which your marginal value for an orange is twenty cents—and can draw point D on my graph. You move to Chicago, the cold winds are blowing, and oranges are coming in from Chile at a dollar apiece. I observe that you now buy only thirty-eight a week—and add point B to my graph. Marginal value started out as a way of thinking about choice; it has now turned into an observable characteristic of a person's tastes.

The argument is important and easy to misunderstand, so it may be worth stating it in a more general form:

A consumer who buys a quantity of a good such that the value to him of the next unit is more than its price is missing an opportunity to get something for less than it is worth to him: He should buy more. A consumer who buys a quantity such that the value of the last unit is less than its price is throwing his money away: He should buy less. So a rational consumer buys the quantity for which marginal value equals price. The quantity he buys at a price is a point on his demand curve, since a demand curve is a graph showing how much he buys at any price. Since he buys the quantity at which marginal value equals price, it is also a point on his marginal value curve.

We have just shown that the same line describes two different things: how much an additional orange is worth (as a function of how many you have), and how many oranges you buy (as a function of their price). The first is a marginal value curve. The second is a demand curve. They mean quite different things—but their graphs are identical.

PRICE, VALUE, DIAMONDS, AND WATER

There is no obvious relation between price (what you must give up to get something) and value (what you are willing to give up to get it), a point nicely summarized in the saying that the best things in life are free. But if you are able to buy as much as you like of something, you will choose, as we have just seen, to consume a quantity such that the last unit is worth exactly its price. So the marginal value of goods, when you have bought as much of them as you wish to buy, is just equal to their price. If the best things in life are free, meaning that you can consume as much as you want of them without giving up anything else (true of air, not true of love), then their marginal value is zero!

This brings us back to the diamond-water paradox. Water is far more useful than diamonds, and far cheaper. The resolution of the paradox is that the total value to us of water is much greater than the total value of diamonds (we would be worse off with diamonds and no water than with water and no diamonds), but the marginal value of water is much less than that of diamonds. Since water is available at a low cost, I use it for all its valuable uses; if I used a little more, it would be used, not to keep me from dying of thirst, but to water the lawn. Diamonds, being rare, get used only for their (few) valuable uses. Price equals marginal value; diamonds cost more than water.

WHAT IS A PRICE WORTH?

Suppose someone argued that "since the value of everything is equal to its price, I am no better off buying things than not buying, so I would be just as happy on Robinson Crusoe's island with nothing for

sale as I am now." He would be confusing marginal value and average value. You are no better off buying the last drop of water at a
price just equal to its value but are far better off buying (at the same
price) all the preceding (and to you more valuable) drops.

Can we make this argument more precise? Can we say how
much better off you are by being able to buy as much water as you
want at $0.01 per gallon or as many eggs as you want at $0.80 per
egg? The answer is shown in Figure 4–2. By buying one egg instead
of none, you receive a marginal value of $1.20 and give up $0.80; you
are better off by $0.40. Buying a second egg provides a further
increase in value of $1.10 at a cost of another $0.80. So buying two
eggs instead of none makes you better off by $0.70.

This does not mean you have $0.70 more than if you bought no
eggs—on the contrary, you have $1.60 less. It means that buying

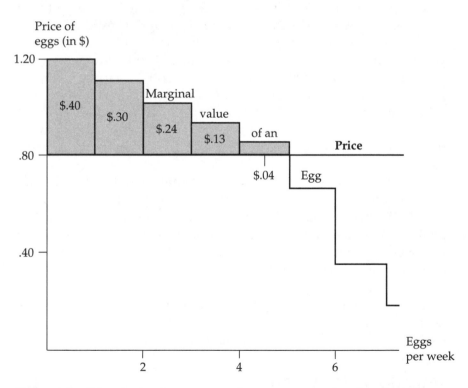

Figure 4-2   Marginal value curve and consumer surplus for a lumpy
good. The shaded area under the marginal value curve and above the
price is consumer surplus: the net benefit from buying that quantity at
that price.

two eggs instead of none makes you as much better off as would the extra goods you would buy if your income were \$0.70 higher than it is. You are indifferent between having your present income and buying two eggs (as well as whatever else you would buy with the income) and having \$0.70 more but being unable to buy any eggs.

Up to five eggs per week, each additional egg you buy makes you better off. Your total gain from consuming five eggs at a price of \$0.80 each instead of consuming no eggs at all is the shaded area on the figure, the sum of the little rectangles. The gain from consuming five eggs is the gain from consuming five instead of four, plus the gain from consuming four instead of three, plus. . . .

Next consider Figure 4–3, where instead of a lumpy good such as eggs we show a continuous good such as wine. If we add up the gain

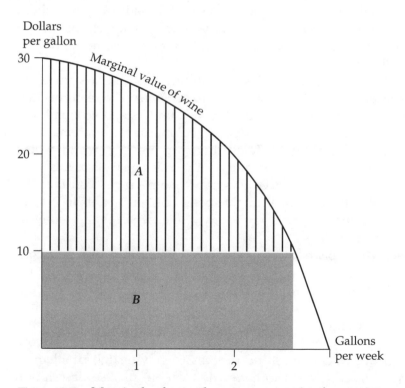

Figure 4-3 Marginal value and consumer surplus for a continuous good. *A* is the consumer surplus from being able to buy all the wine you want at \$10 per gallon. *B* is what you pay for it. *A* + *B* is the total value to you of two gallons per week of wine.

on buying wine, drop by drop, the tiny rectangles exactly fill the region *A*. That is your net gain from being able to buy wine at $10 per gallon.

This area is *consumer surplus*: The net gain to you from what you consume. Think of it as the value of what you buy (*A + B* on the figure) minus what you give up to get it *(B)*. It is a tool of many uses. In later chapters it will help us to measure the real cost of taxes, figure out how to run Disneyland, and decide whether to legalize polygamy.

ECONOMICS AND TIME

It is often convenient to describe consumption in quantities—numbers of apples, gallons of water, and so forth. But consuming a hundred apples in a day is a very different experience from consuming a hundred apples in a year—a fact you can, but had better not, check for yourself. Our quantities are really rates—six apples per week, seven eggs per week. Income and value are measured not in dollars but in dollars per week.

The characters in my stories are extraordinarily shortsighted; all their decisions seem to be oriented to the present. The reason is that they are living in a static world. Once we understand economics in such a world, we can go on to more complicated situations—and will, starting in chapter 12. Until then, we are in a world where tomorrow is always like today and next year is always like this year. In drawing indifference curve diagrams, we need not consider the possibility that the consumer might spend only part of his income in order to save the rest for a rainy day; either it is raining today or there are no rainy days.

Time also appears in economic arguments in a different context. In describing the process of choice, I talk about "doing this, then doing that, then . . ." For example, I talk about increasing consumption from no oranges to one, then from one to two, then from. . . . It sounds as though the process happens over time, but that is an illusion of language. What I am describing is not consumption but calculation—the process of solving the problem of how much of each good to consume. A more precise description would be "First you imagine that you choose to consume no oranges and spend all your money on other things. Then you imagine that you consume one orange instead of none and compare that bundle with the previous one. Then two instead of one.

Then . . ." Finally, after you have figured out what level of consumption you should choose, we turn a switch, the game of life starts, and you put your solution into practice.

MONEY, VALUE, AND RUBBER RULERS

I have insisted several times that economics is not about money; you may therefore wonder why, in talking about prices and values, I put them in dollars. The answer is that I do it because that is the form in which you are used to seeing prices. The arguments of this chapter could be made in potato values just as easily as in dollar values. Indeed potato values are more fundamental than dollar values, as you can easily check by having a hamburger and a plate of french-fried dollars for lunch.

The value to me of one more dollar is the value to me of the goods I would buy with it—which depends on what I already have. This creates a problem for my analysis. As we change the price of one good, we also change the amount of money I have available to spend on all other goods, which changes how much of them I have and thus the value of an additional dollar. We are measuring with a rubber ruler.

Alfred Marshall, who about a hundred years ago invented much of modern economics, described his approach to economic theory in a letter: Work out results mathematically, then convert them to ordinary language; if the second step is impossible, burn the mathematics. One wonders how much of the next century of economic theory went into his fireplace.

In a textbook I once wrote, dealing with the problem of the rubber ruler took two and a half pages of mathematics. Following Marshall's advice, I have translated the explanation into English; it takes the form of the following short dialogue:

Query: "When a new good becomes available, you get consumer surplus by spending money on that good. But do you not lose the consumer surplus on the other goods you are now not buying with that money?"

Response: "If you are consuming many goods, you get the money to buy the new good by giving up a marginal unit of each of the others: the last orange that was barely worth buying, the trip you weren't sure you wanted to take. The marginal unit is worth just what you pay for it—that is why it is marginal—so it generates no surplus."

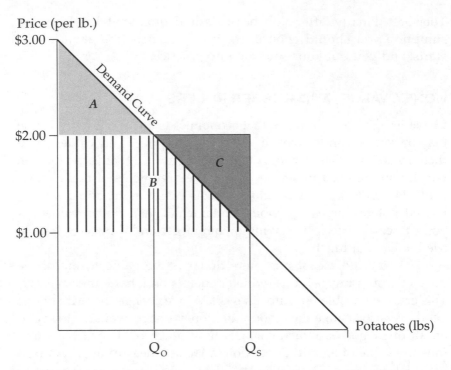

Price (per lb.)

Figure 4-4   Your demand curve for potatoes. A one-dollar subsidy shifts the price from $2 to $1, increasing your consumer surplus by B, costing you $B + C$ in additional taxes, thus making you worse off by C.

POTATOES . . .

In chapter 3, we saw how a potato subsidy could take money from you, give it all back, and yet leave you worse off. We can use the tools of this chapter to get the same result in a different way—which may help us to intuit more clearly why it is true.

Figure 4–4 shows your demand curve for potatoes. To simplify the problem, I assume that potatoes cost $2 a pound to produce and are sold at a price that just covers their cost.

Without the subsidy the price is $2 and your consumer surplus is area A. With the subsidy, the price is $1 and your surplus is $A + B$. So your gain from the subsidy is the difference: area B.

What does the subsidy cost you? Just as in chapter 3, we assume that everyone buys the same quantity of potatoes and pays the same share of taxes, so your taxes are just equal to the cost of the subsidy you are receiving: $1 a pound times the number of pounds of potatoes you are consuming (Q_s). That is, $B + C$ on the figure. You gain B, you lose $B + C$, so your net loss is C.

Where does the loss come from? It comes from consuming potatoes that are worth less to you than they cost to produce. Between Q_0 and Q_s, the value to you of each additional pound of potatoes is between \$1 and \$2, as shown by your marginal value curve—the same line as your demand curve. Because of the subsidy, you are eating potatoes that cost \$2 to produce and are worth less than \$2 to you. C is the resulting net loss.

. . . AND POPCORN

Movie theaters sell popcorn, sodas, and candy at a high price. To most people who have thought about the question, the explanation is obvious. Once you are inside the theater, there is only one place to buy food. The theater has a captive market, and exploits it with high prices.

We now know enough to see why that simple answer is wrong. What you are buying for the price of admission is an environment— an opportunity set. One part of that opportunity set is the opportunity to watch a movie, another part is the opportunity to buy popcorn. How much the second part is worth depends on how much the popcorn costs—a fact the theater owner must take into account in deciding how much to charge for popcorn.

Figure 4–5 shows your demand curve for popcorn. Suppose the theater sells it at a dollar a bag. You buy one bag for a dollar, spending area $B + D$; your consumer surplus is area A. If popcorn costs the theater fifty cents a bag, their cost is D, leaving them B—a profit of fifty cents.

Next suppose they cut the price to fifty cents. Your expenditure is now $D + E$—two bags at fifty cents apiece. Their profit is zero, since they are selling at cost. It looks as though dropping the price lost them fifty cents—area B.

We have forgotten consumer surplus. At the lower price, your consumer surplus is $A + B + C$. The value to you of the environment they are providing has increased by $B + C$, so when they cut the price of popcorn they can raise the admission price by that much without driving you off. They have lost B on popcorn but gained $B + C$ on admission, for a net gain of C.

Suppose the theater decides to push your consumer surplus even higher by giving the popcorn away. At a price of zero, you buy three

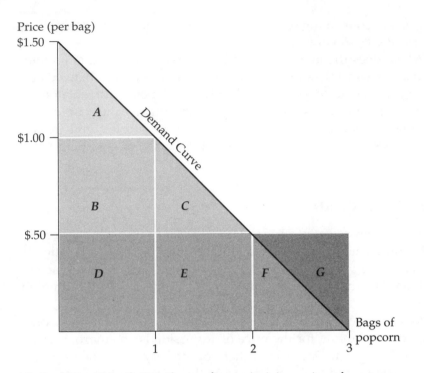

Figure 4-5   Calculating the profit maximizing price of popcorn.

bags. Their loss from producing three bags and giving them away is their cost: $D + E + F + G$. The amount you are willing to pay for admission has increased by the increase in your surplus: $D + E + F$. They are worse off by G.

With a little effort, you should be able to satisfy yourself that the theater maximizes its combined profit, from admission and from popcorn, by selling the popcorn at cost. Any higher price costs more in consumer surplus to you (which translates into admission price to them) than it gains them in profits on the popcorn. Any lower price costs more in loss on the popcorn than it gains in consumer surplus.

Once we have the answer, the explanation is straightforward. Selling above cost means giving up the opportunity to sell you popcorn that is worth more to you than it costs them—and since they are using the admission price to transfer your gains back to them, the result is to make them worse off. Selling below cost means providing you some popcorn that is worth less to you than it costs them—which also makes them worse off. Area G is the net loss, to you plus them, from producing popcorn that is worth less than it costs to produce. It is exactly equivalent to area A on Figure 4–4—the net loss from selling potatoes for less than they cost to produce.

We now have a puzzle. We have used economics to prove that a theater owner maximizes his profits by selling popcorn at cost. So why don't they? Something is wrong somewhere; there must be a mistake either in the proof or in our observation of what theaters actually do. We will return to that puzzle, and two possible solutions, in chapter 10.

Many people, seeing this analysis and this puzzle for the first time, have a simple answer: The argument is fine in theory, but wrong in practice. Real people pay admission for the movie, not the popcorn, so increasing the popcorn price has no effect on what you can collect at the box office.

I have at least one piece of evidence on my side. When movie distributors rent movies to theaters, they sometimes do it not for a flat fee but for a percent of the box office take. Such contracts routinely specify maximum prices at which the theater is allowed to sell refreshments.

If the price of popcorn has no effect on how many people are willing to pay how much for admission tickets, there is no reason why the distributors should care what the theater charges for popcorn. If, on the other hand, my analysis is right, a theater, by raising food prices, transfers income from the box office to the concession stand. If the distributor gets a cut from the box office but not from the concession stand, there is a good reason for him to object. The evidence suggests that it is the prediction of economic theory, not of "common sense," that fits the practical experience of people who make their living in the movie business.

5

BRICKS WITHOUT CLAY: PRODUCTION IN A ONE-INPUT WORLD

The mayor calls a press conference to announce a major coup: He has beaten out three other cities in the competition for a new GM factory. The cost was a package of special tax breaks, a low-interest loan to be financed by city bonds, and the lease of city land on very favorable terms. But it was worth it—all the benefits combined will cost the city no more than $10 million a year, and the new factory will bring $20 million a year into the city.

Questioned by reporters, the mayor expands his estimate of benefits. Not only will GM be spending $20 million a year on payroll and purchases; the people who receive that money, local firms and GM employees, will spend most of what they receive in the city, providing another $18 million of income—to landlords, grocers, and lots of other people. And the people who receive that money will spend it

BRICKS WITHOUT CLAY   55

too. By the time all the effects are added up, the mayor estimates that the new factory will add at least $100 million to the incomes of city residents.

Disentangling truth, fraud, and honest error in this story requires more than one chapter of economics. I will ignore, for the moment, the ingenious (and widely believed) theory of multiplying benefits propounded by the mayor, which seems to imply that one could solve the problems of New York City by dropping a dime in Central Park, enriching all the people through whose hands it passes before it gets out of the city. In this chapter, I focus on a simpler and perhaps more important error—the assumption that spending a dollar in the city is the same thing as benefiting inhabitants of the city by a dollar.

The puzzle I will be trying to solve is a simple one: By how much do producers benefit from the opportunity to sell their goods? The mayor's answer, that benefit is equal to income, cannot be right; getting a job that pays me $50,000 is not the same thing as winning $50,000 in the lottery. The mayor is confusing revenue with profit.

A producer's profit is how much better off he is producing and selling his goods than he would be if he did neither. It is the producer's gain from the opportunity to sell his goods at a price: *producer surplus*, the mirror image of consumer surplus.

We will continue with the tactic of thinking through ideas by considering the simplest case to which they apply. Real producers combine a variety of inputs—labor, raw materials, capital goods, land—to produce their output. Producers that operate that way—firms—will be analyzed in some detail in chapter 9. For the moment, we are considering a simpler case: one-person firms whose only input is their own labor.

Analyzing production by individuals instead of firms not only makes the problem more manageable; it also gives a more fundamental answer. Firms are not people—they cannot eat and drink, feel joy or pain or weariness. They are merely middlemen, passing costs up and down from real people (their employees, stockholders, suppliers) to other real people (customers). So it makes sense to start with human beings dealing directly with each other and only introduce firms as a later complication.

One implication of assuming only a single input to production is that the producer does not care what he produces—only how long it takes and how much he is paid. He is indifferent between an hour spent mowing lawns and an hour spent washing dishes. Otherwise we would be assuming that mowing a lawn cost the producer not only an hour of labor but also something else—perhaps a sunburn.

There are three steps to the logic of simple production. The first is choosing what to produce. The second is deciding how much of it to produce. The third is combining the results of the decisions of many individual producers. Along the way we will learn a little more about what is wrong with mayor's account of his coup.

STEP I: HOW TO SPEND YOUR LIFE

You can produce any of three goods, as shown in Table 5–1: mowed lawns, washed dishes, or meals. The price for a mowed lawn is $10 and you can mow one lawn in an hour, so mowing pays $10 an hour. Washing seventy dishes per hour at $0.10 per dish yields $7 an hour, and cooking two meals per hour at $3 per meal yields $6 an hour. Since the only difference among the alternatives is the implicit wage, you get out the mower.

Table 5-1

	LAWN MOWING	DISH WASHING	COOKING
Output	1 lawn/hour	70 dishes/hour	2 meals/hour
Price	$10/lawn	$0.10/dish	$3/meal
Wage	$10/hour	$7/hour	$6/hour

STEP II: HOW MUCH OF YOUR LIFE TO SPEND

How many lawns do you mow? Figure 5–1a shows the marginal disvalue of labor. Just as the marginal value of oranges depends on how many you have, so the marginal disvalue of working depends on how much work you are doing. If you were enjoying twenty-four hours a day of leisure, it would take only a small payment ($0.50 in the figure) to make you willing to work for a single hour; you would be indifferent between zero hours a day of work and one hour of work plus $0.50. If you were already working ten hours a day, it would take a little over $10 to make you willing to work an additional hour.

The wage is $10 an hour and you are working five hours per day. You would be willing to work an additional hour for an additional payment of about $3; since you can actually get $10 for it, you are better off working the extra hour. The same argument applies to the next hour; it keeps applying as long as the marginal disvalue of labor to you is less than the wage. So you end up working that number of hours for which the two are equal; the number of hours of labor you supply at a wage of $10 is the number at which your marginal disvalue for labor is equal to $10. Your marginal disvalue for labor curve is your supply curve for labor—just as, in chapter 4, your marginal value curve was your demand curve. You work ten hours (and mow ten lawns) a day.

Producer Surplus

The wage is $10 per hour. You are willing to work the first hour for $0.50; since you receive $10 for it, your net gain is $9.50. The next hour is worth a dollar to you; you receive $10 for a gain of $9. Summing these gains over all the hours you work gives us the shaded area of Figure 5–1a, the amount by which you are better off working at $10 an hour than not working at all. Just as consumer surplus was the area under the demand curve (equal to the marginal value curve) and above price, so producer surplus is the area under the wage and above the supply curve (equal to the marginal disvalue curve) for labor.

We now have the supply curve for labor, but what we want is the supply curve for lawns. Since I can mow one lawn per hour, a price of $10 a lawn corresponds to a wage of $10 an hour and a labor supply of ten hours per day corresponds to mowing that many lawns. It appears that the supply curves for lawns and for labor are the same; all I have to do is relabel the vertical axis "price in dollars per lawn" and the horizontal axis "lawns per day."

Appearances are deceiving; there is one important difference between the two supply curves. When the amount I get for mowing a lawn drops below $7, my output of mowed lawns drops to zero; I am better off washing dishes. The resulting supply curve is shown in Figure 5–1b. The shaded area is my producer surplus.

To see why it does not include Z, the area below the line at $7, consider what my surplus would be if I could get $7 for each lawn I mowed. How much better off am I being able to mow lawns at $7 than not mowing lawns? I am not better off at all; at that price, I can do just as well washing dishes.

Cost is opportunity cost: The cost to me of mowing lawns is

Wage ($ per hour)

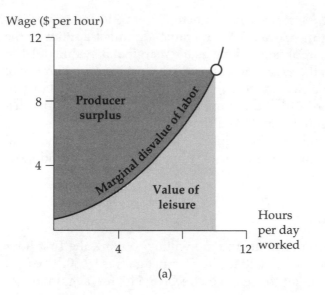

(a)

Price ($ per lawn)

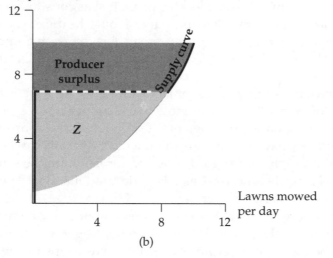

(b)

Figures 5-1a & b   Producer surplus, the marginal disvalue of labor, and the supply curve for lawn mowing. The area above the marginal disvalue curve and below the $10 an hour wage is the producer surplus from being able to work for $10 an hour. The shaded area above the supply curve for lawns and below the price is the producer surplus from being able to mow lawns for $10 per lawn. The supply curve is horizontal at the price at which you switch to your next most profitable option—washing dishes.

whatever I must give up in order to do so. If the best alternative use of my time is leisure, the cost is the value of my leisure. If the best alternative use is washing dishes, the cost is the money I would have gotten by washing dishes.

STEP III: SUMMING PEOPLE UP: THE AGGREGATE SUPPLY CURVE

Producers differ in how good they are at producing different goods and in how willing they are to work, so different people have different supply curves. A producer who is very good at mowing lawns or very bad at doing anything else will mow lawns even at a low price; one who is bad at mowing lawns or good at something else will mow lawns only when the price is high. Figure 5–2 shows the supply curves for two such producers, A(nne) and B(ill), and their combined supply curve.

At prices below $2.50 per lawn, neither Anne nor Bill produces. At prices above $2.50 per lawn but below $5 per lawn, only Anne produces. At a price of $5, Bill enters the market, mowing six lawns per day for a total output (Anne plus Bill) of fifteen. When the price goes from $5 to $6, Anne increases her output by another unit and so does Bill; total output increases to seventeen.

The combined supply curve is a horizontal sum; we are adding up quantities (shown on the horizontal axis) at each price. The same would be true if we were deriving an aggregate demand curve from two or more individual demand curves. All consumers in a market pay the same price, so total quantity demanded at a price is the quantity consumer A demands plus the quantity consumer B demands plus. . . .

As you should be able to see from the figure, the sum of the producer surplus that Bill receives at a price of $6 plus the producer surplus that Anne receives is equal to the producer surplus calculated from the combined supply curve—the area above their combined supply curve and below the horizontal line at $6. The result applies to any number of producers, as does a similar result for the consumer surplus of any number of consumers. So we can find the sum of the surpluses received by consumers or producers by calculating the surplus from their aggregate demand or supply curve just as if it were the demand or supply curve for a single individual.

We have solved our puzzle, at least for the simple economy we are looking at. The benefit to producers of being able to sell their goods at a price is their producer surplus—the area above the supply curve and below the price. It is, at least in principle, measurable,

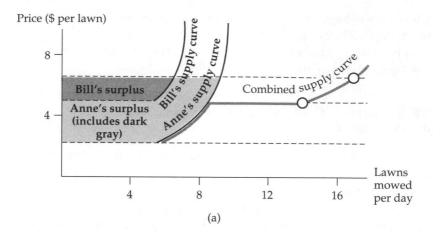

(a)

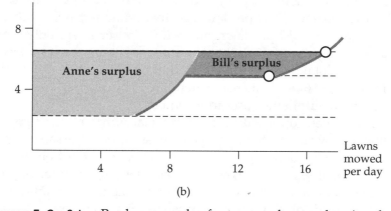

(b)

Figures 5–2a & b   Producer surplus for two producers, showing that the producer surplus calculated from the summed supply curve equals the sum of the producer surpluses from the individual demand curves.

since we can measure supply curves by seeing how much producers are willing to produce at different prices.

Economists rarely have large enough research grants to be able to vary the world price of, say, wheat and see how the wheat farmers of the world respond, so measuring supply curves is easier in books than in the real world. But knowing how we would measure supply curves and producer surplus in principle takes us a long distance toward being able to analyze, on theoretical and empirical grounds, the effect on the welfare of producers of policies such as price controls, tariffs, or taxes.

OOPS: THE BACKWARD-BENDING SUPPLY CURVE FOR LABOR

Look again at Figure 5–1a, and think about what it means. At a wage of $1 an hour, the producer is working two hours per day and earning $2 a day. It may be possible to live on an income of $730 a year, but it is not easy. At a wage of $15 an hour, the same individual chooses to work twelve hours a day and earn $65,700 a year. What is the point of earning that much if, between working, eating, and sleeping, you have practically no time left to enjoy it? There is something wrong somewhere in our analysis.

An increase in wages makes leisure more costly, which is an argument for working more hours at the higher wage. But it also makes the producer wealthier, and so inclined to consume more leisure. If the second effect outweighs the first, the increased wage causes a decrease in hours worked, a backward-bending supply curve for labor, as shown in Figure 5–3.

A backward-bending supply curve for labor is analogous, on the production side, to a curiosity of economic theory called a "Giffen good"—a good whose demand curve slopes in the wrong direction, so that we buy more when its price rises. An example might be beans in a poor society where consumers spend most of their income on (cheap) beans and (expensive) meat. When the price of beans rises, consumers can no longer afford meat, so they buy more beans. The *income effect* of the price increase (an increase in price is equivalent to a decrease in your real income, and poorer people eat more beans) has more than canceled the *substitution effect* (beans are now more expensive relative to meat, which should make you eat fewer beans and more meat).

A Giffen good is a logical possibility, but not a likely one. We divide our consumption expenditures among many goods, so the income effect of a change in the price of one good is usually small. But most of us are specialists in production; we get most of our income from selling one kind of labor, so a change in the price of what we sell has a large effect on our income.

A second reason a Giffen good is unlikely is that it must be an *inferior good*—something (like beans) that we buy less of when we get richer. Inferior goods are the exception, not the rule; when income rises we consume more of most things. Our labor is something that we, as producers, sell, not something we buy, so an increase in its price makes us richer, not poorer, so leisure need only be a normal good in order for the income effect to work against the substitution effect. A Giffen good is only a theoretical curiosity; a backward-bending supply curve for labor may well be a real phenomenon, at least for some ranges of income.

Economic analysis is simpler if demand curves slope down and supply curves slope up than if they insist on wriggling about as in Figure 5–3. Fortunately the argument for upward-sloping supply curves for goods does not depend on upward-sloping supply curves for labor. If individuals sometimes supply less labor, and so mow fewer lawns, as the price of lawn mowing rises, individual supply curves may slope down. But an increase in the price increases the number of people who find that lawn mowing pays better than any other alternative, so the aggregate supply curve for lawns may still slope up. If the production of any one good employs only a small part of the population, even a small rise in the price of a good can induce some people to switch to producing it, so aggregate supply curves are unlikely to slope down.

The analysis in the first part of this chapter (ignoring income effects) would correctly describe a producer whose income from

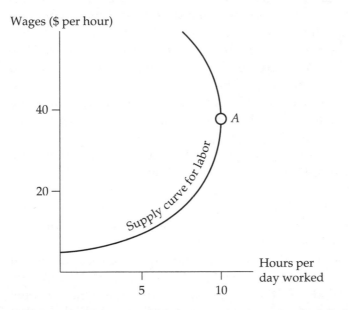

Figure 5–3   A backward-bending supply curve for labor. As the wage increases, the number of hours worked first increases (up to A), then decreases.

other sources was large in comparison to his income from production. Changes in his wage would have only a small effect on his income, so we could legitimately ignore the income effect and consider only the substitution effect. The result would be the curves shown in Figures 5–1a and b and 5–2a and b. It would also correctly describe a producer facing only a temporary change in his wage. He can transfer money from one year to another by saving or borrowing, so the value of money to him depends not on his current income but on some sort of lifetime average—his *permanent income*. His permanent income is changed only very slightly by changes in this week's wage, so the income effect of a temporary wage change is small.

Which way the supply curve for labor sloped was a matter of controversy two hundred years ago, when Adam Smith wrote *The Wealth of Nations*, the book that founded modern economics. Some employers argued that if wages rose their employees would work fewer hours and the national income would fall; Smith argued that higher wages would mean better fed, healthier employees willing and able to work more in exchange for the higher reward. Here and elsewhere Smith argued that what was good for workers was good for England and almost as consistently that what was good for merchants and manufacturers (high tariffs and other special favors from government) was bad for England. He was a defender of capitalism—not of capitalists.

We have been analyzing production using the marginal value curves of chapter 4. We could have done it, if we wished, using the indifference curves of chapter 3. Each producer has indifference curves representing preferences among different bundles of leisure and income, and a budget line showing his ability to transform one into the other. Changes in his wage correspond to changes in the slope of his budget line; if he has no other source of income, all of the budget lines go through the point corresponding to twenty-four hours a day of leisure and no income. The supply curve for labor is calculated by finding the points of tangency between budget lines and indifference curves that show, for each wage, the preferred combination of income and leisure.

Production and consumption are the same problem; this chapter is simply a special case of our previous analysis of consumer choice. We could, if we wished, rewrite it by starting with an individual who owned a good called leisure (twenty-four hours per day) that he could either consume himself or sell at a price (his wage) and for which he had a marginal value curve. The marginal value for leisure curve is the same as the marginal disvalue for labor curve, and the demand curve for leisure is the same as the supply curve for labor, except that in each case the direction of the horizontal axis is reversed—increasing leisure corresponds to decreasing labor.

Our old friend the equimarginal principle—$P = MV$, or "everything is equal at the margin"—applies here as well. The individual works a number of hours such that the disvalue of a little more labor is just equal to the price he is paid for it. In equilibrium, the wage equals the marginal disvalue of labor (marginal value of leisure).

That final result tells us something important about the working of a price system. The cost to me of having my lawn mowed is what I must pay for it. We now know that, at least in the simple world we are discussing, that is also the cost to the man who mows my lawn. I pay him ten dollars in money; he gives up ten dollars' worth of leisure. It follows that the price I pay is an accurate signal of the real cost of producing the service I consume.

6

PTOLEMAIC TRADE THEORY, OR CAN WE BRING THE <u>NEW YORK TIMES</u> INTO THE TWENTIETH CENTURY?

For more than a thousand years, the orthodox view of astronomy was the system devised by Ptolemy in the second century A.D. The earth was at the center of the universe, surrounded by a set of nested crystalline spheres; as the spheres revolved, they carried the moon, the sun, the planets, and the stars around with them. The work of Copernicus and Newton, in the sixteenth and seventeenth centuries, replaced the Ptolemaic system by our present picture—the sun in the center, the planets orbiting around it according to the laws of Newtonian physics.

Most public discussions of trade issues are based on a system of ideas that disappeared from economics about a hundred years after the Copernican revolution eliminated Ptolemy's system from astronomy. It is rather as if the *New York Times* had carried editorials worrying about how the *Apollo* expedition was going to avoid crashing into the first of the crystalline spheres—the one at the orbit of the moon.

Here are three propositions about trade that can be found, implicitly or explicitly, in most popular discussions, whether from left or right.

1:   The reason we have a trade deficit with Japan is that American industry is insufficiently good at producing things—our costs are too high or our quality too low. The reason for that is high taxes, government regulation, and trade unions (right wing) or badly managed corporations and inadequate government support for education and technology (left wing).

2:   If we imposed a tariff and the Japanese did not, our trade balance with Japan would improve. The main reason not to is the fear that the Japanese would retaliate by imposing a tariff on us.

3:   A trade surplus is good ("favorable balance of trade"); a trade deficit is bad ("unfavorable balance of trade"). Since one country's surplus is another country's deficit, this implies a world of continual competition, in which every country tries to improve its trade balance at the expense of other countries—to become more "competitive."

All three propositions would seem obvious to a mercantilist economist in 1760 or a newspaper writer in 1996. All three have been known to be false since David Ricardo published *The Principles of Political Economy* in 1817.

The first step toward a better understanding of trade is to work out where gains from trade come from—how it is that an exchange can make both parties better off. We start with a simple case: I have a hundred apples, you have a hundred oranges. If both of us are fond of both apples and oranges, but less fond the more we eat, it is likely that an exchange of fifty of my apples for fifty of your oranges will benefit us both.

Declining marginal value motivates our exchange. My hundredth apple is worth less to me than my first orange, your hundredth orange is worth less to you than your first apple, so when we trade one apple for one orange, both of us gain. We do it again. We continue until there are no more trades that both of us are willing to make.

Another possible motivation is different tastes. This time each of us starts with fifty apples and fifty oranges. I hate apples; you are allergic to oranges. I trade all of my apples for all of your oranges; we are both better off.

One can even construct situations in which we start with the same goods and the same tastes, but still gain from trade. Each of us has four bottles of beer and four apples. It takes eight apples to make an apple pie and eight bottles to get properly drunk. Four apples will make too small a pie and four bottles will get me just drunk enough to burn it. I trade my beer for your apples—making both of us better off.

All these are examples of one very general principle. If the relative values of goods are different to different people, both can gain by exchange.

TRADE WITH PRODUCTION

It takes me an hour to cook dinner and half an hour to clean up afterwards. My roommate is better at cooking but worse at washing dishes; he can cook dinner in half an hour but takes an hour to clean up. We take turns with the chores; each of us cooks half the time and cleans up half the time. Every two days each of us spends an hour and a half on cooking and cleaning.

I propose a deal: I will do all the cleaning if he does all the cooking. Each of us now spends only an hour every two days on the chores. We are both better off. We have the same quantity of meals and cleanliness, and it is costing us less work to get it.

Why does the trade make us better off? The obvious answer is because I am doing the chore I am better at and he is doing the chore he is better at.

My current roommate moves out of town. His replacement turns out to be an efficiency expert and a whiz in the kitchen. It takes him only ten minutes to prepare dinner and twenty more to clean up. He is better than I am at everything—does it follow that there is no longer any gain to trading chores?

I make the same offer as before—I do all the cleaning, he does all the cooking. Before making that trade, I was spending an hour and a half every two days on chores and he was spending half an hour. After the trade, he is cooking two dinners, which takes him twenty minutes, and I am cleaning up twice, which takes me an hour. We are both better off.

I am hiring him to cook—which he does better than I do. He is hiring me to clean up—which I do worse than he does. The first makes sense, but how can he gain by hiring me to do a job he is better at than I am?

He can clean up in less time than I can, but time is not what we are trading, so costs in time are not what determine gains from trade. Consider again my exchange with my first roommate. In the time it takes me to cook one dinner I can clean up two; that is the cost to me of cooking measured in cleaning. In the time it takes him to cook one dinner he can clean up half a dinner; the cost to him of one meal is half a cleanup. Meals cost him half a cleanup and cost me two cleanups, so he is better at cooking—can cook meals more cheaply— than I. He sells me meals and I pay him by cleaning up.

We could just as accurately say that the cost to me of cleaning up is half a meal cooked, the cost to him is two meals cooked. I am better than he is at cleaning up, so I sell him cleanups—and he pays with meals. The transaction makes equally good sense either way. From my standpoint I am buying meals and paying in cleanups. From his standpoint he is buying cleanups and paying in meals.

Now consider my second and more talented roommate. His costs measured in time are lower, but his costs measured in meals or cleanups are exactly the same. He, too, can cook a meal in the time it takes him to clean up half a meal, or clean up one meal in the time it takes him to cook two. Just as in the previous case, I am better at producing one service, he is better at producing the other, so we both benefit by trade.

This way of looking at gains from trade has one very important consequence—a consequence that makes nonsense out of most public discussions of "competitiveness." Since the cost of producing one good is measured in other goods, I cannot be better than you at everything. If I am better at cleaning up (in terms of meals), then I must be worse at producing meals (in terms of cleaning up). What matters is relative cost. If

$$\frac{\text{Time to Clean Up After Dinner}}{\text{Time to Cook a Meal}} \text{ is larger for me than for you, then}$$

$$\frac{\text{Time to Cook a Meal}}{\text{Time to Clean Up After Dinner}} \text{ must be larger for you than for me.}$$

OUT OF THE KITCHEN AND INTO THE PACIFIC

What we have just worked through is called the "principle of comparative advantage." Two individuals, or two nations, can both gain by trade if each produces goods for which it has comparative advantage. Nation A has comparative advantage over Nation B in producing a good if the cost of producing that good in A relative to the cost of producing other goods in A is lower than the cost of producing that good in B relative to the cost of producing other goods in B.

The error of confusing absolute advantage ("He can do everything better than I can") with comparative advantage shows up in the claim that because some other country has lower wages, higher productivity, lower taxes, or some other advantage, it can undersell our domestic manufacturers on everything, putting our producers and workers out of work. This is used as an argument for protective tariffs—taxes on imports designed to keep them from competing with domestically produced goods.

There are a number of things wrong with this argument. To begin with, if we were importing lots of things from Japan and exporting nothing to them (and if no other countries were involved), we would be getting a free ride on the work and capital of the Japanese. They would be providing us with cars, stereos, computers, toys, and textiles, and we would be giving them dollars in exchange—pieces of green paper that cost us very little to produce. A good deal for us, but not for them.

Here, as in many other cases, thinking in terms of money obscures what is really happening. Trade is ultimately goods for goods—although that may be less obvious when several countries are involved, since the Japanese can use the dollars they get from us to buy goods from the Germans, who in turn send the dollars back to get goods from us. If we measure cost in goods, the Japanese cannot be better at producing everything. If it costs them fewer computers to produce a car (translation: If the cost in Japan of all the inputs used to produce a car divided by the cost in Japan of all the inputs used to produce a computer is smaller than the corresponding ratio in the United States), then it costs them more cars to produce a computer. If they trade their cars for our computers, both sides benefit. Put more formally, if:

$$\frac{\text{Cost of Making a Car in Japan}}{\text{Cost of Making a Computer in Japan}} < \frac{\text{Cost of Making a Car in the U.S.}}{\text{Cost of Making a Computer in the U.S.}}$$

then:

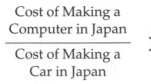

$$\frac{\text{Cost of Making a Computer in Japan}}{\text{Cost of Making a Car in Japan}} > \frac{\text{Cost of Making a Computer in the U.S.}}{\text{Cost of Making a Car in the U.S.}}$$

Japan has comparative advantage in making cars; the United States has comparative advantage in making computers.

If you still find the claim that tariffs protect American workers from being replaced by foreign workers plausible, consider the following fable.

Growing Hondas

There are two ways we can produce automobiles. We can build them in Detroit or we can grow them in Iowa. Everyone knows how we build automobiles. To grow automobiles, we first grow the raw material from which they are made—wheat. We put the wheat on ships and send the ships out into the Pacific. They come back with Hondas on them.

From our standpoint, growing Hondas is just as much a form of production—using American farmworkers instead of American autoworkers—as building them. What happens on the other side of the Pacific is irrelevant; the effect would be just the same for us if there really were a gigantic machine sitting somewhere between Hawaii and Japan turning wheat into automobiles. Tariffs are indeed a way of protecting American workers—from other American workers.

In chapter 19, we will return to the subject of tariffs in order to show why American tariffs usually make America worse off and in what special cases they do not. At that point, we will also explore the question of why tariffs exist and why particular industries succeed in getting them.

TRADE BALANCES AND EXCHANGE RATES

Having served our apprenticeship trading apples for oranges and meals for cleaning, we are now ready to see how the logic of comparative advantage works itself out in modern international trade. Consider the claim that the United States is not competitive because our production costs are too high relative to the cost of producing similar goods abroad. American costs are in dollars and Japanese costs are in yen. In order to compare them, we must first know how many yen you can get for a dollar—the exchange rate. Until we know how the exchange rate is determined, we cannot know whether to blame the high cost of an American car in Japan (measured in yen) on the number of dollars it takes to produce a car or the number of yen it takes to buy a dollar.

How is the exchange rate determined? Some people wish to trade dollars for yen; others to trade yen for dollars. If more yen are supplied than demanded, the price falls; if fewer, the price rises. When the two numbers are equal, the price is at its equilibrium level, just as on any other market.

Why do people want to trade dollars for yen? To simplify the analysis, we start in a world without capital flows—the Japanese do not want to buy U.S. government debt, or U.S. land, or shares in U.S. corporations, nor do Americans want to buy similar assets in Japan. The only use the Japanese have for dollars is to buy American goods; the only use Americans have for yen is to buy Japanese goods.

Suppose that, at the current exchange rate, most goods are cheaper in Japan than in the United States—America is "not competitive." Many Americans want to trade dollars for yen in order to buy Japanese goods, but very few Japanese want to sell yen for dollars, since practically nothing in America is worth buying. The supply of yen is much lower than the demand, so the price of yen goes up. Yen now trade for more dollars than before, and dollars for fewer yen.

The fewer yen you get for a dollar, the more expensive Japanese goods are to Americans, since Americans have dollars and Japanese goods are priced in yen. The more dollars you get for a yen, the less expensive American goods are to the Japanese. The exchange rate continues to move until prices are, on average, about the same in both countries—more precisely, until the quantity of dollars offered for sale by Americans equals the quantity that Japanese wish to buy. Since the only reason people in one country want the other country's money is to buy goods, the dollar value of U.S. imports (the number of dollars we are selling for yen) is now the same as the dollar value of U.S. exports (the number of dollars they are buying with yen). Americans are exporting those goods in which we have a comparative advantage (our production cost for those goods, relative to our production cost for other goods, is low compared to the corresponding ratio in Japan) and importing those goods in which the Japanese have a comparative advantage.

Suppose the United States imposes a tariff: Anyone who buys

goods abroad and imports them must pay 10 percent of their price to the government. Japanese goods are now more expensive to Americans, so we buy fewer of them, so our demand for the yen we buy them with falls. The price of yen measured in dollars falls, which makes Japanese goods less expensive to us and American goods more expensive to the Japanese. The process continues until trade is again in balance. The total volume of trade is less than before, since the government is now taxing it, but the balance of trade has not changed.

The same thing happens if the quality of American goods improves or their price in dollars falls, making American goods, at the old exchange rate, more attractive than before to Japanese buyers. Again, the result is not an imbalance of trade but a change in the exchange rate. Improved production makes a country richer, but it does not make it more competitive.

If trade automatically balances, how can it be that, as the newspapers keep assuring us, the United States has a trade deficit? To answer that question, we must drop the assumption that the only reason Japanese want dollars is to buy U.S. goods.

The United States is an attractive place to invest. Foreigners wish to acquire American assets: shares of stock, land, government bonds. To do so, they need dollars. Demand for dollars on the dollar-yen market consists in part of demand by Japanese who want dollars to buy American goods and in part of demand by Japanese who want them to buy land or stock. At the equilibrium exchange rate, American imports (supply of dollars) equal American exports plus Japanese investment (demand for dollars). America now has a trade deficit: Our imports are more than our exports.

From the standpoint of a firm trying to export American goods, the reason for the trade deficit is that its costs are too high. But that reason confuses a cause with an effect. The fact that our dollar costs are high compared to Japan's yen costs is a statement not about our costs but about the exchange rate. The real reason for the trade deficit is the capital inflow; indeed, the capital inflow and the trade deficit are simply two sides of an accounting identity. If the exchange rate were not at a level at which the United States imported more than it exported, there would be no surplus of dollars in Japanese hands with which to buy capital assets from Americans.

One implication of this analysis is that "trade deficit" and "unfavorable balance of payments" are misleading terms. There is nothing inherently bad about an inflow of capital. The United States had a capital inflow, and consequently an "unfavorable balance of payments," through much of the nineteenth century; we were building our canals and railroads with European capital.

If capital is flowing into the United States because foreigners think America is a safe and prosperous place to invest, then the trade deficit is no more a problem now than it was 150 years ago. If capital is flowing into the United States because Americans prefer to live on borrowed money and let their children worry about the bill, then that is a problem; but the trade deficit is the symptom, not the disease.

BILATERAL MONOPOLY: THE SERPENT IN THE GARDEN

So far, our discussion has dealt with gains from trade and where they come from. We now turn to a darker subject—the problem of how to divide up the gain.

My horse is worth $100 to me and $200 to you. If I sell it to you for $100, you get all the benefit; if I sell it for $200, I do. Anywhere in the bargaining range between these two extremes we divide the $100 surplus between us.

If I convince you that I will not take any price below $199, it is in your interest to pay that; gaining $1 is better than gaining nothing. If you convince me that you will not pay more than $101, it is in my interest to sell it for that—for the same reason. Both of us are likely to spend substantial real resources—time and energy, among other things—trying to persuade each other that our bargaining positions are real.

When I set up the problem, I (the author of this book) told you (the reader of this book) how much the horse was worth to each of us, but the you and I inside the problem do not have that information. Each of us has to guess how much the horse is worth to the other—and each has an incentive to try to make the other guess wrong. If you manage to persuade me that the horse is worth only $101 to you, there is no point in my trying to hold out for more.

There is a risk to such deceptions. If I persuade you that the horse is really worth more than $200 to me, you stop trying to buy it. If you persuade me that it is worth less than $100 to you, I stop trying to sell it. In either case, the deal falls through and the $100 gain disappears.

Strikes and Wars—Errors or Experiments?

Consider a strike. When it is over, union and management have agreed to some contract. Both the stockholders whose interest management is supposed to represent and the workers whose interest the union is supposed to represent would be better off if they agreed, on the first day of bargaining, to whatever contract they will eventually sign, avoiding the cost of the strike. The reason they do not is that the union is trying to persuade management that it will only accept a contract very favorable to it and management is trying to persuade the union that no such contract will be offered. Each tries to make its bargaining position persuasive by demonstrating that it is willing to accept large costs—in the form of a strike—rather than give in.

Much the same is true of wars. When the smoke clears, there will be a peace treaty; one side or the other will have won, or some compromise will have been accepted by both. If the peace treaty were signed immediately after the declaration of war and just before the first shot was fired, there would be an enormous savings in human life and material damage. The failure of the nations involved to do it that way may in part be the result of differing factual beliefs; if each believes that its tanks and planes are better and its soldiers braver, then the two sides will honestly disagree about who is going to win and hence about what the terms of the peace treaty will be. The war is an (expensive) experiment to settle a disagreement about the military power of the two sides.

But there are other reasons why wars occur. Even if both sides agree on the military situation, they may have different opinions about how high a price each is willing to pay for victory. It is said that when the Japanese government consulted its admiralty on the prospects of a war with the United States, the admiralty replied that they could provide a year of victories, hold on for another year, and would then start losing—a reasonably accurate prediction. The Japanese attacked anyway, in the belief that the United States—about to become engaged in a more difficult and important war in Europe—would agree to a negotiated peace sometime in the first two years.

While bilateral monopoly bargaining is a common and important element in real-world economies, it is not the dominant form of trade. There are, fortunately, other mechanisms for setting the terms of trade that lead to less ambiguous results and lower transaction costs.

GETTING "RIPPED OFF"

There seems to be a widespread belief that if someone sells something to you for more than he could have—if, for example, he could make a profit selling it to you for $5 but charges $15—he is mistreating you, "ripping you off" in current jargon. This is an oddly one-sided way of looking at such a situation. If you pay $15 for the good, it is presumably worth at least that much to you. If it costs him $5 and is worth $15 to you, then there is a $10 gain when you buy it; your claim that he ought to sell it to you for $5 amounts to claiming that you are entitled to the whole benefit. It would make just as much sense to argue that he should get all the benefit, that if you buy a good for $5 for which you would have been willing to pay $15, you are ripping him off. Yet I know very few people who, if they see a price of $5 on a new book by their favorite author for which they would gladly pay $15, feel obliged to volunteer the higher price—or even to offer to split the difference.

As it happens, substantial bargaining ranges are not typical of most transactions, for the same reasons that bilateral monopoly is not the dominant form of trade. Most goods are sold at about cost, for reasons we will explore in the next few chapters. But bilateral monopolies and bargaining ranges do exist.

I give speeches and write articles on a variety of topics: legal, economic, political, and historical. Sometimes I do it for free. That is no reason why I should not charge for my services if I can. When someone is willing to pay me $500 for a speech I would be willing to give for free, that is evidence that giving the speech produces a net gain of at least $500. I feel no obligation to turn all of that gain over to my audience.

ARBITRAGE, TRANSACTION COSTS, AND CONSISTENT PRICES

Several times so far, I have claimed that money is not really essential to economics—yet I continue to use money in my examples. One reason to do so should by now be clear—stating prices in cleanups and meals cooked is slower and clumsier than stating them in dollars. If we were willing to put up with that inconvenience, everything I have done using money prices could have been done instead with prices measured in apples. Once you have the price of everything in terms of apples, you have the price of everything in terms of any good. If a peach exchanges for four apples and four apples exchange for eight cookies, then the cookie price of a peach is eight.

There are two ways of seeing why this is true. The simpler is to observe that someone who has cookies and wants peaches will never pay more than eight cookies for a peach, since he could always trade eight cookies for four apples and then exchange the four apples for a peach. Someone who has a peach and wants cookies will never accept fewer than eight cookies for his peach, since he could always trade it for four apples and then trade the four apples for eight cookies. If nobody who is buying peaches will pay more than eight cookies and nobody selling them will accept less, the price of a peach (in cookies) must be eight. So once we know the price of all goods in terms of one (in this example apples), we can calculate the price of each good in terms of any other.

This argument depends on an assumption that has so far been implicit in our analysis—that we can ignore all costs of buying and selling other than the price paid. That is a reasonable approximation for much economic activity, but not all. Imagine that you have twenty automobiles and want a house. The cookie price of an automobile is forty thousand; the cookie price of a house is eight hundred thousand. It seems, from the discussion of the previous paragraph, that all you have to do to get your house is trade automobiles for cookies and then cookies for the house.

But where will you put eight hundred thousand cookies while you wait for the seller of the house to come collect them? How long will it take you to count them out to him? What condition will the cookies be in by the time you finish?

This brings us to the second reason why relative prices must be consistent. Trading huge quantities of apples, cookies, peaches, or whatever may be very costly for you and me. It is far less costly for those in the business of such trading—people who routinely buy and sell carload lots of apples, wheat, pork bellies, and many other outlandish things and who make their exchanges not by physically moving the goods around but merely by changing the pieces of paper saying who owns what, while the goods sit still. For such professional traders, transaction costs really are close to zero. And such traders, in the process of making their living, force prices into a consistent pattern. The way they do it is called *arbitrage*. It is a way in which a few very skilled people make very large amounts of money.

To see how, imagine that we start with an inconsistent structure of prices. A peach trades for 2 apples and an apple for 4 cookies, but the price of a peach in cookies is 10. A professional trader in the peach-cookie-apple market appears. He starts with 10,000 peaches. He trades them for 100,000 cookies (the price of a peach is 10 cookies), buys 25,000 apples with the 100,000 cookies (the price of an apple is 4 cookies), trades the apples for 12,500 peaches (the price of a peach in apples is 2). He has started with 10,000 peaches, shuffled some pieces of paper representing ownership of peaches, apples, and cookies, and ended up with 2,500 peaches more than he started with! By repeating the cycle again and again, he can end up with as many peaches—and exchange them for as much of anything else—as he wants.

So far, I have ignored the effect of such arbitrage on the prices of the goods traded. But if you can get peaches for nothing simply by shuffling a few pieces of paper around, there is an almost unlimited number of people willing to do it. When the number of traders—or the quantities each trades—becomes large enough, the effect is to change relative prices.

Everyone is trying to sell peaches for cookies. The result is to drive down the price—the number of cookies you must pay to get a peach. Everyone is trying to buy apples with cookies. The result is to drive up the price of apples measured in cookies. As prices change in this way, the profit from arbitrage becomes smaller and smaller. If the traders have no transaction costs at all, the process continues until there is no profit. When that point is reached, relative prices will be perfectly consistent—you get the same number of cookies for your peach whether you trade directly or via apples. If the traders have some transaction costs, the result is almost the same but not quite; discrepancies in relative prices can remain as long as they are small enough so that it does not pay traders to engage in the arbitrage trades that would eliminate them.

In our world, prices for one good are rarely stated in terms of another, so there is little room for arbitrage on the peach-cookie market. But prices of one currency are often stated in another, so there is a market, and money to be made, arbitraging pounds to lire to dollars to yen to pounds. And there are still greater opportunities in more complicated forms of arbitrage, where the first person who notes that two bundles of financial assets are equivalent but their prices are not equal can make a considerable amount of money correcting the discrepancy.

7

PUTTING IT TOGETHER:
PRICE THEORY IN A
SIMPLE ECONOMY

Sometimes it seems that everyone is an economist. My father-in-law, for example, would not seriously consider challenging my views on physics, a subject in which I acquired a doctorate before switching to economics—although, as a geologist, he actually knows something about physics. But he has no reservations about preferring his views on foreign trade to mine, despite the fact I have taught and published in economics for more than twenty years.

Economics sounds seductively simple. "Competition," "efficiency," "supply and demand" are familiar words and seem to have obvious meanings. The subject—prices, wages, goods, and services—is all about us. It is only too easy to slip from "I am familiar with" to "I understand." Not only geologists but radio commentators, editorial writers, preachers, and politicians succumb to the temptation, make up their own economics on the spot, and proceed to tell the rest of us, with great confidence, what everything means, why everything happens, and what we should all do about it.

I hope I have by now convinced you that that approach does not work. There is real, nonobvious content to economics that you cannot simply make up as you go along. Like the similar approach that some people take to medicine, it is likely to lead to conclusions that are not only wrong, but dangerously wrong.

Up to this point, we have been doing economics in pieces—although I have tried to choose pieces complete enough to provide answers to interesting questions. We are now ready to put it together. By the time we are halfway through this chapter, we will have assembled an entire economy—although a simple one. Once we see how it all goes together, we will devote the rest of the chapter to putting our new toy through its paces—answering such real-world questions as how much taxes really cost to whom and what the effect of landlord-tenant regulation is on landlords and tenants.

PART 1: X MARKS THE SPOT

In chapters 4 and 5, we worked out the logic of demand and supply curves—curves showing, at any price, how much an individual consumes or produces. We saw that the market supply curve was simply the horizontal sum of individual supply curves: how much I want to produce, plus how much you want to produce, plus how much he wants to produce. The same logic gives market demand as a horizontal sum of individual demand curves.

It may have occurred to you that supply and demand are not, cannot be, separate problems. There is no way to consume something unless someone produces it, or sell something unless someone buys it. Somehow, quantity supplied and quantity demanded must end up equal. We are now ready to see how.

Figure 7–1a shows supply and demand curves for widgets, an imaginary commodity consumed mostly by economics professors. The vertical axis is price, the horizontal axis is quantity; any point on the diagram represents a quantity and a price.

Suppose widgets cost $10 apiece. At that price, producers wish to produce and sell more widgets than consumers want to buy. Producers with widgets they cannot sell are willing to cut their price to get rid of them. Price falls—and continues to fall as long as quantity supplied is greater than quantity demanded.

What if, instead of $10, the initial price was $5? At that price,

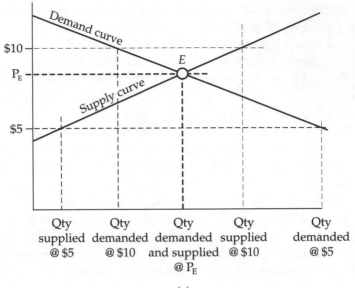

(a)

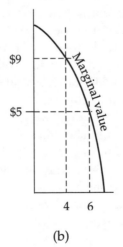

(b)

Figures 7-1a & b   Market equilibrium. At point E, price $= P_E$; quantity demanded equals quantity supplied. At lower prices, less is supplied; individuals are consuming quantities for which $M_V > P$, as shown in Figure 7–2, and so are willing to offer a higher price for additional quantities.

consumers want to buy more than producers want to sell. Some consumers find that they cannot buy as many widgets as they want. Figure 7–1b shows the marginal value curve of one such consumer. At $5 a widget he would like to buy six widgets but can only find four for sale. He is willing to pay anything up to $9 for one more widget, since that is its marginal value. He, and other consumers with the same problem, bid the price up.

If the price is below P_E, it will be driven up; if it is above P_E, it will be driven down. P_E, the price at the point where the two curves cross, is the *equilibrium price*—the price at which quantity supplied equals quantity demanded.

The idea of *equilibrium* is common to many different sciences. There are three varieties, easily illustrated with a pencil. Hold the pencil by the point, with the eraser hanging down. It is in *stable* equilibrium—if someone nudges the eraser end to one side, it swings back. Point E is a stable equilibrium. Balance the pencil on its point on your finger. It is in *unstable* equilibrium—if someone nudges it, it will fall over (when I try the experiment, it falls over even without nudging—I never was good at balancing). Lay the pencil (a round one) down on the table. It is in *metastable* equilibrium—nudge it and it rolls over partway and remains in its new position. One sometimes encounters people, human or feline, in metastable equilibrium.

Shifting Curves

Much confusion can be avoided by distinguishing carefully between *changes in demand* (the demand curve shifting) and changes in *quantity demanded*, and similarly for *supply* and *quantity supplied*. In Figure 7–2, for example, demand changes, which changes price, which changes the quantity supplied. But supply has not changed; the supply curve is the same after the change as before.

Being careful with such distinctions can help you avoid some of the worst absurdities of newspaper economics. Consider the following: *"The demand for memory chips increased, which drove up the price, which drove up the supply, which brought the price back down."*

This is the change illustrated in Figure 7–2. An increase in demand (the demand curve shifts out) raises price; the increased price reduces quantity demanded below what it would have been if the demand curve had shifted but the price had remained the same (Q_3). The new quantity demanded (Q_2) is less than Q_3 but more than

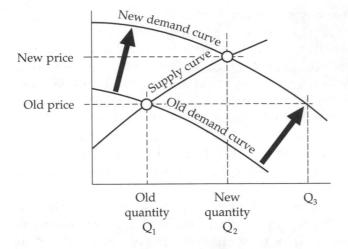

Figure 7-2   The effects of shifts in supply and demand curves.

the old quantity demanded (Q_1). Q_2 must be greater than Q_1 because quantity demanded is equal to quantity supplied, the supply curve has not shifted, and a higher price applied to the same supply curve results in a larger quantity supplied.

Elasticity: A Brief Digression

The effect on price and quantity of shifts in supply and demand curves depends on the shape of the curves—in particular on their *elasticity*, which measures how rapidly quantity changes as you change price. Elasticity is one if a 1 percent increase in price results in a 1 percent increase in quantity supplied, two if it results in a 2 percent increase in quantity. More formally, the elasticity of a supply curve at a price is defined as the percentage increase in quantity divided by the percentage increase in price, for a very small price change.

Supply (or demand) is very elastic if a small change in price results in a large change in quantity and very inelastic if a large change in price results in only a small change in quantity. The limiting cases are *perfectly elastic* (a horizontal supply or demand curve) and *perfectly inelastic* (a vertical curve). One of the differences between economics as done by economists and economics as done by journalists and politicians is that the latter often speak as though almost all supply and demand curves were perfectly inelastic—they ignore the effect of price on quantity.

This is the same disagreement discussed earlier as "needs" versus "wants." The noneconomist thinks of the demand for water as "the amount of water we need" and assumes that the alternative to having that amount of water is dying of thirst. But only a tiny fraction, less than one gallon in a thousand, of the water we consume is drunk. While the demand for drinking water is highly inelastic over a wide range of prices, demand for other uses is not. If the price of water doubles, it pays farmers to switch to trickle irrigation, chemical firms to use less water in their manufacturing processes, and homeowners to fix leaky faucets. Nobody dies of thirst, but total consumption of water drops.

One familiar example of what is wrong with the popular picture of an economy is the game Monopoly. In the economy it models, where you stay is determined by a die roll, not by the rent; quantity demanded is unaffected by price. You never have to worry that putting a hotel on Park Place, and thus raising the cost of a visit to the square from $35 to $1500, might drive away some potential customers.

Who Pays Taxes?

We are now ready to start on one of the questions frequently asked of economists; the number of pages it has taken us to get this far may explain why answers that fit a thirty-second news story are generally wrong. The question is, "Who really pays taxes?" When a government imposes a tax on some good, does the money come out of the profits of those who produce it or do the producers pass it along to the consumers in higher prices?

Suppose the tax is $1 per widget; for every widget sold, the producer must pay the government $1. The result is to shift the supply curve up by $1, from S_1 to S_2, as shown in Figure 7–3a.

Why? What matters to the producer is how much he gets, not how much the consumer pays. If he gets $6 a widget, of which he must hand over $1 to the government, his return for each widget sold is the same as if he were selling them at $5 per widget. So he produces the same quantity of widgets at $6 per widget after the tax is imposed as he would have produced at $5 before, and similarly for all other prices. Each quantity on the new supply curve corresponds to a price $1 higher than on the old; the supply curve shifts up by $1.

This does not mean that the market price goes up $1. If it did, producers would produce the same amount as before the tax and

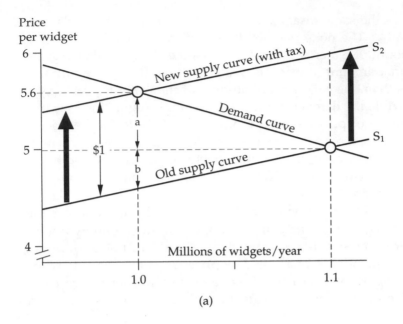

Price
per widget

6

5.6

5

$1

a

b

New supply curve (with tax)

Demand curve

Old supply curve

S₂

S₁

4

Millions of widgets/year

1.0

1.1

(a)

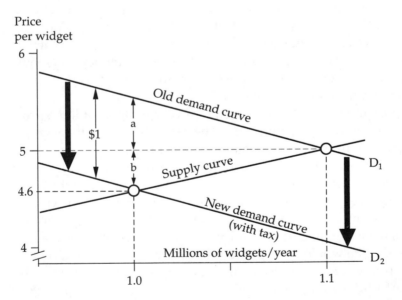

Price
per widget

6

5

$1

a

b

4.6

4

Old demand curve

Supply curve

New demand curve
(with tax)

D₁

D₂

Millions of widgets/year

1.0

1.1

(b)

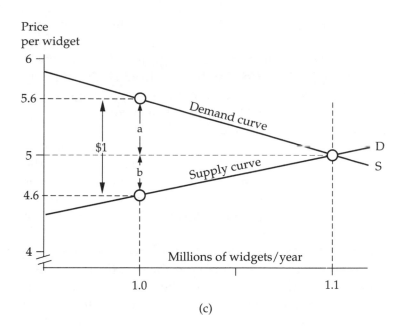

Figures 7-3a, b, c   The effect of a $1 tax on widgets. Figure 7–3a shows the effect of a tax paid by the producer; the supply curve shifts up from S_1 to S_2. Figure 7–3b shows the effect of a tax paid by the consumer. Figure 7–3c shows the same situation, with S depending on price received by the producer (market price minus any tax on producers) and D on price paid by the consumer (market price plus any tax on consumers). The difference between the two prices is the tax.

consumers would consume less than before, making quantity supplied greater than quantity demanded. If, on the other hand, price did not rise at all, quantity demanded would be the same as before the tax, quantity supplied would be less (since producers would be getting a dollar less per widget), so quantity supplied would be less than quantity demanded. As you can see on Figure 7–3a, the price rises, but by less than a dollar. All of the tax is paid by the producer in the literal sense that the producer hands the government the money, but in fact the price paid by the consumer has gone up by a and the price received by the producer (net of tax) has gone down by b, where $a + b$ adds up to the full amount of the tax.

Suppose that, instead of taxing producers, the government decides to tax consumers: For every widget you buy, you must pay the government $1. The result is shown in Figure 7–3b. This time it is the demand curve that is shifted by the tax—from D_1 down to D_2. Widgets at $5 with no tax cost you the same amount as widgets at $4 with a $1 tax, payable by the consumer; either way you give up, for each widget purchased, the opportunity to buy $5 worth of something else. Since the cost to you is the same in both cases, you buy the same quantity in both cases—and so does everyone else. So the total quantity demanded is the same at a price of $4 with the tax as it would be without the tax at a price of $5, and similarly for all other prices. The demand curve shifts down by $1—the amount of the tax.

Looking at Figure 7–3b, you can see that the tax lowers the price received by the producer by b and increases the cost (including tax) to the consumer by a—and that a and b are the same as on the previous figure. If we ignore the old supply curve on one figure and the old demand curve on the other, Figure 7–3b is simply 7–3a shifted down by $1. On Figure 7–3a, the price shown on the vertical axis is price after tax, since the tax is paid by the producer; on 7–3b, it is price before tax, since the tax is paid by the consumer. The difference between price before tax and price after tax is the amount of the tax: $1.

A third way of describing the same situation is shown in Figure 7–3c. Here supply is shown as a function of price received, demand as a function of price paid. Before the tax was instituted, market equilibrium occurred at a quantity (1.1 million widgets per year) for which price received was equal to price paid; after the tax was instituted, market equilibrium occurs at a quantity (1 million widgets per year) for which price received is a dollar less than price paid, with the difference going to the government.

Figures 7–3a, b, and c are all essentially the same; the only difference is what is shown on the vertical axis. They are the same not because I happen to have drawn them that way but because they have to be drawn that way; all three describe the same situation. The cost of widgets to the consumers (which is what matters to them), the amount received by the producers per widget sold (which is what matters to them), and the quantity of widgets sold are all the same whether the tax is "paid by" producers or consumers. How the burden of the tax is really distributed is entirely unaffected by who actually hands over the money to the government!

And for the Real Cost of Taxes . . .

The previous section started with the question of who really pays taxes. It seems we now have the answer. Using a supply-demand diagram, we can show how much of the tax is passed along to the consumer in the form of higher prices and how much appears as a reduction in the (after-tax) price received by the producer. In any particular case, the answer depends on the relative elasticity of the supply and demand curves—on how rapidly quantity demanded and quantity supplied change with price, as indicated by the slopes of the curves S and D on our diagrams. If supply is much more elastic than demand, most of the tax is passed on to consumers; if demand is much more elastic than supply, most of it is passed on to producers.

We have answered *a* question, but not quite the right question. We know how much the tax increases the price paid by the consumer and how much it decreases the price received by the producer, but that is not the same thing as how much worse off it makes them.

Consider the effect of a tax of $1,000 per widget. Production and consumption of widgets drop to zero. The government receives nothing; producers and consumers pay nothing. Does that mean that a tax of $1,000 per widget costs consumers (and producers) nothing? Obviously not. The tax costs consumers whatever benefit they previously received from consuming 1,100,000 untaxed widgets at a price of $5 each and costs producers whatever benefit they received from selling those widgets. The cost to consumers of a tax includes both the extra money they pay for goods they continue to buy and the lost benefit from goods no longer worth buying.

What we left out of our analysis of the cost of a $1 tax on widgets was consumer (and producer) surplus—whose function is to measure the net benefit of being able to buy (sell) goods. Before the tax, the consumer could purchase (and the producer sell) as many widgets as he wanted at $5 apiece; afterwards the cost to the consumer was $5.60 per widget and the revenue received by the producer was $4.60 per widget. The cost of the tax to producers and consumers is the difference between their surplus in the first case and his consumer surplus in the second, shown in Figure 7–4.

The entire area under the demand curve and above $5 is consumer surplus before the tax. The area under the demand curve and above $5.60 is consumer surplus after the tax. The shaded area above $5 is the difference between the two—the cost of the tax to consumers. It is made up of two parts—a rectangle (increased cost per

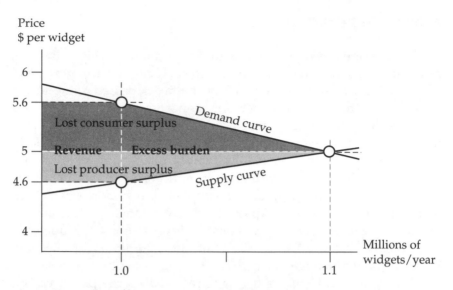

Figure 7-4   The effect on surplus of a $1 tax on widgets. The dark shaded area is lost consumer surplus, the lightly shaded area lost producer surplus. Lost surplus equals revenue collected (the two rectangles) plus excess burden (the two triangles).

widget times number of widgets purchased) plus a triangle (lost consumer surplus on widgets no longer bought because of the tax).

Similarly, the shaded area below $5 is the cost of the tax to producers—their loss of producer surplus. It, too, consists of a rectangle (lost revenue on the widgets still being produced) plus a triangle (lost producer surplus on widgets no longer sold because of the tax).

If we sum the two rectangles, we have the tax per widget (the difference between cost per widget to consumers and revenue per widget to producers) times the number of widgets produced—the total *revenue* produced by the tax. If we sum the two triangles, we have the *excess burden* of the tax—a loss for producers and consumers with no corresponding gain for anyone.

Figures 7–5a and b show that the relation between revenue and excess burden depends in part on the shape of the demand curve. The steeper the demand curve (the more *inelastic* demand is), the less a given tax reduces quantity and thus the lower the ratio of excess burden to revenue. In the limiting case of perfectly inelastic demand, there would be no reduction in consumption and no excess burden. The same argument applies to the supply curve as well.

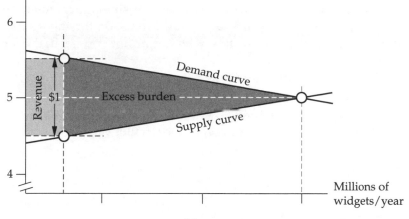

(a)

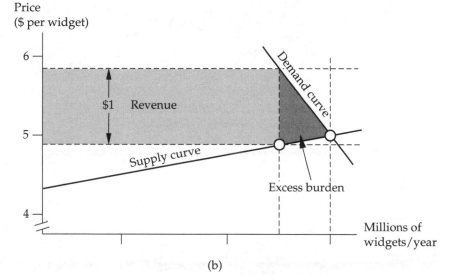

(b)

Figures 7-5a & b   The effect of elasticity of the demand curve on the relation between revenue and excess burden. A very elastic demand curve (Figure 7–5a) produces a high ratio of excess burden to revenue; a very inelastic demand curve Figure 7–5b) produces a low ratio.

This has sometimes been offered as an argument for taxing necessities, on the theory that demand for necessities is inelastic. An obvious objection is that taxes on necessities hurt the poor. A less obvious objection is that necessities and luxuries, as conventionally defined, may not correspond very closely to goods with inelastic and elastic demands. Cigarettes are usually considered a luxury, but their demand curve seems to be quite inelastic. A similar argument on the supply side is used to justify taxing land rents, on the theory that the supply of land is very inelastic—whether or not you tax it, the land is still there.

Elasticities of both supply and demand are usually greater in the long run than in the short. If the price of gasoline rises, the immediate response of the consumer is to drive less. Given more time to adjust, he can arrange a car pool, buy a smaller car, or move closer to

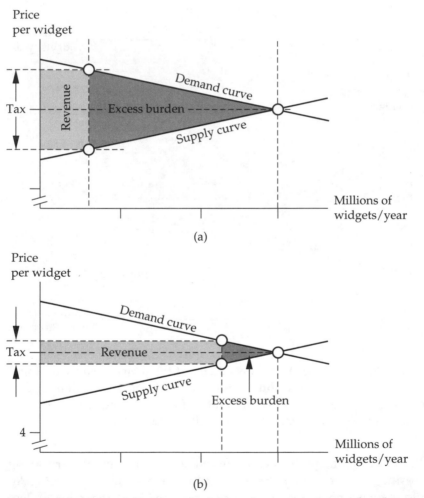

(a)

(b)

Figures 7-6a & b   A large tax (7–6a) produces more excess burden per dollar of revenue than a small tax (7–6b).

his job. If the price of heating oil rises, he can adjust, in the short run, only by turning down his thermostat. In the long run, he can improve the insulation of his house or move to a warmer climate.

If the price at which a producer can sell his goods falls, he may still be better off producing than scrapping his factory. But it is no longer worth replacing machines that wear out, so output gradually falls. If price rises, the producer's short-run response is limited to trying to squeeze more output from the existing factory. In the longer run, he can build a bigger factory.

For all of these reasons, elasticities of supply and demand are usually greater in the longer run. High elasticity implies high excess burden, so the excess burden of a tax is likely to become larger as time goes on. One example is the window tax in London some centuries ago, which led to a style of houses with few windows. Another is a tax on houses in New Orleans based on the number of stories at the front of the house. One of the architectural oddities of New Orleans is the camelback style of house—one story in front, two in back. In the long run, dark houses in London and higher building costs in New Orleans were part of the excess burden of those taxes.

A lower tax rate costs less in excess burden per dollar collected, as can be seen in Figures 7–6a and b. This is an argument in favor of spreading taxation over many goods—for instance, by a general sales tax—instead of collecting most of the revenue from taxes on a few goods. An argument on the other side is that the administrative cost of collecting a tax, which we have so far ignored, may be lower if only a few goods are being taxed.

LANDLORDS AND TENANTS: AN APPLICATION OF PRICE THEORY

The government of Santa Monica announces that, in the interest of social justice, every landlord must pay each of his tenants $10 a month. In the short run, this is a simple transfer from landlords to tenants. In the longer run, long enough to allow rents to adjust to the new law, the analysis is more complicated.

From the standpoint of the landlord, the transfer is a tax of $10 a month on each apartment rented. Just as in our previous example, the supply curve shifts up by the amount of the tax; at a rent of $510 per apartment per month, the quantity of apartments offered to rent is the same as it would have been before at a rent of $500 per month.

From the standpoint of the tenant, the $10 is a subsidy—a negative tax. The demand curve shifts up by $10. Whatever quantity of housing each tenant would have chosen to rent before if the rent was $500 per month (instead of buying a house, sharing an apartment with a friend, or moving to Chicago), that is now the quantity he will choose to rent if the rent is $510, since $510 in rent minus $10 from the landlord is a net cost to him of $500.

Figure 7–7a shows the result; for simplicity I am treating housing as if it were a simple continuous commodity like water, and defining price and quantity in terms of some standard-sized apartment. Since both curves shift up by $10, their intersection shifts up by $10 as well. The new equilibrium rent is precisely $10 higher than the old. The law neither benefits the tenant nor hurts the landlord.

Next consider a more realistic regulation. The city council decides that the terms of some existing leases are unfair to tenants and announces that in the future landlords must give tenants six months' notice before evicting them, even if the tenants have agreed in the lease to some shorter period. Again we consider the effect after enough time has passed to let rents reach their new equilibrium.

The new rule increases operating costs by making it harder to evict undesirable tenants. From the standpoint of the landlord, it is like a tax. Suppose it is equivalent to a tax of $10: Landlords are indifferent between having to provide each tenant with six months' notice and having to pay a $10 a month tax on each apartment. The supply curve for apartments shifts up by $10, as shown in Figure 7–7b.

The additional security is worth something to the tenants. Suppose it is worth $5 a month; a tenant is indifferent to paying $500 a month for an apartment without six months' tenure and paying $505 for one with the additional security. The demand curve shifts up by $5, as shown in Figure 7–7b.

Looking at the figure, you can see that the new price is higher than the old by more than $5 and less than $10. The exact change depends on the slope of the curves, but (as you should, with a little effort, be able to prove) the increase must be more than the smaller shift and less than the larger. Since the law increases costs to landlords by more than it increases rents, landlords are worse off. Since it increases the value of the apartment to tenants by less than it increases rents, tenants are also worse off!

I have assumed that the requirement costs the landlords more than it is worth to the tenants. What if we assume instead that the

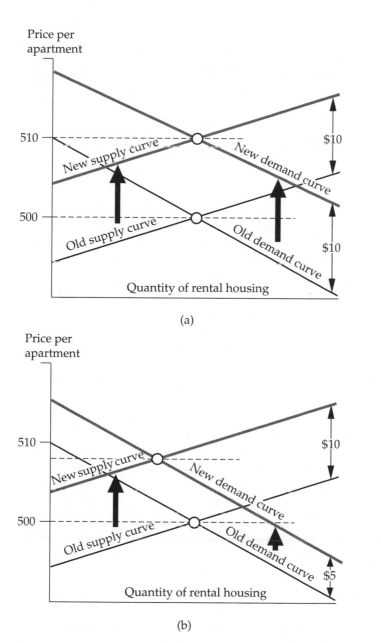

(a)

(b)

Figures 7–7a & b   Effect of regulations on the rental market. Figure 7–7a shows the effect of a compulsory $10 transfer from landlords to tenants. Figure 7–7b shows the effect of requiring landlords to provide tenants with six months' notice. The requirement is equivalent to a $10 tax on landlords and a $5 subsidy to tenants.

law imposes a cost of $5 (shifting the supply curve up by $5) and a benefit of $10 (shifting the demand curve up by $10)? The increase in rent is again between $5 and $10. Both parties are better off as a result of the law—the landlord gets an increase in rent greater than the increase in his costs, while the tenant pays an increase in rent less than the value to him of the improved contract.

In this case, however, the law is unnecessary. If there is no law setting the terms for rental contracts, a landlord who charges $500 a month will find it in his interest to offer his tenant the alternative of the same apartment with six months' security at, say, $509 a month. The tenant will accept the offer, since he prefers $509 with security to $500 without. The landlord will be better off, since the security costs him only $5 a month. All rental contracts will provide for six months' notice before eviction.

The argument is not limited to this particular issue. It pays the landlord to include in the lease contract any terms that are worth more to the tenant than they cost him—and adjust the rent accordingly. Requiring him to include additional terms, terms that cost more than they are worth, hurts both landlord and tenant—once we take account of the effect of the requirement on rents.

In proving this result, I made a number of simplifying assumptions. One was that the cost per apartment imposed by the regulation did not depend on how many apartments the landlord was renting out; the requirement shifted the supply curve up by the same amount all along its length. I made a similar assumption for the tenants—that security was worth the same amount per apartment independent of how much apartment was consumed. Dropping these assumptions makes the analysis more complicated. One can construct situations where the requirement shifts the curves in a way that benefits tenants at the expense of landlords or landlords at the expense of tenants, but there is no particular reason to expect either to happen.

A second assumption was that the regulation had the same effect on all landlords and on all tenants. Dropping this assumption changes the results somewhat. Imagine that you are unusually good at recognizing good tenants. Offering six months' security costs you nothing—you never rent an apartment to anyone you will ever want to evict. If there is no legal restriction on contracts, you find that by offering security you can get a rent of $505 a month instead of $500; since the security costs you nothing, you do so. After the law changes to force all landlords to offer security, the market rent for apartments (with the required six months' security) is more than $505 (as shown in Figure 7–7b). The restriction has forced your competitors to add a feature to their product (security) that was expensive for them to produce but inexpensive for you. Their higher costs shifted the market supply curve and increased the market price, benefiting you.

One could construct similar cases involving tenants. The interesting point to note is that the effect of legal restrictions on contracts between landlords and tenants is not, as one might at first expect, a redistribution from one group (landlords) to another (tenants). If the groups are uniform, restrictions typically either have no effect or injure everyone. If the members of the groups differ from each other, the restriction may also redistribute within the groups—benefiting some members of one or both of the groups at the expense of other members of the same group.

At first glance, much of economics seems to be simply plausible talk about familiar subjects. That is an illusion. So far in this chapter, I have given proofs of two surprising results—that it does not matter whether a tax is collected from producers or consumers and that restrictions on rental contracts in favor of tenants are likely to hurt both tenants and landlords.

The second proof is a sketch of a much more general result—the desirability of freedom of contract. As a general rule, with some exceptions, legal restrictions on the terms of contracts are more likely to injure both parties than to benefit one at the expense of the other.

This result is relevant not only to public policy but also to private profit. Suppose you are a businessman or an attorney negotiating a contract. It is tempting to go through the contract term by term, trying in each case to get whatever term is most favorable to you or your client.

But a more profitable strategy may be to go through looking for the contract terms that maximize the combined gain to both parties. Only when you get to the final term—the price—do you shift back to trying to make it as favorable as possible, thus collecting as much as possible of the gain produced by your well-designed contract. Most of your job is maximizing the size of the pie. The bigger the pie, the bigger you can make the slices for both sides.

PART 2: ODDS, ENDS, AND PROFUNDITIES

We have achieved the main objectives of this chapter—showing how supply and demand go together to determine price and quantity, and applying that knowledge to analyze real-world issues. Having done so, it is now time to clarify a few points and warn against some common misunderstandings.

Mechanism Versus Equilibrium

At a price of $1, purchasers of eggs wish to buy 1,000 eggs per week and producers wish to produce 900. What happens?

Step 1: Consumers bid against each other until they have driven the price up to $1.25; at that price, they only want to buy 900 eggs.

Step 2: At the new price, producers want to produce 980 eggs per week. They do so. They cannot sell that many at that price. Price falls to $1.05; at that price, consumers will buy 980 eggs.

Step 3: At $1.05, producers only want to produce 910 eggs per week. They do so. Consumers bid against each other . . .

This is a poor approach to solving this sort of problem. We are stuck in an infinite series that may never converge; with some demand and supply curves, the swings in price could get wider and wider. Furthermore, we are assuming that producers and consumers foolishly base their decisions on what the price was instead of trying to estimate what it is going to be. The alternative approach goes as follows:

If quantity supplied is greater than quantity demanded, the price will fall; if less, the price will rise. Price will therefore tend toward the point at which the two are equal. This is the equilibrium price—the intersection of supply and demand.

Shortages, Surpluses, and How to Make Them

To most people, a shortage is a fact of nature—there just isn't enough. To an economist, it has almost nothing to do with nature. Diamonds are in very short supply—yet there is no diamond shortage. Water is plentiful; the average American consumes, directly or indirectly, more than 1,000 gallons per day. Yet there are water shortages.

The mistake is in assuming that "enough" is a fact of nature—that we need a particular amount of water, diamonds, oil, or whatever. How much of something we choose to consume depends on its price. The amount we think we need is simply the amount we are used to consuming at the price we are used to paying. A shortage occurs not when the amount available is small but when it is less than the amount we want; since the latter depends on price, a shortage simply means that a price is too low—below the level where quantity supplied would equal quantity demanded. Usually this is the result of either government price control (gas and oil prices in the early seventies) or the refusal by government to charge the market price for something it supplies (water). Sometimes it is the result of producers who misestimate demand and are unwilling or unable to adjust price or output quickly.

An interesting example of a stable supply-demand disequilibrium (a surplus rather than a shortage) occurred many years ago in Hong Kong. Rickshaws are small carts drawn by one person and used to transport another—a sort of human-powered taxi that used to be common in Hong Kong. Drivers seemed to spend most of their time sitting by the curb waiting for customers—quantity supplied was much larger than quantity demanded. Why?

Many of the customers were tourists from countries where the wage level was much higher than in Hong Kong. The price it seemed natural to them to offer was far above the price at which supply would have equaled demand. Drivers were attracted into the rickshaw business until the daily income (one-fourth of the day working for a high hourly payment, three-fourths of the day sitting around) was comparable to that of other Hong Kong jobs. The tourist who paid $4HK for a ride that represented $1HK worth of labor was worse off by $3HK than if he had paid the lower price—but there was no corresponding gain to the recipients; $4HK was a fair price for their time—an hour pulling a rickshaw plus three hours waiting for the next customer.

The Invisible Demand Curve

A careless reading of an economics textbook gives the impression that economists go around measuring supply and demand curves and calculating prices and quantities from them. That is wrong. Supply curves and demand curves are not so much facts to be observed as analytical tools, ways of understanding the mechanism by which prices are determined.

Indeed, demand and supply curves are in many contexts unobservable. When the price of a good changes, it is for a reason—either demand or supply (or both) has shifted. Unless we know the reason for the change, and thus which curve has shifted, we cannot tell whether the new price and quantity are on the old demand curve (and a new supply curve) or on the old supply curve (and a new demand curve).

Demand or Supply?

One of the early puzzles in economics was whether price was determined by the value of a good to the purchaser (demand) or the cost of production (supply). We now know that the answer is "both." Price and quantity are determined by the point where the two curves cross. As Alfred Marshall put it, asking whether demand or supply determines price is like asking which blade of the scissors cuts the paper.

Not only is price determined by both value to the consumer and cost of production, price is equal to both—provided that by "value" and "cost" we mean "marginal value" and "marginal cost."

A rational consumer increases the amount he consumes until his marginal value for an additional unit is just equal to its price. We saw that in chapter 4, when we derived the demand curve from the marginal value curve. So price equals value—not because value determines price but because price (at which the good is available) determines quantity (that the consumer chooses to consume) and quantity consumed determines (marginal) value.

A rational producer expands output until his marginal cost of production is equal to the price he can sell his goods for. We saw that in chapter 5. So price equals cost—not because cost determines price but because price (at which he can sell the good) determines quantity (that he produces), which determines (marginal) cost.

In considering a single consumer or a single producer, we may take price as given, since his consumption or production is unlikely to influence it significantly. Considering the entire industry (made up of many producers) and the entire demand curve (made up of many individual demand curves), this is no longer true. The market price is that price at which quantity demanded equals quantity supplied. At the quantity demanded and supplied at that price, price equals marginal cost equals marginal value. Demand and supply curves jointly determine price and quantity; quantity (plus demand and supply curves) determines marginal value and marginal cost.

TO THINK ABOUT

Social Security taxes are paid half by the employer and half by the worker. How would the effect of the tax change if it were collected entirely from the worker or entirely from the employer? Why do you think Social Security is set up this way?

8

THE BIG PICTURE

SOLVING AN ECONOMY

An economy is a complicated interdependent system. In the previous chapter, we solved the system for a single good. In this chapter, we will try to generalize that solution to an entire economy.

Putting It Together: The First Try

Each individual, considered as a consumer, is described by his preferences—how he would choose between any alternative bundles of goods. Think of preferences as the generalization of the indifference curves of chapter 3 to a world of many goods. Each individual, considered as a producer, is described by his production function—his ability to convert his labor into goods. Think of a production function as a generalization of the table in chapter 5 that showed how many lawns, meals, or clean dishes could be produced in an hour. The preferences of consumers (and their incomes) give us demand curves, the preferences of producers (between leisure and income) plus production functions give us supply curves, the inter-sections of supply and demand curves give us prices (and quanti-ties), and we are finished. We have derived prices and quantities from preferences and production functions.

It is not so simple. The intersection of supply and demand curves gives us prices. Prices (of the goods the individuals produce and sell) give us incomes. But we needed incomes to start with, since they are one of the things that determine demand curves!

In thinking about what determines the price of one good, we usually treat all other prices as given. We cannot follow the same procedure in understanding the whole interdependent system. Each price depends on all other prices, directly, because the price of one good to a consumer may affect his demand curve for other goods, and indirectly, since the price at which a producer can sell his goods affects his income from producing them, which in turn affects his supply and demand curves for other goods.

Nailing Jelly to a Wall

The interdependence of the different elements that make up the economic system is not wholly new; it is a more complicated exam-ple of the difficulty we encountered in the egg market of chapter 7. I tried to solve that problem step-by-step, each time solving one part while holding everything else fixed. The tangle that resulted was a (simple!) example of what happens when you try to solve an inter-acting system one piece at a time while ignoring the effect on all the other pieces.

The solution was to ignore the mechanism and instead find the equilibrium: the price and quantity combination for which quantity supplied equals quantity demanded. In the more complicated case of the whole economy, we follow the same procedure.

Putting It Together: The Second Try

Our problem is to start with individual preferences and produc-tive abilities and find a complete set of equilibrium prices and quan-tities. The first step is to consider some list of prices—a price for every good. This initial list is simply a first guess, a set of prices cho-sen at random.

The quantity supplied of any one good by any one producer is determined by the prices of the goods the producer would like to buy (that is why he wants money) and the prices of other goods that he could produce instead (and preferences and productive abilities, which we know), so we can calculate quantity supplied by each producer and sum to find total quantity supplied of every good. Since income is determined by the prices of the goods we produce and the quantities we produce of them, we can calculate every producer's income. Since the quantity demanded by a consumer of any particular good is determined by income (of the consumer, which he gets as a producer) and prices (of other goods), we can calculate all demand curves; since quantity demanded of any good is determined by the demand curve and the price of that good, we can calculate the quantity demanded of every good.

So, starting with preferences, productive abilities, and a list of prices, we can calculate all quantities supplied and demanded and compare the quantity demanded of every good with the quantity supplied. If the two are equal (for every good), we have the right list of prices—the list that describes an equilibrium of the system. If they are not equal, we pick another list of prices and go through the calculation again. We continue until we find the right list of prices. The logical sequence is diagrammed in Figure 8–1.

This is a slow way of finding the right answer, rather like putting a thousand monkeys at a thousand typewriters and waiting for one of them to type out *Hamlet* by pure chance. After the first million years, your best result might be "To be or not to be, that is the grglflx." There are faster ways of solving n equations in n unknowns, which is how a mathematician would describe what we are doing.

Our egg example, for example, involved two equations in two unknowns (quantity and price). A problem with two unknowns can be solved in two dimensions, so we were able to solve the problem graphically by finding the point where two lines (the supply and demand curves) intersected.

I have gone through right and wrong ways of solving an economy so fast that you may have lost the former in the latter. I will therefore repeat the very simple result.

To solve an economy, find that set of prices such that quantity demanded equals quantity supplied for all goods and services.

That simple result—contrasted with the previous four chapters— may remind you of the mountain that gave birth to a mouse. But without those chapters, we would not have known how prices and preferences generate supply and demand curves, nor how supply and demand curves in turn determine prices.

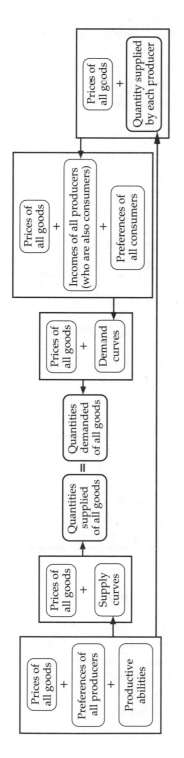

Figure 8-1   How to solve an economy. Starting with prices of all goods, productive abilities, and preferences of all consumers, derive quantities supplied and demanded. If they are equal for all goods, the initial set of prices describes a possible market equilibrium—a solution for that economy.

Solving even a very simple real-world economy would involve thousands of equations; in practice, the problem is insoluble even with advanced mathematics and modern computers. But the point of the analysis is not to solve an economy; even if we knew how to solve the equations we could not write them down in the first place, since we do not know everyone's preferences and abilities. What we observe are prices and quantities; we see the solution, not the problem. The point of the analysis is to learn how the system is interrelated, so that we can understand how any particular change (a tariff, a tax, a law) affects the whole system. Also for the fun of understanding the logical structure of the intricate web of exchange that surrounds and sustains us.

Your response may be that we do not understand a system if our "solution" requires information and calculating abilities we do not have. But economists do not claim to know what people's objectives are, only some of the consequences of people rationally pursuing them.

If you think economics is useless if it cannot actually solve an economy—predict what the entire set of prices and quantities is going to be—consider what we have already done. The book so far contains at least four strikingly counterintuitive results: (1) that a theater owner maximizes his profit by selling popcorn at cost, (2) that for a nation or individual to be better at producing one thing is logically equivalent to its being worse at producing something else, (3) that the costs imposed by taxes on producers and consumers are unaffected by who pays the taxes, and (4) that legal restrictions on leases "in favor of" tenants are likely either to have no effect or hurt both tenants and landlords. Not one of those conclusions depended on our knowing real-world demand or supply curves, nor the preferences and productive abilities from which those curves might have been derived.

PARTIAL AND GENERAL EQUILIBRIUM

The economics we did in chapter 7 was *partial equilibrium* theory: analyzing the effect of changes in the market for one good while ignoring effects on most other goods. The economics in this chapter, solving the whole interdependent economy as a single problem, is *general equilibrium* theory. Most economic analysis, in this book and elsewhere, is done as partial equilibrium. Why do we do it that way—and believe the results?

Consider a change that shifts the demand or supply curve for one good, changing its price. If a consumer is now spending more (or less) on the good whose price has changed, he must be spending less (or more) on all other goods. So the quantity demanded of those goods has changed. So assuming that only the good whose curve has shifted is affected by the change is wrong.

It is wrong, but not very wrong. In most cases, such effects are spread among a large number of other goods, each of which is only slightly affected (this is not true in the special case of two goods that are close substitutes, such as butter and margarine, or close complements, such as cars and gasoline, which is why such goods get treated together even in a partial equilibrium analysis). Small changes in prices produce very small effects on total surplus—the sum of consumer and producer surplus. Roughly speaking, a $0.10 increase in price produces not one-tenth the effect of a $1 increase but one-hundredth.

Why? When a price goes up, most of the resulting loss in consumer's surplus is a gain in producer surplus; only the lost surplus due to the reduction in quantity, the surplus on the units no longer produced because of the higher price, is a net loss. Since the reduction in quantity associated with a price increase of $1 is about ten times as great as that associated with a price increase of $0.10 (exactly ten times if the relevant curve is a straight line) and since the average consumer surplus per unit on the lost consumption is also about ten times as high, the product is a hundred times as great.

A change in the market for one good produces changes in the market for other goods. This matters if the result is a change of $1 in the price of one other good. It matters less if the result is a change of $0.10 in ten other goods and still less if is a $0.01 change in each of a hundred other goods. Since such effects are typically spread over thousands of goods, it is usually legitimate to ignore them. This is one justification for using partial equilibrium analysis. The *reason* for doing so is that, as you have probably realized at this point, general equilibrium analysis is usually much harder.

IS THIS CHAPTER NECESSARY?

I have spent much of this chapter showing that the way in which we have been doing economics is not quite correct, explaining what the correct way would be, and then explaining why I am going to keep on using the not quite correct approach. Leaving out the chapter would have saved both of us time and trouble. The reason I did not do so is that I believe lying is bad pedagogy. It is my obligation to point out problems in the ideas I am presenting instead of passing quietly over them in the hope that you will not notice. In the rest of this book, I will limit myself to partial equilibrium theory; the purpose of this chapter was to explain why doing so will usually give the right answer.

HALFTIME

WHAT WE HAVE DONE SO FAR

I started this book by defining economics in terms of rationality. The connection between that definition and the arguments of the next seven chapters may not always have been obvious, since I usually did not bother interrupting the analysis to point out what was being applied where. We have now finished learning to understand a simple economy and are about to launch into a sea of complications, so this is a convenient place to look back and trace out some of the links.

The central assumption of rationality, that people tend to choose the correct means to achieve their objectives, has been applied repeatedly. In the analysis of production, for example, we first figured out which good it was in the individual's interest to produce, then concluded that that was the good he would produce. We went on to figure out how much it was in his interest to produce, given his preferences, and again concluded that that was what he would do. Similarly, in the analysis of consumption, the demand curve was equal to the marginal value curve because the individual took the actions that maximized his net benefit. In the analysis of trade, each individual made only exchanges that benefited him.

The assumption that individual objectives are reasonably simple has been used implicitly several times. In discussing consumer behavior in chapter 3, for example, I assumed that the only reason someone wanted money was for the goods it would buy, and that a consumer in an unchanging world would therefore spend his entire income each year. But one could imagine an individual who liked the idea of living below his income—forever—and so chose to buy fewer goods than he might, while accumulating an ever increasing pile of money. That may seem irrational to you, but remember that we have no way of knowing what people *should* want. Economics deals with the consequences of what they *do* want.

In discussing price indices, I again assumed that one desired money only for what it could buy: I assumed that how well off you were depended only on what bundles of goods you could buy. But suppose that at some point in your life you fell in love with the idea of being a millionaire. What you wanted was not a particular level of consumption but the knowledge that you "had a million dollars." Doubling all incomes and prices would leave the bundles of goods available to you unaffected but make it considerably easier for you to reach that goal. I ignored the possibility of such behavior not because it was irrational in the normal sense of the word but because it violated the assumption that individual objectives were reasonably simple.

Revealed preference appeared in the argument linking the marginal value curve with the demand curve; your values were revealed by how much you bought at a price. That was how we got to consumer surplus. Consumer surplus was combined with rationality in our proof that a profit-maximizing theater owner would sell popcorn at cost. In classroom discussions of the popcorn problem, I find that many students are unwilling to accept the argument; they believe that consumers (irrationally!) ignore the price of popcorn and simply decide whether or not the movie is worth the price. Perhaps so. The applicability of economics to any form of behavior is an empirical question. What I demonstrated was that if the assumptions of economics apply to popcorn in movie theaters, then the obvious explanation of why it was expensive was wrong.

Rationality appeared a second time in the popcorn problem, applied to the theater owner rather than to his customers. If the theater owner maximizes his profits by selling his popcorn at cost, then rationality implies that that is what he will do. The observation that theater owners apparently sell popcorn for considerably more than it costs them to produce it provides us with a puzzle. One possible conclusion is that economics is wrong. In chapter 10, I hope to persuade you that there are more plausible solutions to the puzzle.

The same assumptions will continue to be applied throughout the rest of the book, as I expand and apply the ideas. One of the things I have learned from writing books is that economics is more complicated than I thought it was. In such an intricately interrelated system of ideas, pointing out every connection would make it almost impossible to follow the analysis. Much of the job of tracing out how and where the different strands are connected you will have to do for yourself.

That is not entirely a bad thing. It has been my experience that I only understand something when I have figured it out for myself. Reading a book can tell you the answer. But until you have fitted the logical pattern together yourself, inside your own head, what you have read is only words.

IN SEARCH OF THE REAL WORLD

9

BOSSES, WORKERS, AND OTHER COMPLICATIONS

The obvious way to coordinate the work of lots of people is to have someone at the top giving orders. We have been discussing a less obvious, but often better, way—voluntary exchange on a market. Much of the economy is coordinated that way—but not all. Seen from the outside, a firm is simply one more market participant, buying and selling like a private individual. But internally, it is a miniature command economy: employers giving orders to supervisors who give orders to workers. The capitalist system of coordination by trade seems to be largely populated by indigestible lumps of socialism called corporations.

This raises three puzzles. The first is why corporations exist—why there is a role for coordination by command even in a market economy. The second is how corporations are controlled—what they try to achieve and why. The third is how the existence of corporations can be incorporated into economic theory—how the analysis of a market populated by individuals can be rewritten with these more complicated actors.

Why Are Firms?

I am looking for a job. There are twenty universities as well suited to me as UCLA and a hundred economists as suitable for UCLA as I am. I accept a job at UCLA, move to southern California, buy a house, and spend a year or two learning to know and work with my colleagues and discovering how to teach UCLA undergraduates (slip lecture cassettes into their Walkmen). When I came to UCLA, my salary was $60,000 a year. Two years later, I am just as productive as expected and enjoy UCLA exactly as much as I expected to. But a problem arises.

The chairman of the department realizes that if I was willing to come for $60,000, I would probably stay even if he reduced my salary to $55,000—after all, there is no way I can get my moving expenses back. He calls me into his office to discuss the tight state of the department's budget.

I am glad to have a chance to talk with the chairman, for I, too, have been considering the situation. For my first two years, my productivity was reduced by the need to learn the ropes. My employers must expect to make enough off me in future years to make up for that loss. Now that I have an opportunity to talk to the chairman, I will explain that, after considering the difficulty of the work I am doing, I believe I am entitled to a substantial raise. After all, there is no way he can get back the money he has lost on me during the first two years.

The competitive market on which I was hired turned into a bilateral monopoly, with potential bargaining costs, once I and my employer had made costly adjustments to each other. The obvious solution is long-term contracting. When I come to UCLA, it is with an agreement specifying my salary for some years into the future.

This solution is itself costly—it constrains us even if circumstances change so that the contract *should* be renegotiated. There is no easy way to distinguish renegotiation motivated by changed circumstances from renegotiation designed to exploit a bilateral monopoly. We could try to make the salary contingent on relevant circumstances (cost of living, university budget, alternative job offers), but there will never be enough small print to cover all of them.

Similar problems exist in other contexts where individuals adapt to each other in order to engage in joint production. Imagine an assembly line on which every worker was an independent subcontractor. At a critical point in production, perhaps the peak of seasonal demand, a single key worker could threaten to shut down production by leaving unless his share of revenue was drastically increased. Here again, a long-term contract, specifying what each participant agrees to contribute and what the penalties are for default, is one solution.

A firm is simply an elaborate long-term contract, part of which is an agreement by employees to do what they are told, within limits, for a stated number of hours a day in exchange for a fixed payment. Its function is to eliminate the transaction costs of using trade to coordinate individuals engaged in interdependent production.

Trade has costs—but so does command. The central problem of the firm is summed up in the Latin phrase *qui custodiet ipsos custodes?*—"Who guards the guardians?" Since the workers receive a fixed wage, their objective is to earn it in the most enjoyable way possible—not necessarily the same behavior that maximizes profits. It is necessary to hire supervisors to make sure the workers do their job. Who, then, is to watch the supervisors? Who is to watch him?

One answer is to have the top supervisor be the *residual claimant*—the person who receives the firm's net revenue as his income. He watches the supervisors below him, they watch the ones below them, and so on. The residual claimant does not have to be watched in order to make him act in the interest of the firm—his interest and the firm's interest are the same.

I have described a firm run by its owner. That is a sensible arrangement if the hardest worker to supervise is the top supervisor; since he is the residual claimant, he supervises himself. But in some firms, the hardest—and most important—person to supervise is not the top manager but some skilled worker on whose output the firm depends—an inventor, for instance, with a firm built around him to support his genius (Browning, Ruger, Dolby). It may make sense for him to be the residual claimant—the owner—and for the top manager to be an employee; that is how such firms are sometimes organized. In other firms, there may be a group of skilled workers who can most easily be supervised by each other: a law partnership, for example.

Another common arrangement is a joint stock corporation, owned neither by its managers nor its workers but by the stockholders who provide much of its capital, and controlled by managers chosen by a board elected by the stockholders.

Even Homer Nods: Smith and the Corporation

Adam Smith, who in the eighteenth century produced the most influential economics book ever written, argued that large joint stock corporations were almost hopelessly incompetent. With ownership widely dispersed, everybody's business is nobody's business; the managers can do what they like with the stockholders' money. Smith predicted that corporations would succeed only with government support, except in a few fields that required lots of capital and very little skill, such as banking and insurance.

He was wrong. Even with no special support from government (save for the privilege of limited liability)—even with special taxes imposed on them—corporations successfully compete with owner-run firms and partnerships in a wide range of fields. At least part of his mistake was failing to predict the benign effects of the takeover bid.

You notice that a corporation is being mismanaged. You buy as much stock as possible—enough to let you take over the corporation, fire most of its executives, and install competent replacements. Earnings shoot up. The market value of your stock shoots up. You sell out and look for another badly managed firm. Such raids are discouraged by securities regulation and corporate managements, but they (and their threat, which helps keep managers honest) may be the reason for the success of the corporation in the modern world.

The arguments that show corporations cannot work apply with still greater force to democratic government—there too, everybody's business is nobody's business. Most voters do not even know the names of most of the politicians who "represent" them. We cannot use takeover bids, or the threat of takeover bids, to keep our government honest and efficient, since votes are not associated with transferable shares—but one can imagine a world where they were.

Each citizen owns one citizenship, which includes one vote. If the country is badly run, someone buys a vast number of citizenships, elects a competent government, and makes a fortune reselling the citizenships at a higher price. The country need not be emptied in the interim; the entrepreneur can always rent his citizenships out between the time he buys them and the time he sells them.

THE THEORY OF THE FIRM

We now know why firms exist, what they try to do (maximize profits), and why. The next step is to incorporate them into our picture of the economy. Like individuals, they appear on both sides of the market— buying and selling. Unlike individuals, their purchases are not for consumption—firms do not eat meals or watch movies—but production.

Up to this point, all production has used a single input—the producer's labor. It is now time to drop that assumption. A firm uses multiple inputs—raw materials, labor, capital goods, land—to produce its output. It must decide what particular bundle of inputs to use, how much output to produce, and what price to sell it for.

PART I: FROM PRODUCTION FUNCTION TO COST CURVE

A sensible first step, on the principle of dividing hard problems into manageable pieces, is to pick a quantity (a thousand television sets), consider all ways of producing that quantity, and select the least expensive. Repeat the calculation for every level of output the firm might want to produce. The result is a total cost curve, showing how much it costs to produce any quantity of output using the least expensive combination of inputs. Once a firm knows its total cost curve, the next step is to calculate what quantity of output maximizes profit: the difference between total cost and total revenue. The firm maximizes its profit by producing that quantity in the least costly way.

We now have a simple description of how a firm acts. The next step is to apply that in two directions: to the firm's behavior as a buyer of inputs and as a producer of output.

The Input Market

I Knew I Had an Equimarginal Principle Lying Around Here Somewhere. The argument that led us to the equimarginal principle in consumption applies in production as well, if we replace marginal value with *marginal product*. The marginal product of an input is the rate at which output increases as the quantity of that input increases, all other inputs held constant. Think of it as the increase in output resulting from one additional unit of input. If adding one worker to a factory employing a thousand, while keeping all other inputs fixed, results in an additional two cars per year, then the marginal product of labor in that factory is two cars per man-year.

How can you produce two more cars with no more steel? Perhaps the additional labor can be used to improve quality control, so that fewer cars have to be scrapped. Or perhaps it makes possible a more labor-intensive production process that produces cars with slightly less steel in them.

If we consider large changes in inputs, this becomes less plausible—it is hard to see how one could produce cars with no raw materials at all, however much labor one used. This is an example of the *law of diminishing returns,* which plays the same role in production as the law of declining marginal value in consumption. If you hold all inputs but one constant and increase that one, eventually its marginal product begins to decline. Each additional man-year of labor increases the number of cars produced by less and less. However much fertilizer you use, you cannot grow the world's supply of wheat in a flowerpot. In just the same way, as you hold all other consumption goods fixed and increase one, eventually the value of each additional unit becomes less and less. I will not trade my life for any number of ice cream cones.

We define the *marginal revenue product* (MRP) of an input as its marginal product multiplied by the revenue the firm gets for each additional unit produced. If an automobile sells for $10,000 and an additional ton of steel increases output by half an automobile, then the marginal revenue product of steel is $5,000 per ton.

Suppose steel costs only $4,000 per ton. If the firm uses an additional two tons of steel while holding all other inputs constant, its production cost increases by $8,000, its output increases by one automobile, its revenue increases by $10,000, and its profit increases by $2,000. As long as the cost of steel is lower than its marginal revenue product, profit can be increased by using more steel. So the firm continues to increase its use of steel until the marginal revenue product of steel equals its price: $MRP = P$. The argument should be familiar—it is the same one used in chapter 4 to show that $MV = P$.

The same relation holds for all inputs, so the marginal revenue product of each is proportional to its price. Once a firm has adjusted its purchases to earn the highest possible profit, an additional dollar's worth of any input produces the same increase in output—one dollar's worth. This is our old friend the equimarginal principle, applied to production instead of consumption.

Firms buy some of their inputs from other firms, but if we go down enough layers we eventually reach a human being—a worker selling his labor, for example. In a simple economy, the price a worker gets for his labor is the value to the consumer of the goods that labor produces. In an economy with firms, wage equals marginal revenue product, so the price a worker receives for his labor from a firm is the value to consumers of the additional goods produced by that labor. The connection is more complicated, especially when the labor passes through multiple firms on its way to the consumer, but the result is still the same. The wage a worker receives measures the value of his work to the human beings who ultimately benefit by it.

Warning. You should not interpret anything I have said as implying that an actual firm, say General Motors, has a list somewhere describing every possible way of producing every conceivable quantity of output and a room full of computers busy twenty-four hours a day figuring the least costly way of doing so. GM is profoundly uninterested in the cost of producing seven automobiles per year or seven billion, and equally uninterested in the possibility of making them out of bubble gum, cardboard, or the labor services of phrenologists.

The fundamental assumption of economics is that people tend to end up making the right decision, which in this case means producing goods at the lowest possible cost. To figure out what that decision is, we imagine how it would be made by a firm with complete information and unlimited ability to process it. In practice, the decision is made by a much more limited process involving a large element of trial and error—but we expect that it will tend to produce the same result. If it does not, and some other practical method does, then some other firm will produce cars at lower cost than GM. Eventually GM will either imitate its competitor's method or go out of business.

Getting Personal. Big firms are distant, abstract, abstruse. It may be easier to understand their production function by thinking of yours, or mine. I, too, use inputs: my own labor, paper, electric power, computer disks, and many others. I produce outputs—including this book. Like the firm, I have to decide how best to trade off different inputs with different costs in the process of finding the best way of producing my output.

Consider the decision of whether to clean up my office. The cost is several hours, perhaps days, of time and effort spent now. The benefit is not spending an extra five minutes every time I want to find anything. Cleaning up my office is a capital investment, made now in exchange for a future return. Pretty clearly, it is worth making. If I want to convince people that I am rational, I had better keep the door closed.

The Output Market: Cost Curves

A production function shows all of the ways of producing output; a total cost function shows the cost of the cheapest way. Think of it as the production function for producing automobiles (or anything else) using only one input—money. The single input is used to hire labor and machinery, buy steel, glass, and rubber, produce automobiles.

From a total cost function, showing how much it costs to produce any number of automobiles, we can deduce a marginal cost function—the extra cost of producing one more automobile. It plays the same role in the production decision of the firm that marginal disvalue plays in the production decision of the individual producer.

Looking at Figure 9–1, you may have noticed that I have drawn marginal cost intersecting average cost at its lowest point. There is a reason for that. If marginal cost is above average cost, that means that additional units cost more to produce than the average of the units already produced, so additional production pulls up average

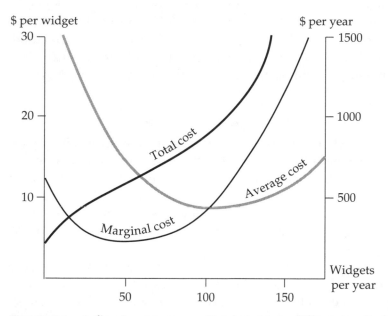

Figure 9-1   A firm's cost curves. Total cost is in different units from marginal and average cost, so the former uses the right vertical axis and the left.

cost. If marginal cost is below average cost, increased production adds units that cost less than the average, pulling the average down. The same thing would happen if you calculated the average height of a basketball team and then decided to average in the coach.

Before the two curves cross, marginal cost is below average cost, so average cost is falling. After they cross, marginal cost is above average cost, so average cost is rising. Since average cost is falling before the intersection and rising after, the intersection is at the minimum of average cost.

At this point that result may seem academic in the worst sense of the term, the sort of thing useful only for creating questions for multiple choice exams—which are useful only because they are easier to grade than real exams. In chapter 16, the fact that marginal cost intersects average cost at the latter's minimum turns out to be a key element in the proof of one of the most surprising, and important, results in all of economics. Stay tuned.

Why Do Cost Curves Look like That?

Average cost curves in economics books usually have the shape shown in the figure—starting high, falling to some minimum, then rising again. The reason is the shifting balance between economies and diseconomies of scale.

Economies of scale are ways in which large firms can produce more cheaply than small ones. One source of such economies is mass production; a firm producing a million widgets per year can set up assembly lines, buy special widget-making machinery, and so forth. Another source may be economies of scale in administration; a large firm can have one executive to deal with advertising and another with personnel. Economies of scale are usually important only up to some maximum size; that is why a large firm, such as GM or U.S. Steel, does not consist of one gigantic factory, as it would if such a factory could produce at a substantially lower cost than several large factories.

There are also diseconomies of scale. One important source of them has already been discussed: the conflict of interest between employees and owners. This problem is "solved" by supervisors who watch the employees, give raises to those who work hard, and fire those who do not. Since such monitoring is neither costless nor perfectly effective, every additional layer increases costs and reduces performance. The more layers there are, the more the employees find themselves pursuing, not the interest of the firm, but what they think the person above them thinks the person above him thinks is the interest of the firm. Seen from this standpoint, the ideal arrangement is the one-person firm; if its sole employee chooses to slack off, he, being also the owner of the firm, pays all of the cost in reduced profits.

Once, when choosing a publisher, I had offers from two firms, one substantially larger and more prestigious than the other. I ended up choosing the smaller firm, in large part because in dealing with it I felt as though I was conversing with human beings, not training manuals on how to deal with authors. I suspect that the people I dealt with at the smaller firm were several layers closer to the top than their opposite numbers at the larger firm. My editor there, to whom I owe one of the economics jokes in this book, is now a vice president.

If there were only economies of scale, we would expect to see an economy with one firm per industry. If there were only diseconomies of scale, we would expect an economy of one-person firms, cooperating by trading goods and services with each other. What we actually see is an economy with a wide range of firm sizes, reflecting differences in the point at which diseconomies of scale begin to outweigh economies of scale in different industries.

How to Make Money

The firm's profit is the difference between what it takes in (*total revenue*—the quantity produced times the price for which it is sold) and what it spends (total cost). As long as the price it sells one more car for is higher than the cost of producing that car, the firm increases its profit by producing another car. It keeps doing so until it reaches a level of output at which the cost of producing one more car is equal to the price it can be sold for: marginal cost equals price.

What if the price is so low that there is no quantity of output for which the firm can cover its cost—price is below average cost everywhere? If the firm tries to "maximize" its profit by producing where $MC = P$, the gain on units produced at a cost below the price they sell for will be more than wiped out by the loss on earlier units, produced at a cost higher than they can be sold for; the maximum profit is negative. The firm is better off shutting down.

We now know, for any price, how much a firm will produce. It

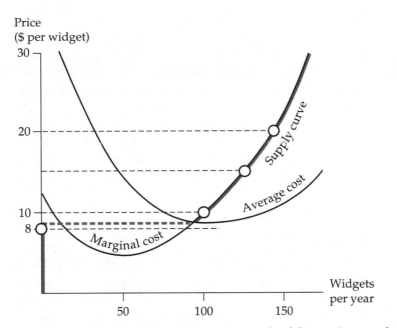

Figure 9-2   The quantity produced at each of four prices, and the resulting supply curve. As long as price is above the minimum of average cost, the firm maximizes its profit by producing a quantity for which $P = MC$. At lower prices, it shuts down and produces nothing. So the supply curve S is the marginal cost curve above its intersection with average cost.

produces nothing if the price is below the minimum of average cost. If price is above minimum average cost, the firm maximizes profit by producing the quantity for which marginal cost equals price. The firm's supply curve is the marginal cost curve above its intersection with average cost. Figure 9–2 shows a series of different prices, and for each, the quantity the firm chooses to produce.

The individual producer of chapter 5 also had a supply curve that was equal to a marginal cost curve—the marginal cost to him of his own time. I explained the horizontal segment of a firm's supply curve by saying that below some price, the profit from producing is negative, so it is better not to produce. I explained the horizontal segment of the individual supply curve by the existence of a price for one good below which the producer is better off producing something else.

The two explanations are the same. One cost of using your time to mow lawns is that you are not cooking meals at the same time. How great is that cost? It is equal to what you could make by cooking meals. If the hourly return from mowing is less than the hourly return from cooking, then mowing produces a negative profit—when the opportunity cost of not cooking is taken into account. In chapter 5, it was convenient to think of the "cost of working" as the "disvalue of labor"—sore muscles, boredom, and the like. But that is only one example of a more general sort of cost. The cost of mowing lawns is whatever you give up in order to do so, whether that is the pleasure of lying in bed reading science fiction or the income from washing dishes.

Industry Supply Curve: First Try

From the standpoint of one firm in a large industry, the price at which it buys its inputs is given, since the amount it buys is not enough to have a significant effect. That is not true from the standpoint of the industry as a whole. If one farmer doubles the amount of wheat he plants, he need not worry about the effect of that decision on the price of fertilizer or the wages of farm laborers, but if every farmer doubles his planting, fertilizer prices and farm wages are likely to rise.

Once we take account of these effects, it is no longer true, as it was in chapter 5, that the industry supply curve is simply the horizontal sum of the individual supply curves of the producers. Each firm calculates its supply curve with the price of inputs held fixed. But for the industry as a whole, increased production means higher prices of inputs, shifting up every firm's supply curve. In order to induce the auto industry to produce more cars, the price must rise not only enough to move each firm out along its supply curve but also enough more to make up for the increased price the firms must pay for steel due to the increased demand due to the increased production of automobiles.

This raises an interesting problem with regard to producer surplus. Back in chapter 5, the producer surplus calculated from the summed supply curves of several producers was simply the sum of producer surplus calculated for each producer. That was an important result, since it meant that to calculate the overall effect on producers of something—a tax or a regulation, say—all we needed was the supply curve for the industry.

That no longer works here. The supply curve for an industry is

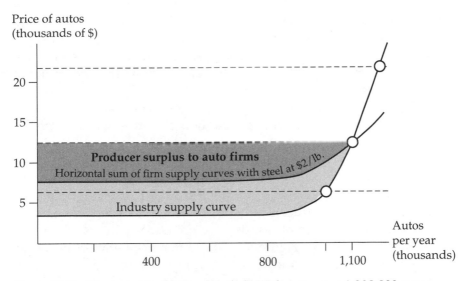

Figure 9-3   Firm and industry surplus. With output at 1,300,000 autos per year and steel at $2 per pound, producer surplus calculated from the firm supply curves (dark gray is less than producer surplus calculated from the industry supply curve (dark and light gray).

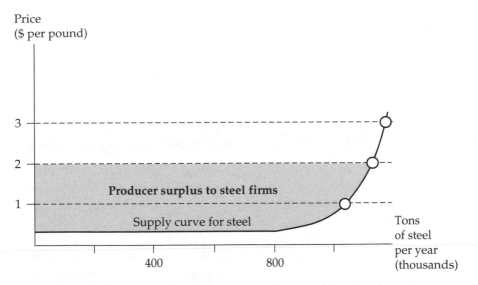

Figure 9-4   Industry surplus going to producers of inputs. As auto output increases, the industry's increased consumption of steel bids up the price, generating producer surplus for the steel producers.

no longer the sum of the supply curves of the firms—it rises more steeply, because of the effect of increased output on the price of inputs, as shown in Figure 9–3. The producer surplus of the industry is greater than the producer surplus of the firms that make it up! What have we missed?

The answer is in Figure 9–4. The auto firms on Figure 9–3 are not the only producers who benefit from their output—there are also the producers of steel. If more cars are produced, more steel will be required to produce them—increasing its price. If we had drawn the figures precisely and to scale, using actual production functions, the shaded area in Figure 9–4, representing the producer surplus received by the producers of steel when auto production is at 1,100,000 and the price of iron is $2 a pound, would just equal the lightly shaded area in Figure 9–2, the difference between producer surplus calculated from the industry supply curve and producer surplus calculated from the firm supply curves. Some of the producer surplus received by the automobile industry is being passed through the automobile firms to the firms (and ultimately the individuals) that produce their inputs.

FREE ENTRY: THE SOAP BUBBLE ECONOMY

So far in the analysis we have held the number of firms in the industry fixed. But in an ordinary competitive industry, firms are soap bubbles, popping into and out of existence. High prices make it worth starting new firms, low prices make it worth shutting down old ones.

When price increases, some of the resulting increase in output comes from new firms started to take advantage of the higher price. This is the same situation we encountered in chapter 5, when we noted that as the price of a good increases, more and more people find that they are better off producing it than producing anything else, so a higher price results in output from new producers as well as increased output by those already producing that good.

If all firms, actual and potential, have the same cost curves, the result is a very simple supply curve for the industry. If existing firms are making positive profits—if their total revenue is larger than their total cost—it pays new firms to come into existence, driving down the price. If existing firms are making negative profits, it pays some to go out of business, driving up the price.

There is only one possible equilibrium—the price at which revenue exactly covers cost. If revenue exactly covers cost, average cost must be equal to price. We already know that each firm is producing an output for which marginal cost equals price. So the equilibrium of the whole industry occurs where price, marginal cost, and average cost are all equal.

If the firm produces where marginal cost equals average cost, then, as we saw earlier in the chapter, average cost is at its minimum. So in equilibrium each firm produces at minimum average cost and sells its product for a price that just covers all costs. The supply curve for the industry is simply a horizontal line at price equal to minimum average cost. Increases in demand increase the number of firms and the quantity of output, with price unaffected.

You may be puzzled by the assertion that new firms come into existence as soon as existing firms start making a profit; surely entrepreneurs require not merely some profit but enough to reimburse them for the time and trouble of starting a new firm. But profit is defined as revenue minus cost, and cost, for economists if not for accountants, includes the cost to the entrepreneur of his own time and trouble. If firms are making positive profits, that means that they are more than repaying their owners for the costs of starting them.

What about a company owned by its stockholders? For accounting purposes, its profit is what is left after paying for labor, raw materials, and interest on loans; it is what the stockholders get in exchange for their investment. But for economic purposes, capital provided by the stockholders is an input, and its opportunity cost—what the stockholders could have gotten by investing the same money elsewhere—is one of the costs of production. So the firm makes an economic profit only if it makes enough to pay the stockholders more than the normal market return on their investment. If so, that is a good reason for new firms to enter the industry.

TWO ROADS TO AN UPWARD-SLOPED SUPPLY CURVE

The supply curves in chapters 5 and 7 sloped up; more output required higher prices. The last few paragraphs, however, seem to imply a horizontal supply curve. If new firms start producing every time price rises above minimum average cost, we should be able to get unlimited output at a constant price. What have I left out?

I have left out the effect of increases in the size of the industry on the price of its inputs. If the output of automobiles increases, so does the demand for steel, autoworkers, and Detroit real estate. As the demand for these things increases, their prices rise. As the price of the inputs increases, so does average cost; the result is a rising supply curve.

In a competitive industry with free entry, profit is competed down to zero, so firms receive no producer surplus. But if the industry supply curve slopes up, the industry as a whole must have producer surplus. The explanation is that all of the producer surplus passes through the firms to the suppliers of their inputs. If the suppliers are themselves competitive firms with free entry, it passes through them to their suppliers, until it eventually ends up in the hands of the ultimate suppliers—workers renting out their labor, landowners renting out their land, and so forth.

So far we have assumed that all firms are identical. Another way of getting upward-sloping supply curves is by assuming that some firms are better at producing than others. As output price rises, worse and worse firms are pulled into the market. The price, at any level of production, must be high enough to cover the costs of the highest-cost firm that is producing—the *marginal firm;* otherwise it will not produce. It must not be high enough to cover the costs of the next higher cost firm, the most efficient potential firm that is *not* producing—otherwise that firm would enter the market too.

These two ways of getting upward-sloping supply curves are really the same. The reason input costs eventually rise with increasing demand for inputs is that there is not an unlimited supply of identical inputs. There are only so many skilled automakers willing to work for $12 an hour. To get more, you must pay more, inducing those presently employed to work more hours and luring additional workers into the industry. The same applies to land, raw materials, and capital goods. The reason firms do not all have the same cost curves is that some possess inputs that others lack—a particularly skilled manager, an unusually good machine, a favorable location. It is because of the limited supply of those particular inputs that increased production must use worse machines, less skillful managers, worse locations—or pay more in order to attract high-quality inputs away from wherever they are presently being used.

So long as the scarce inputs belong to the firm—consisting, for instance, of the talents of the firm's proprietor or real estate belonging to a corporation—the distinction between a better production function and scarce assets may not be very important. Seen one way, the firm receives positive profits from its operations and turns them over to its owners; seen the other, its profits are zero, but its owners receive income on scarce resources that they rent to the firm. It is a more important distinction when the scarce asset belongs to the firm's landlord or one of its employees. When the relevant contracts are next renegotiated, the firm is likely to find that its positive profit was purely a short-run phenomenon.

THE MYTH OF CORPORATE TAX

Quite a lot of political demagoguery depends on not noticing that benefits to an industry pass through the firms to individuals. "Producers" are identified with firms, heartless corporations. Who can object to taxes or regulations that impose costs on them—why not starve the greedy corporations to feed the people?

But corporations lack not only hearts but also stomachs, which makes it difficult to starve them. Costs imposed upon corporations are passed on to some human being, whether worker, customer, supplier, or stockholder. There is no point in arguing about whether or not to tax corporations—corporations have no consumption to give up, and so cannot be taxed. We can only tax people through corporations.

SUMMING IT UP

We have spent much of this chapter deriving the supply curve for an industry of many firms; the process has contained enough complications and detours that you may well have lost track of just how we did it. This is a convenient place to recapitulate.

We start with a production function—a description of what quantity of output can be produced with any bundle of inputs. We calculate a total cost curve by finding the cost of the least expensive bundle of inputs necessary to produce each level of output. From that total cost curve—total cost of production as a function of quantity produced—we calculate average cost and marginal cost curves. From those we calculate a supply curve for the firm; each firm maximizes its profit by producing that quantity for which marginal cost equals price—unless, at that quantity, price is still below average cost, in which case the firm produces nothing and exits the industry.

Once we have the supply curve for the firm, we are ready to find the supply curve for the industry. If new firms are free to enter the industry, equilibrium profit must be zero, since positive profit attracts firms into the industry, driving down the market price, while nega-tive profit drives firms out, raising the market price. In the simplest case—identical firms able to buy all the inputs they want without affecting their price—the result is a horizontal supply curve for the industry's output at a price equal to the minimum average cost of the firm. In more complicated cases, the result is a rising supply curve. Price is still equal to minimum average cost—or if firms are not iden-tical, it is between the minimum average cost of the highest-cost firm that is producing and the minimum average cost of the lowest-cost firm that is not.

Industry Equilibrium and Benevolent Dictation

The outcome we have just described—competitive equilibrium with free entry—has some interesting features. Suppose you were appointed industry czar and told to produce the same output at the lowest possible cost. You would arrange things just as they are arranged in this solution—with each firm producing at minimum average cost.

A second interesting feature is that the price of a good to a con-sumer is equal to the cost of producing it: $P = MC$. A consumer will buy a good only if it is worth at least that much to him—in which case it is, in some sense, worth producing. Both of these points will be discussed in more detail in chapter 16.

PRODUCTION AND EXPLOITATION

There is a sense in which nothing is produced. The laws of physics tell us that the sum total of mass and energy can be neither increased nor reduced. What we call "production" is the rearrangement of mat-ter and energy from less useful to more useful (to us) forms.

It is sometimes said that middlemen—retailers and whole-salers—merely move things about while absorbing some of the value that other people have produced. But all *anyone* does is to move things about—to rearrange from less to more useful. The producer rearranges iron ore and other inputs into automobiles; the retailer rearranges automobiles on a lot into automobiles paired up with par-ticular customers. Both increase the value of what they work on and collect their income out of that increase.

It is often said that some participants in the economy exploit others—most commonly that employers exploit workers. Two different definitions of exploitation are implicit—simultaneously—in such discussions. The first is that I exploit you if I benefit by your existence. In this sense, I hope to exploit my wife and she hopes to exploit me; so far we have both succeeded. If that is what exploitation means, then it is the reason that humans are social animals and not, like cats, solitary ones.

The friends who rent our third floor are enthusiastic gardeners; we are not. We get free gardening; they get free use of a yard to garden in. Who is exploiting whom?

The second definition is that I exploit you if I gain *and you lose* by our association. The connection between the two can be made either by claiming that the world is a zero-sum game in which one person can gain only at another person's expense, or by arguing that if I gain by our association you deserve to have the gain given to you, so my refusal to give it to you injures you. The former argument is implausible. The second has a curious asymmetry. If I give you all the gain, you have now gained by our association and should give it all back to me. It may be more sensible to keep "exploitation" out of discussions of economics and reserve it for political invective.

10

MONOPOLY FOR FUN
AND PROFIT

The industries in chapter 9 were made up of lots of firms, each producing only a small fraction of industry output. Such a firm is a *price taker*—it takes the market price as given and assumes it can sell as much as it wants at that price. This is a pretty good description of the wheat industry and the paper industry, and quite a lot of others, but not so good for car makers, or local telephone service, or the one general store in a small town. Such firms are *price searchers*—they can sell goods at a considerable range of prices, although they sell fewer goods the more they charge. Suppose you are running such a firm— suppose, to make matters simple, you are the only firm in your industry. How should you act, what price should you charge, so as to maximize your profit?

This question is relevant to CEOs of multibillion-dollar firms, but also to me. There are other authors who write about economics. But, as I hope you have discovered by now, none of them write quite the same sort of book I do. So if you define my market narrowly—as a certain sort of economics writing—the one-man firm writing this book is a monopoly.

The first issue facing me (actually my publishers, but I am assuming HarperCollins out of existence for purposes of this example) is what price to charge. If I were in a perfectly competitive industry, that would be easy—there is no point to charging less than the market price, and I cannot sell anything if I charge more. But as a monopoly I face a more complicated situation. The higher my price, the fewer books I will sell.

Revenue is quantity times price; if I sell a hundred thousand books at $10 apiece, I collect a million dollars. What I want to maximize is not revenue but profit, however, and books cost something to produce. Suppose, for simplicity, that the marginal cost of producing this book is $10 a copy. That is the extra cost of producing one more copy—it does not include my time and trouble writing the book or the expenses of editing, typesetting, and the like. Assume those additional costs (called *fixed costs* because they do not depend on how many copies of the book are produced) total $100,000.

In the previous chapter, I argued that firms in a competitive industry would maximize their profit by charging a price equal to marginal cost. If I imitate them by charging $10 for the book, I will lose $100,000—not a very attractive outcome. Suppose I instead charge $15 a book. At that price, as shown on the demand curve of Figure 10–1, I sell only seventy-five thousand books. But since I am now getting more for each book than it costs me to produce it, there is something left over to go to fixed costs—$375,000 left over, to be precise. After paying $100,000 of fixed cost, I have a little over a quarter of a million left.

This is an improvement over selling at marginal cost—but can I do better? One way of finding out would be to redo the calculation for lots of different prices and find the one that maximizes my profit. A more organized procedure is to calculate *marginal revenue*—the increase in revenue for each additional book sold—as a function of how many books I am selling. As long as marginal revenue is larger than marginal cost, each additional book sold increases my profit. So I keep increasing quantity until I reach the point where marginal cost equals marginal revenue. I sell fifty thousand books at $20 apiece, receive $1,000,000, deduct $500,000 in production cost and $100,000 in fixed cost, and am left with a $400,000 profit—and eager to write a sequel.

This procedure for maximizing profit should sound familiar; setting marginal cost equal to marginal revenue is exactly what the firms of the previous chapter did. The difference is that a firm in a

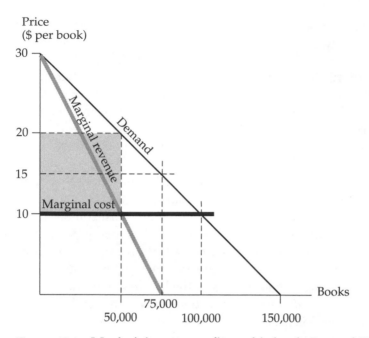

Figure 10-1   Maximizing my profit on this book. Beyond 50,000, each additional book increases revenue by less than it increases cost, so sales beyond that point would reduce profit. The gray square is my gross profit of $500,000; subtracting fixed cost gives me a net profit of $400,000.

competitive industry can sell as many units as it wants at the market price, so the additional revenue from selling one more unit is simply the price it sells for. A monopoly, on the other hand, can increase sales only by cutting price. So the marginal revenue from selling one more book is the price I sell that book for minus the loss in revenue from having to cut my price a little on all the other books I sell in order to sell one more. That is why the marginal revenue curve on Figure 10–1 is below the demand curve; at any quantity, marginal revenue is less than price.

In Figure 10–1, the demand curve is a straight line. It happens that for a straight-line demand curve, marginal revenue is also a straight line, running from the vertical intercept of demand (the price at which quantity demanded is zero) to one-half the horizontal intercept (half the quantity that would be demanded at a price of zero), as shown in the figure. This fact is of no significance at all for economics, since there is no reason to expect real-world demand curves to be straight lines, but it is very convenient for drawing figures.

I have been assuming so far that all copies of my book will be sold at the same price—that is why, when I lowered the price to sell an additional book, I also had to lower it on the copies that would have sold at a higher price. This suggests an obvious strategy for increasing my profit—sell at different prices to different customers, charging a higher price to those willing to pay it.

There are practical problems with such *price discrimination*, although not necessarily insoluble ones. If I announce that the first fifty thousand copies of my book will cost $20 each and after that I will drop my price to $15, everyone may decide to wait—with the result that I will sell no copies at all. I could try to sell at a high price to particularly well-dressed customers, on the theory that they are probably well off enough to be willing to pay it, but if they catch on they may start taking off their ties before they come into the bookstore. Even if I have some reliable way of telling how rich people are—perhaps a friend who works for the IRS—I still have to worry about poor people buying the book at a low price and reselling it to rich people.

One solution popular in the book industry is to produce two versions of the product, one of somewhat higher quality than the other, and to sell the higher-quality version (called a hardcover) at a price that more than covers the increased production cost. Now customers self-select. The ones who really want the book, and would be willing to pay a higher price even for the paperback, are also the ones who will prefer the hardcover. For some kinds of books, such as entertainment fiction by popular authors, higher quality is combined with earlier publication. Only a few of us have enough willpower, when a new Dick Francis or the latest volume of a David Drake series comes out in hardcover, to wait for the paperback.

The same tactic can be used in other industries. The price difference between tourist and first class, or between the economy and the luxury version of a car, may reflect differences in production cost—but it may also be a way of getting more money out of those willing to spend more. Sometimes the source of the price difference is unambiguous—because there are no differential costs. A few years back, Intel was selling 386 microprocessors in two versions, one with and one without a numeric coprocessor. The price difference between the two might have reflected a difference in production costs—but not when the less expensive chip was being made from the more expensive by disabling the coprocessor.

A more familiar example is the policy of charging less for children than for adults at movie theaters. A child takes up as much space as an adult—one seat—and may well impose higher costs, in noise and mess, on the theater and the other patrons. Why, then, do theaters often charge lower prices for children? The obvious answer is that children are usually poorer than adults; a price the theater can get adults to pay is likely to discourage children from coming—or parents with several children from bringing them.

A similar example is the youth fare that airlines used to offer: a low-cost standby ticket, offered only to those under a certain age. The lower fare reflected in part the advantage to the airlines of using standby passengers to fill empty seats, but that does not explain the age limit. The obvious explanation is that making the fare available to everyone might have resulted in a substantial number of customers "trading down"—buying a cheap standby ticket instead of an expensive regular one. The airlines hoped that making it available to youths would result in their buying a cheap standby ticket on an airplane instead of taking the bus, driving, or hitching.

Another way of separating customers by willingness to pay is to sell at different prices through different channels. An example is the Book-of-the-Month Club. A publisher who gives a special rate to a book club is getting customers most of whom would not otherwise have bought the book; since most of those who are willing to buy the book at the regular rate are not members of the club, he is only stealing a few sales from himself.

A more recent example of the same approach is the practice of selling computers with lots of "free" software already on them. Many of the purchasers are people to whom the software is worth something, but not enough to make them willing to buy it—and most of the people the software producer wants to sell to already have a computer.

A firm that wants to engage in price discrimination faces two practical problems. The first is the problem of distinguishing customers who will buy the good at a high price from those who will not. In the examples I have given, that is done indirectly—by dress, taste, membership in a discount book club, or the like. A more direct solution is said to be used by some optometrists. When the customer asks how much a new pair of glasses will cost, the optometrist replies, "sixty dollars." If the customer does not flinch, he adds "for the lenses." If the customer still does not flinch, he adds, "each."

This account of selling glasses may be apocryphal, but something rather similar is standard business practice in selling houses. When I asked a realtor to find a house for me to buy, one of her first questions was, "How much do you want to spend?" To an economist, this seems an odd question; how much I want to spend, on houses or anything else, depends on what I can get for my money. But realtors get a commission calculated as a fixed fraction of the price of each house they sell—so it is in their interest to get the customer to buy the most expensive house he can afford. One obvious way of doing it is to first find out how much the customer is willing to pay, then select houses to show him accordingly.

The second problem is preventing resale. It does no good to offer your product at a low price to poor customers if they turn around and resell it to rich ones. This is why discriminatory pricing is so often observed for goods consumed on the producer's premises— transportation, movies, medical treatment. If Ford sells cars at a high price to rich customers and at a low price to poor ones, Rockefeller can send his chauffeur to buy a car for him. There is little point in having the chauffeur take a trip for Rockefeller or see a movie for him.

So far, we have been talking about how to charge different prices to different customers. There is another form of price discrimination that does not depend on differences among customers—indeed, that works best if all customers are identical. It is time to abandon books and shift to something tastier.

DOUGH FROM COOKIES

You have a thousand customers for your cookie bakery, all identical. The demand curve you face is simply the demand curve of a single customer (Figure 10–2) multiplied by a thousand. Each additional cookie costs you $0.40 to make. You are an expert at making cookies from dough and are trying to use economics to figure out how to reverse the process.

The figure shows your first attempt—sell cookies at the price ($0.70) that maximizes your profit, where marginal revenue equals marginal cost. The lightly shaded area is your gross profit on each customer ($0.30 per cookie, equal to price minus marginal cost, times six cookies per customer). To find your net profit you would have to subtract fixed cost, but that does not depend on how you price your cookies or how many you sell, so we can ignore it at this point. It becomes relevant only if it turns out that fixed cost is greater than gross profit, making net profit negative—in which case you should go out of business.

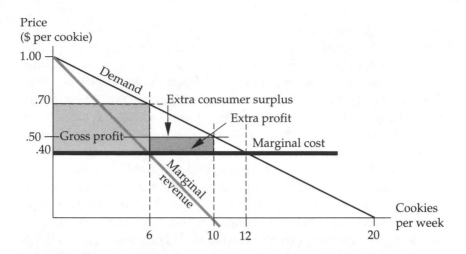

Figure 10-2　Discriminatory pricing in the cookie industry—first try. The profit-maximizing single price is $0.70 per cookie. The firm charges each customer that price for the first six cookies but sells additional cookies for $0.50 per cookie, increasing its profit by the shaded area.

Looking at the figure, you notice that, up to a quantity of twelve cookies per week, additional cookies are worth more to the customer than they cost to produce. It seems a pity to lose those additional sales—and the money that could be made on them. You get an idea:

> As a special favor to our customers, and in order to celebrate the tercentennial of the invention of the cookie, we are cutting our prices. For the first six cookies per week purchased by each customer, the old price of $0.70 remains in effect, but additional cookies may be purchased for only $0.50 each.

The result is shown on the figure. Each customer buys ten cookies: six at $0.70 each and four more at the reduced price of $0.50. The customers are better off than before by the additional consumer surplus on the extra cookies; you are better off by the profit on the additional cookies.

You are doing pretty well, but that is no reason to rest on your laurels. Figure 10-3a shows the more elaborate price schedule released for the next year. The first cookie a customer buys costs $0.95, the next $0.90, and so on down the demand curve. The shaded

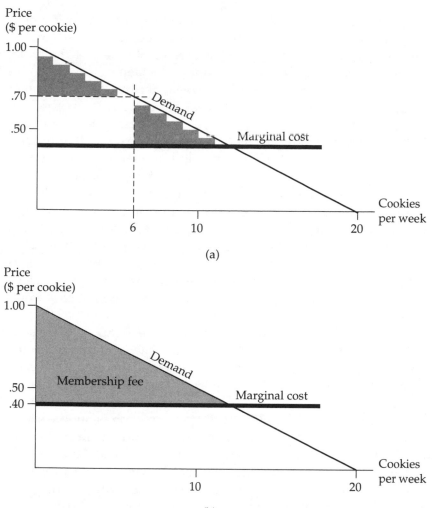

Figures 10-3a & b   Discriminatory pricing in the cookie industry—improved versions. In Figure 10–3a, cookies are sold on a sliding scale starting at $0.95 per cookie. In Figure 10–3b, the price is $0.40 per cookie, but cookies are sold only to customers who pay $3.60 for membership in the cookie club.

area is the increase in profit above what you could make if you charged the same price for every cookie.

Figure 10–3a is very close to *perfect discriminatory pricing*—a price schedule that transfers all consumer surplus to the producer. There is an easier way to do the same thing. The next year, you announce a new pricing policy, shown in Figure 10-3b. Cookies will no longer be sold to the general public—only to members of the cookie club. Members can buy cookies at cost—$0.40 per cookie—and may buy as many as they wish at that price. The membership fee for the cookie club is $3.60 a week. That, by a curious coincidence, is just equal to the consumer surplus received by a consumer free to buy as many cookies as he wants at a price of $0.40 a cookie. This *two-part price* (membership plus per-cookie charge) first maximizes the sum of consumer and producer surplus by inducing the consumer to buy every cookie that is worth at least as much to him as it costs to produce, then transfers the entire consumer surplus to the producer.

Since all consumer surplus is transferred to the producer, he gets the sum of what would normally be consumer and producer surplus. He maximizes that sum by setting price equal to marginal cost. If he charged more than that, he would be losing the opportunity to sell to customers who valued a cookie at more than it cost him to produce it. If he charged less, he would be selling cookies that were not worth what they cost. A price either above or below marginal cost would reduce total surplus—and thus his profit.

If you think this sounds familiar, you are right. It is the same argument used at the end of chapter 4 to show why movie theaters should sell popcorn at cost. It is also a pricing strategy used by sellers of telephone services, electricity, and a variety of other goods and services.

One problem with discriminatory pricing is preventing resale. It occurs here when a cookie club member buys forty-eight cookies per week, eats twelve, and sells thirty-six to friends who have not paid for membership in the cookie club. That is why two-part (or more generally multipart) pricing is more practical with electricity or health spa services than with cookies. Perhaps you had better warn your customers that, due to the risk of lurking cookie monsters, the cookies you sell should all be consumed on the premises.

So far all your customers have been identical—at least in their demand for cookies. Your latest market research study reveals a disturbing new trend; customers are splitting into two different groups. Half retain their old demand curve (D_A on Figure 10–4), but the other half, frightened by the new blockbuster movie *The Cookie That Ate the World*, are no longer as fond of cookies as they used to be (D_B).

If you retain your old pricing system, customers of type A will continue to join the club and buy the cookies, but customers of type B will find that the cookie club costs more than it is worth and refuse to join. You can do somewhat better by cutting the membership fee to

Price
($ per cookie)

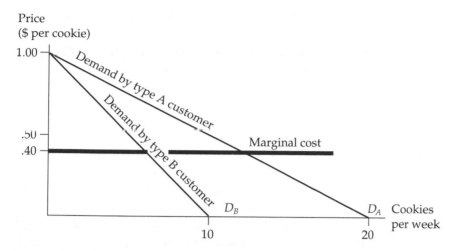

Figure 10-4 **The case of nonidentical customers.** D_A is the demand curve for type A customers; D_B is the demand curve for type B customers.

$2.40 a week (the consumer surplus for type B consumers) and getting everyone to join. But that still leaves the type A customers with surplus that obviously ought to go to you.

One solution would be to figure out which customers are of which type, raise the membership fee to $3.60, and offer a "special discount membership" to the type B customers. An alternative is to let the customers tell you which group they are in by how many cookies they buy. By raising the per-cookie price while cutting the membership fee, you can raise the cost to type A customers—who are the ones willing to pay more—while keeping the type B customers.

It is straightforward to calculate that a price of $0.50 per cookie and a membership fee of $1.667 produces a larger total profit than a price of $0.40 and a membership fee of $2.40. You are charging your customers more than the marginal cost of producing cookies, with the result that you are no longer maximizing the total surplus—but you are no longer able to collect all of the surplus, and the higher price increases the share that goes to you.

We finally have a possible solution to the popcorn puzzle. In my previous discussion, I assumed that theater customers were all identical; if that assumption holds, so does the conclusion—that the theater should sell popcorn at marginal cost and make its profit on admission tickets. But if customers are not identical and if those who are willing to pay a high price for a ticket tend to be the ones who buy a lot of popcorn, then the combination of cheap tickets and expensive popcorn may be an indirect way of charging a high admission price to those willing to pay it without driving away those who are not.

DON'T TRY THIS IN THE WHEAT BUSINESS

The ability of a firm to engage in successful discriminatory pricing depends on its having some degree of monopoly power. In a market with many firms producing virtually identical products, price discrimination is impractical; if one firm tries to sell the product at an especially high price to rich customers, or customers who very much want the product, another will find it in its interest to lure those customers away with a lower price. Airlines do not want their own customers to trade down to a cheaper ticket—but Delta has no objection to getting a customer to give up a first-class ticket on United in order to buy a tourist ticket on Delta.

My examples of discriminatory pricing have all involved some element of monopoly. Youth fares existed at a time when airline fares were controlled by the Civil Aeronautics Board (CAB), a regulatory agency that provided government enforcement for a private cartel, keeping rates up and new firms out; they have since disappeared along with airline regulation. Copyright laws (and the economics of publishing) give each book publisher a monopoly—not of books but of a particular book. So publishers are price searchers; each knows that some customers are willing to pay a high price, while others will buy the book only if they can get it at a low price. Movie theaters have an element of monopoly, at least in areas where they are scarce enough that a customer cannot conveniently pick among several showing the same film.

WHY IS A MONOPOLY?

Why do monopolies exist? Why, if revenue is greater than cost, do not other firms choose to start producing the same product?

One answer may be that if they do, the monopolist will call the police. The original meaning of *monopoly* was an exclusive right to sell something. Typically such monopolies were either sold by the government as a way of raising money or given to people the government liked, such as relatives of the king's mistresses. Monopolies of this sort are still common. An example is the post office: the Private Express Statutes make direct competition illegal.

A second possibility is a *natural monopoly*. This occurs when, because of economies of scale, a firm large enough to produce the total output of the industry has a lower average cost than any smaller firm. If such a large firm is formed and sells at a price above its average cost but below the average cost of a smaller firm, smaller firms will not find it worth their while to enter the market.

Most people who think about natural monopolies imagine gigantic firms such as Bell Telephone or GM. It is widely believed that such firms, by taking advantage of mass production, can produce more cheaply than any smaller firm and that free competition thus leads to monopoly. As George Orwell put it, "The trouble with competitions is that somebody wins them."

This is a better description of athletics than of economics. While economies of scale exist, they are usually swamped by diseconomies of scale, costs due to the increasing distance between the president and the factory floor, at a size well below the size of an entire industry. Big natural monopolies are uncommon. GM is a very large firm but it is far too small to monopolize the world auto industry.

My monopoly over the production of a certain kind of writing is a better example of natural monopoly than the situation of Bell or GM. It is due not to the huge scale of production but to the specialized nature of the product. Similar monopolies would be your favorite thriller writer or Aiello's, the only Italian restaurant in the town of Whitney Point, New York (and the best for many miles around—free plug). Such small monopolies are not only much more common than big ones, they are also much more important to you. It is unlikely that you will ever be the head of GM or U.S. Steel, and if you are, you may find your monopoly power surprisingly limited. It is much more likely that you will find yourself selling a specialized product in a particular geographical area, and so functioning as a price searcher facing a downward-sloped demand curve.

Artificial Monopoly

Suppose economies and diseconomies of scale roughly balance so that, over a wide range of production, big firms and small firms can produce at about the same cost. It is widely believed that such a situation is likely to lead to an *artificial monopoly;* the usual example is the Standard Oil Trust under John D. Rockefeller.

I am Rockefeller and have somehow gotten control of 90 percent of the petroleum industry. My firm, Standard Oil, has immense revenues, from which it accumulates great wealth; its resources are far larger than the resources of any smaller oil company or even all of them put together. As long as other firms exist and compete with me, I can earn only the normal return on my capital—economic profit equals zero.

I decide to drive out my competitors by cutting prices below average cost. Both I and my competitors lose money; since I have more money to lose, they go under first. I now raise prices to a monopoly level. If any new firm considers entering the market to take advantage of the high prices, I point out what happened to my previous competitors and threaten to repeat the performance if necessary.

This argument is an example of the careless use of verbal analysis. "Both I and my competitors are losing money" sounds as though we are losing the same amount of money. We are not. If I am selling 90 percent of all petroleum, a particular competitor is selling 1 percent, and we both sell at the same price and have the same average cost, I lose $90 for every $1 he loses.

My situation is worse than that. By cutting prices, I have caused the quantity demanded to increase; if I want to keep the price down, I must increase my production—and losses—accordingly. So I must actually lose (say) $95 for every $1 my competitor loses. My competitor, who is not trying to hold down the price, may be able to reduce his losses and increase mine by cutting his production, forcing me to sell still more oil at a loss. He can cut his losses by mothballing older refineries, running some plants half-time, and failing to replace employees who move or retire. For every $95 I lose, he loses (say) $0.50.

But although I am bigger and richer than he is, I am not infinitely bigger and richer; I am ninety times as big and about ninety times as rich. I am losing money more than ninety times as fast as he is; if I keep trying to drive him out by selling below cost, it is I, not he, who will go bankrupt first. Despite the widespread belief that Rockefeller maintained his position by selling oil below cost in order to drive competitors out of business, a careful study of the record of the antitrust case that led to the breaking up of Standard Oil found no evidence that he had ever done so. The story appears to be the historian's equivalent of an urban myth.

In one case, a Standard Oil official threatened to cut prices if a smaller firm, Cornplanter Oil, did not stop expanding and cutting into Standard's business. Here is the reply Cornplanter's manager gave, according to his own testimony:

> Well, I says, "Mr. Moffett, I am very glad you put it that way, because if it is up to you the only way you can get it is to cut the market, and if you cut the market I will cut you for 200 miles around, and I will make you sell the stuff," and I says, "I don't want a bigger picnic than that; sell it if you want to" and I bid him good day and left. That was the end of that.
>
> —Quoted in John S. McGee, "Predatory Price Cutting: The Standard Oil (NJ) Case," *Journal of Law and Economics,* vol. 2 (October 1958), p. 137.

In addition to predatory pricing, a variety of other tactics have been suggested for a firm trying to get and maintain an artificial monopoly. One is for the firm to buy out all of its competitors; it has been argued that this, rather than predatory pricing, is how Rockefeller maintained his position. The problem is that if every time someone builds a new refinery Rockefeller has to buy him out, starting refineries becomes a very profitable business, and Rockefeller ends up with more refineries than he has any use for.

It is hard to prove that none of these tactics can ever work. If Rockefeller can convince potential competitors that he is willing to lose an almost unlimited amount of money keeping them out, it is possible that no one will ever call his bluff—in which case it will cost him nothing. One can only say that the advantage in such a game seems to lie with the small firm, not the large, and that the bulk of the economic and historical evidence suggests that the artificial monopoly is largely or entirely a work of fiction. It exists in history books and antitrust law but is and always has been rare or nonexistent in the real world, possibly because most of the tactics it is supposed to use to maintain its monopoly do not work.

One consequence of the myth may be to encourage monopoly. Selling below cost is a poor way of driving your competitors out of business but a good way for a new firm to persuade customers to try its products. Under present antitrust law, a firm that does so risks being accused by its competitors of unfair competition and forced to raise its price. Laws that make life hard for new firms—or old firms entering new markets—reduce competition and encourage monopoly, even if they are called antitrust laws.

The Mickey Mouse Monopoly

Over the years, Disneyland has used various combinations of an entry fee plus per-ride charges to price its services. When I was last there, the per-ride charges were zero—the admission ticket provided unlimited rides. On earlier visits, tickets were required for individual rides.

How should Disney decide what combination of entry fee and per-ride ticket price to charge in order to maximize profit? To answer that question, we need to know how the amount people will pay for admission is affected by the price of the rides. Fortunately, we do. Consumer surplus is the value of access to an opportunity set—which is what Disney is selling. Anything that increases the customer's consumer surplus from a particular ride by a dollar also increases by a dollar the price that Disney can charge that customer without driving him away.

If the consumers are all identical, Disney follows the same strategy as the cookie club. He prices the ride at the level that maximizes total surplus, and then converts all of the consumer surplus into producer surplus at the admission gate. If the marginal cost of one more person using a ride is zero, an admission ticket should entitle the customer to unlimited free rides. If it costs twenty cents more electricity to operate the ride with one more seat filled, then that should be the price of the ride. Charging a price equal to marginal cost means that the customer consumes an additional ride if and only if its value to him is more than its cost to Disney—which is the right rule for maximizing the combined gain to Disney and its customers.

There are at least two important complications we would have to add if we were really running Disneyland. One is that customers are not identical. If, on average, customers who are willing to pay a high admission price are also ones who go on a lot of rides, then a high price for rides is an indirect way of charging a high total price (rides plus admission) to those willing to pay it.

The second complication is that some rides may be used to capacity. If they are, my decision to go on one more ride lengthens the line of people waiting for it, imposing costs (in waiting time) on everyone behind me in line—with the result that someone else decides not to take it.

Why should Disney care how long the customers have to stand in line? How long they have to stand in line is one of the things affecting the value to them of visiting Disneyland, hence how much they will pay for admission. By going on one more ride, you impose a cost directly on other customers and indirectly on Disney; Disney should take that cost into account in deciding what price to charge for the ride. It turns out that (assuming all customers are identical, and ignoring random fluctuations in demand for rides) the optimal price is the one that just reduces the line to zero. You may find it easier to figure out why that is true after you finish chapter 17.

THE POPCORN PROBLEM

In the discussion of popcorn at the end of chapter 4, I showed that if customers are identical, theaters should sell popcorn at cost. One explanation of what we observe is that they do—that the high price of popcorn (and candy and soda) reflects high costs. Since the theater is selling food for only twenty minutes or so every two hours, perhaps its operating costs are much higher than those of other sellers.

In this chapter I suggested an alternative explanation. If popcorn is expensive, the poor student who is just barely willing to pay $5 to see the movie will either do without or smuggle in his own, while the affluent student (or the one trying to impress a new date) will still come, despite the cost of lots of expensive popcorn. The combination of cheap tickets and expensive popcorn is a way of keeping the business of the poor student while making as much as possible out of the rich one.

How could one find out which explanation is right? Discriminatory pricing is possible only if the seller has a considerable degree of monopoly; in a competitive industry, if you charge richer customers a higher price, some other firm will undercut you. In a small town, only one movie theater is showing a particular movie at a particular time. In a large city, customers can choose among many theaters showing the same film. If the discriminatory pricing explanation is correct, we would expect the difference between the price of popcorn or candy in a movie theater and its price elsewhere to be larger in small towns than in big cities. If, on the other hand, the difference reflects a difference in cost, we would expect the opposite result, since both labor and real estate—the two things that contribute to the high cost of a food concession in a theater—are usually more expensive in cities.

FOR FURTHER READING

I am not the first economist to think of applying economic theory to the Magic Kingdom—nor do I invent all of my clever titles for myself. One of them was stolen from Walter Oi, "A Disneyland Dilemma: Two-Part Tariffs for a Mickey Mouse Monopoly," *Quarterly Journal of Economics*, vol. 85 (February 1971), pp. 77–96.

11

HARD PROBLEMS: GAME THEORY, STRATEGIC BEHAVIOR, AND OLIGOPOLY

"There are two kinds of people in the world: Johnny von Neumann and the rest of us."
—Attributed to Eugene Wigner, a Nobel Prize-winning physicist

So far in this book I have almost entirely ignored an important feature of human interaction and many markets—bargaining, threats, bluffs, the whole gamut of strategic behavior. That is one of the reasons why much of economic theory seems such a bloodless abstraction. We are used to seeing human society as a clash of wills, whether in the boardroom, on the battlefield, or in our favorite soap opera.

Economics presents it instead in terms of solitary individuals or small teams of producers, each calmly maximizing against an essentially nonhuman environment, an opportunity set rather than a population of self-willed human beings.

There is a reason for doing economics this way. The analysis of strategic behavior is an extraordinarily difficult problem. John von Neumann, arguably one of the smartest men of this century, created a whole new branch of mathematics in the process of failing to solve it. The work of his successors, while often ingenious and mathematically sophisticated, has not brought us much closer to being able to say what people will or should do in such situations. Seen from one side, what is striking about price theory is the unrealistic picture it presents of the world around us. Seen from the other, one of its most impressive accomplishments is to explain a considerable part of what is going on in real markets while avoiding, with considerable ingenuity, any situation involving strategic behavior.

This chapter is a brief detour into the twilight zone.

BILATERAL MONOPOLY, NUCLEAR DOOM, AND BARROOM BRAWLS

I have the world's only apple and you are the only person in the world not allergic to apples. The apple is worth nothing to me and one dollar to you. If I sell it to you for a dollar, I am better off by a dollar and you, having paid exactly what the apple is worth, are just as well off as if you had not bought it. If I give it to you, I gain nothing and you gain a dollar. Any price between one and zero represents some division of the dollar gain between us. If we cannot agree on a price, I keep the apple and the potential gain from the trade is lost.

This game, called "bilateral monopoly," nicely encapsulates the combination of common interest and conflict of interest, cooperation and competition, typical of many human interactions. The players have a common interest in reaching agreement but a conflict over what the terms of the agreement will be. The United States and the Soviet Union had a common interest in preserving peace but a conflict over the terms of peace. Husband and wife have a common interest in preserving a happy and harmonious marriage but innumerable conflicts over how their limited resources are to be spent on things that each values.

One way to win is to somehow commit oneself, make it impossible to back down. A child with good strategic instincts might announce, "I promise not to let you have more than twenty cents of the dollar, cross my heart and hope to die." If the second player believes that the oath is binding—that the first player will not back down because no share of the dollar is worth the shame of breaking the oath—the strategy works. The second player goes home with twenty cents and a resolution that next time he will get his promise out first.

The strategy of commitment is not limited to children. Its most dramatic embodiment is the doomsday machine, an idea dreamed up by Herman Kahn and later dramatized in the movie *Doctor Strangelove*.

The United States decides to end all worries about Soviet aggression once and for all. It builds a hundred cobalt bombs, buries them in the Rocky Mountains, and attaches a fancy Geiger counter. If they go off, the cobalt bombs produce enough fallout to eliminate all human life anywhere on earth. The Geiger counter is the trigger, set to explode the bombs if it senses the radiation from a Soviet attack.

We now have the ultimate deterrent. In an improved version, dubbed by Kahn the Doomsday-in-a-Hurry Machine, the triggering device is equipped to detect a wide range of activities and respond accordingly—blow up the world if the Soviets invade West Berlin, or West Germany, or anywhere at all—thus saving us the cost of a conventional as well as a nuclear defense.

A doomsday machine has some downside risk. In *Doctor Strangelove*, it is the Russians who build one. They decide to save the announcement for the premier's birthday. While they are waiting, a lunatic American air force officer launches a nuclear strike against the Soviet Union.

The doomsday machine was not entirely imaginary. During most of the cold war, the chief defense of the United States against a Soviet nuclear attack was the threat of massive retaliation. If the attack had happened despite the threat, our retaliation would have done us little good, and might well have made us even worse off, by increasing fallout and climactic effects. Nonetheless, it would probably have happened. The people controlling the relevant buttons—bomber pilots, air force officers in missile silos, nuclear submarine captains— had been trained to obey orders. They were particularly unlikely to disobey the order to retaliate against an enemy who had just killed large numbers of their friends and family.

Our nuclear arsenal was a doomsday machine, with human beings rather than Geiger counters as the trigger. So was theirs. Both worked, with the result that neither was used. Kahn invented the idea of a doomsday machine not because he wanted the United States to build one but because both we and the Soviet Union already had.

Between "cross my heart and hope to die" and nuclear annihilation, there is a wide range of situations where threat and commitment play a key role. Even before the invention of nuclear weapons, warfare was often a losing game for both sides. A leader who could persuade the other side that he was nonetheless willing to play, whether because he was a madman, a fanatic, or merely an optimist, was in a strong bargaining position. They might call his bluff—but it might not be a bluff.

There are many examples of the same logic on a smaller scale. Consider a barroom quarrel that starts with two customers arguing about baseball teams and ends with one dead and the other standing there with a broken bottle in his hand and a dazed expression on his face. Seen from one standpoint, this is irrational and therefore uneconomic behavior; the killer regrets what he has done as soon as he does it, so he obviously cannot have acted to maximize his own welfare. Seen from another standpoint, it is the working out of a rational commitment to irrational action—the equivalent, on a small scale, of a doomsday machine going off.

Suppose I am strong, fierce, and known to have a short temper with people who do not do what I want. I benefit from that reputation; people are careful not to do things that offend me. Actually beating someone up is expensive; he might fight back, and I might get arrested. But if my reputation is bad enough, I may not have to beat anyone up.

To maintain that reputation, I train myself to be short-tempered. I tell myself, and others, that I am a real he-man, and he-men don't let other people push them around. I gradually expand my definition of "push me around" until it is equivalent to "don't do what I want."

We usually describe this as an aggressive personality, but it may make more sense to think of it as a deliberate strategy rationally adopted. Once the strategy is in place, I am no longer free to choose the optimal response in each situation; I have invested too much in my own self-image to be able to back down. In just the same way, the United States, having constructed a system of massive retaliation to deter attack, is not free to change its mind in the ten minutes between the detection of enemy missiles and the deadline for firing our own. Not backing down once deterrence has failed may be irrational, but putting yourself in a situation where you cannot back down is not.

Most of the time I get my own way; once in a while I have to pay for it. I have no monopoly on my strategy; there are other short-tempered people in the world. I get into a conversation in a bar. The other guy fails to show adequate deference to my opinions. I start pushing. He pushes back. When it is over, one of us is dead.

HAWKS, DOVES, AND BARNYARD BRAWLS

In chapter 1, I offered one example of the close relation between economics and evolutionary biology. My explanation of barroom brawls is another. It is the equivalent, for humans, of what sociobiologists call a "hawk-dove equilibrium."

Suppose there are two varieties of a species of bird, differentiated only by their willingness to fight. When two birds find the same piece of food, the "hawk" variety always fights, the "dove" always flees. If almost all the birds were doves, being a hawk would be profitable, since hawks would almost always get disputed bits of food without having to fight for them. If hawks do better at food gathering than doves, they will be more successful in producing and raising offspring, so the number of hawks will increase.

As the number of hawks increases, the payoff to being a hawk falls; more and more often the opponent turns out to be another hawk, and the result is a fight that does both birds more damage than the food is worth. At some ratio of hawks to doves, we reach an equilibrium where each strategy is equally successful.

The logic is exactly the same if we substitute aggressive personalities for hawks. If almost nobody follows the aggressive strategy, it is a profitable one—so more and more people choose to follow it. The risk of lethal brawls rises and the payoff to being a he-man falls. Equilibrium is reached when the loss from opponents who do not back down just balances the gain from opponents who do, making the alternative strategies—hawk and dove, he-man and wimp—equally profitable.

THE ECONOMICS OF VIRTUE

So far I have assumed that human association, like most animal associations, is involuntary; the he-man is part of your environment, not someone you chose to associate with. As long as that is the case, there is a payoff to having an aggressive personality—as long as there are not too many of you.

That is not true for voluntary associations—business partnerships, employer-employee relations, marriage. When choosing someone to associate with, the aggressive personality goes at the bottom of the list—which means fewer job opportunities, and a worse chance of getting married.

In a society of voluntary association, there is a payoff to a different commitment strategy. Someone known to be considerate, courteous, the sort of person who never takes advantage of other people, who would never steal even if nobody was watching, is a desirable employer, employee, partner, or spouse. To the extent that other people can correctly read your personality, it is in your selfish interest to train yourself to be a nice guy. Hiring honest people saves not only the cost of theft but also the cost of guarding against theft—and that saving will show up in the difference between what honest and dishonest people get paid.

Here again, we would expect something like a hawk-dove equilibrium, although for a different reason. If almost everyone is honest, it is not worth paying much attention to how honest any particular person is, so a strategy of hypocrisy—appearing to be honest but cheating when you think you can get away with it—is profitable. As the number of hypocrites increases, so does the care other people take to identify them. The equilibrium ratio of hypocrites to honest men is reached when the two strategies have the same payoff.

This approach to understanding why people are—or are not—nice has an interesting implication. Being a bad person, an aggressive personality, is profitable in involuntary interactions. Being a good person is profitable in voluntary interactions. We would expect to see nicer people—more honesty and fewer bullies—in a society where most interactions are voluntary than in one where most are involuntary.

Prisoner's Dilemma

Two men are arrested for a burglary. The district attorney puts them in separate cells. He goes first to Joe. He tells him that if he confesses and Mike does not, the DA will drop the burglary charge and let Joe off with a slap on the wrist—three months for trespass. If Mike also confesses, the DA cannot drop the charge but he will ask the judge for leniency; Mike and Joe will get two years each.

If Joe refuses to confess, the DA will not feel so friendly. If Mike confesses, Joe will be convicted and the DA will ask for the maximum possible sentence. If neither confesses, the DA cannot convict them of the robbery, but he will press for a six-month sentence for trespass, resisting arrest, and vagrancy.

After explaining all of this to Joe, the DA goes to Mike's cell and gives the same speech, with names reversed. Table 11–1 shows the matrix of outcomes facing Joe and Mike.

Joe reasons as follows:

If Mike confesses and I don't, I get five years; if I confess too, I get two years. If Mike is going to confess, I had better confess too.

If neither of us confesses, I go to jail for six months. If Mike stays silent and I confess, I get only three months. So if Mike is going to stay silent, I am better off confessing. In fact, whatever Mike does I am better off confessing.

Table 11-1   **The payoff matrix for prisoner's dilemma. Each cell of the table shows the result of choices by the two prisoners; Joe's sentence is first, Mike's second.**

MIKE

		Confess	Say Nothing
JOE	Confess	2 years, 2 years	3 months, 5 years
	Say Nothing	5 years, 3 months	6 months, 6 months

Joe calls for the guard and asks to speak to the DA. It takes a while; Mike has made the same calculation, reached the same conclusion, and is in the middle of dictating his confession.

Both players have acted rationally and both are, as a result, worse off. By confessing, they each get two years; if they had kept their mouths shut, they each would have gotten six months. That seems an odd consequence for rational behavior.

The explanation is that Joe is choosing only his strategy, not Mike's. If Joe could choose between the lower right-hand cell of the matrix and the upper left-hand cell, he would choose the former; so would Mike. But those are not the choices they are offered. Joe is choosing a column, and the left-hand column dominates the right-hand column; it is better whichever row Mike chooses. Mike is choosing a row, and the top row dominates the bottom.

We have been here before. In chapter 1, I pointed out that rationality is an assumption about individuals, not about groups. The Prisoner's Dilemma demonstrates that for a group of two. Prisoners confess for the same reason that armies run away and people take shortcuts across park grass.

Many people find such results deeply counterintuitive. Armies do not always run away, in part because generals have developed ways of changing the structure of rewards and punishments facing their soldiers. Burning your bridges behind you is one solution; shooting soldiers who run away in battle is another. Similarly, criminals go to considerable effort to raise the cost to their co-workers of squealing and lower the cost of going to jail for refusing to squeal.

None of that refutes the logic of the prisoner's dilemma; it merely means that real prisoners and real soldiers are sometimes playing other games. When the net payoffs to squealing, or running, have the structure shown in Table 11–1, the logic of the game is compelling. Prisoners confess and soldiers run.

Democracy Writ Small

Suppose we change bilateral monopoly by adding one more player and a decision rule for dividing the dollar—majority vote. We now have a new game: three-person majority rule. What happens?

Anne and Bill agree to split the dollar fifty-fifty, leaving nothing for Charles; two votes are a majority. Before the final decision, Charles proposes to Anne that she and he split the dollar sixty-forty, leaving Bill out. Forty cents is better than nothing, so it is worth his while to make the offer; sixty cents is better than fifty, so she accepts.

The game is not over. Bill would rather have forty cents than nothing, so he proposes a forty-sixty split with Charles; Charles prefers sixty to forty, so accepts. As is by now clear, this process can go on for a long time, perhaps forever. Each proposed division dominates the one before, but is itself dominated by another proposal.

Domination, in this context, is a very simple concept. One division dominates another if it is preferred by enough people to make it happen. Since, in this game, we make decisions by majority vote, a new division dominates an old one if two people prefer it.

A Small Victory

The objective of game theory is to solve a game—to figure out how the players ought to play it. Its record so far is one success and a few very partial successes.

The success is by von Neumann, who found a solution for all two-player fixed-sum games—games, such as chess or poker, where the interests of the players are diametrically opposed. If anything that benefits me hurts you and there is no third player for us to gang up against, then there is no room for threats or promises, so two-player fixed-sum games offer very little opportunity for strategic behavior.

The von Neumann solution is a strategy, a complete description of how to play the game, for each player and an outcome—say "Anne wins five dollars, Bill loses five dollars." By playing her strategy, Anne guarantees that she will do at least that well—win at least five dollars. By playing his, Bill guarantees that she will do no better, and thus that he will lose no more than five dollars.

Von Neumann proved that any two-person fixed-sum game had such a solution, and showed how, in principle, one would find it—given enough computing power and unlimited time. He also did his part to deal with the former proviso; one of the other things von Neumann helped invent was cybernetics, the mathematical basis for modern computers.

Unfortunately, most interesting games are not two-player fixed-sum. Bilateral monopoly is two-player but not fixed-sum, since some outcomes—blowing up the world in the nuclear variant, for instance—make both players worse off. And many of the other games we would like solutions for, including most of politics, economics, and diplomacy, involve more than two players; three-person majority vote is a simple example of the resulting problem.

Von Neumann also suggested a definition for a solution to a many-player game: a solution is a set of outcomes such that every outcome not in the solution is dominated by one in the solution, and no outcome in the solution dominates another in the solution. An example for majority vote would be the set of three outcomes (.50, .50, 0), (0, .50, .50), (.50, 0, .50). Each involves two players evenly splitting the dollar, with a third left out. As you can check for yourself, any other division is dominated by one of these, and no one of these dominates another.

One problem with this definition of a "solution" is that it does not tell us which of the three will happen. Indeed, it does not even tell us that one of the three will happen—because this game has other solutions. Consider, for example, the infinite set of outcomes defined by $(.90 - x, x, .10)$—all the outcomes in which Charles gets ten cents and the rest of the dollar is divided in some way between Anne and Bill. As you can check for yourself, this set of outcomes is also a von Neumann solution. So is the set defined by $(.91 - x, x, .09)$. And there are lots more.

One von Neumann solution to a many-player game may contain many, even an infinite number, of outcomes, and there may be many, even an infinite number, of different solutions. That does not get us very far toward figuring out what will actually happen when three or more people interact.

Game theorists since von Neumann have come up with other approaches to solving such games, but none of them is very satisfactory. One of the more popular ones is . . .

Nash Equilibrium

Consider a many-player game played over and over. Each player keeps changing his strategy until no further change will make him better off. Equilibrium is reached when each player has chosen a strategy that is optimal for him, given the strategies that the other players are following.

A simple example is the game of choosing which side of the road to drive on. The United States is in a Nash equilibrium; everyone drives on the right. Since everyone else drives on the right, my driving on the left would impose very large costs on me (as well as others), so it is in my interest to drive on the right too.

In England, everyone drives on the left. Since in most other countries people drive on the right, cars have to be specially manufactured with steering wheels on the right side for the English market. Foreign tourists driving in England are at risk of drifting into the wrong lane—especially, in my experience, when making turns—with serious adverse consequences.

If English drivers all switched to driving on the right, they might be better off. But any English driver who tried to make the switch on his own initiative would be very much worse off. A Nash equilibrium is stable against individual action even when it leads to an undesirable outcome.

A Nash equilibrium may not be stable against joint action by many people—as Sweden demonstrated when it switched to driving on the right. Some Nash equilibria are even unstable against joint action by any two people. Consider a prison guard with one bullet in his gun, facing a mob of convicts escaping from death row. Any one convict is better off surrendering. Any two convicts are better off charging the guard.

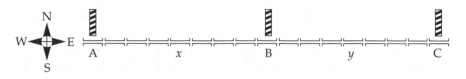

Figure 11–1   The street of barbers. There is one barbershop every eight blocks.

GAMES ECONOMISTS PLAY

Despite its frivolous name, the purpose of game theory is both serious and ambitious: to understand all behavior that has the structure of a game. That includes most of the subject matter of economics, political science, international relations, interpersonal relations, sociology, and quite a lot more. In economics alone, there are many applications, but this is already a long chapter, so I shall limit myself to two: monopolistic competition and oligopoly, two quite different ways of analyzing situations somewhere between monopoly and perfect competition.

The Street of Barbers

Figure 11–1 shows a street with barbershops distributed along it. Since all of the barbers are equally skilled (at both cutting and gossiping), the only things determining which shop a customer goes to are how much it costs and how far it is from his home.

All the barbers are initially charging the same price—say $8. Everyone goes to the closest barbershop; shop B, for example, gets all of the customers between points x and y. The owner of B faces the same situation as an ordinary monopolist. If he cuts his price below $8, he gains a few customers west of D_x and east of E_y who find the lower price makes up for the longer walk. If he raises his price above $8, he loses a few customers. Like any single price monopolist, he maximizes his profit at a price for which $MC = MR$. Every other barber makes a similar calculation, so the pattern of prices is stable only if $8 happens to be the profit-maximizing price.

Suppose $8 is the price for which marginal cost equals marginal revenue; further suppose that at that price barbershops are profitable. There is nothing to stop more barbers from entering the market. As they do so, they drive down the average distance between shops, the number of customers per shop, and the profit per shop. As these change, so does the profit-maximizing price.

Equilibrium is reached at a density and price that satisfy two conditions: marginal cost equals marginal revenue and economic profit equals zero. It is a Nash equilibrium; each barber is maximizing his profit, given what the other barbers are doing. It sounds odd to describe zero as a maximum, but it is the highest profit that the individual barber, like the individual firm in a competitive industry, can get.

Cybernetic Barbershops

Monopolistic competition exists in an industry, such as the street of barbers, where many firms produce products that are close but not perfect substitutes. Each firm has some degree of monopoly power, so profit is maximized where marginal revenue equals marginal cost, but there is open entry, so profits are driven to zero, just as with perfect competition.

This is a common situation in industries where geographic location of seller and buyer is important—goods and services that must be transported from the producer to the consumer and those, such as haircuts or movies, for which the consumer must be transported to the producer—but it is not limited to such industries. Consider the market for microcomputers. Any firm that wishes is free to enter, and many have done so. Their products differ substantially. As the price of one computer goes up, customers least locked into that particular brand shift to another, so quantity demanded falls. But over a considerable range of prices, the company can sell at least some computers to some customers—just as a barbershop can raise its price and still retain the customers who live next door to it. There is undoubtedly some price at which I would abandon my Macintosh for a PC—but Apple has not yet gotten to it.

If profits are positive, new firms enter the industry; if they are negative, some existing firms exit. If one type of computer is particularly profitable, other manufacturers will introduce similar designs—just as high profits on one part of the street of barbers give barbershops elsewhere on the street an incentive to move closer.

When Apple first introduced the Macintosh, it was the only mass-market machine designed around an intuitive, graphic, object-oriented interface. Over the next few years it became clear that there were a lot of customers living on that particular part of the street of computers—a lot of users who, once introduced to such a computer, preferred it to more conventional designs. In 1988, IBM moved its barbershop, introducing a new line of computers and a new operating system based on the same ideas; at about the same time, and with greater success, Microsoft introduced operating system software (Windows) designed to make DOS computers work more like Macintoshes.

One reason IBM chose to move may have been that its own part of the street was getting crowded. By the time IBM finally abandoned the PC line, a large majority of IBM-compatible computers were being made by companies other than IBM.

Neither Fish nor Fowl: The Woes of an Oligopolist

You have suddenly and unexpectedly become CEO of a large firm—one of the main players in the vibrant toothpaste market. Unfortunately, your previous career as a playboy has provided few relevant skills, and there has scarcely been enough time between burying your uncle and moving into his old office to get an MBA.

Fortunately, you came across this book. At this point in reading it, however, you are feeling distinctly left out. If the toothpaste industry were perfectly competitive, the book would provide you not only advice but a useful excuse to explain to the other members of your family why you are earning them only a normal return on their capital. If it were a monopoly, you would have not only advice but a chance of monopoly profits. Unfortunately, with six established firms and a few more test-marketing their products, you fit neither pattern. Nor do you fit the category of monopolistic competition; despite the best efforts of your advertising staff, customers remain convinced that one tube of toothpaste is very much the same as another.

It is not very helpful to tell you the name of what you have inherited—an oligopoly, a firm with some but not many competitors. It may be more helpful to use economics to think through the problems and possibilities of your situation.

The basic problem is very simple. If all the firms reduce their output, price will rise, producing a monopoly profit for the firms to share. But high prices make it profitable for everyone to produce and sell more toothpaste, driving prices back down. What you need is some way of getting all the firms to hold down their production while at the same time keeping new firms from being drawn into the industry by the opportunity to share in the profits.

Your previous life may not have trained you to run a company, but it has given you lots of experience in persuading people. To your great surprise, you succeed in persuading the other six firms to form a cartel—an association of firms to set prices and output. Since the industry is now, in effect, a monopoly, you calculate the price and output that maximize monopoly profit and instruct each firm to sell its share of that output at that price.

Your next problem is how to keep out new entrants. You arrange a meeting with the CEOs of the firms that have been test-marketing their own products to warn them that if they enter they will regret it—the cartel will dissolve itself, prices will plunge, and they will never make back their investment. Your guests are unimpressed. They point out that threats are cheap—but once they have entered, carrying out the threat will destroy you as well as them. You will be better off admitting them to the cartel and a share of the profits.

One way to change the situation is to create an entry barrier—some additional cost to new firms that will make entering the industry unprofitable. Consider the trucking industry under Interstate Commerce Commission (ICC) regulation. In order for a new carrier to be allowed to operate on an existing route, it had to get a certificate from the ICC saying that its services were needed. Existing carriers would of course argue that they already provided adequate service. The result would be an expensive and time-consuming dispute before the commission. Perhaps you could persuade the FDA that while firms already in the toothpaste industry obviously know their business, new firms should be required to demonstrate, beyond any reasonable doubt, the safety and effectiveness of their product before being allowed to sell it.

If that attempt fails, another approach to preventing entry is to build the economic equivalent of a doomsday machine. Suppose you could sign legally binding contracts guaranteeing your customers a low price if any more firms enter the industry. Having done so, you could then point out to potential new firms that if they do enter the industry there will be no monopoly profit for anyone.

It may seem surprising that eliminating some of your options—in effect tying your own hands—can make you better off, but it is true. The situation is precisely analogous to our earlier examples of commitment—doomsday machines of one sort or another. Just as in those cases, the player who commits himself is taking a risk that the other player may somehow misread the situation, call the bluff, and discover that it is no bluff.

Having successfully regulated or bluffed potential competitors out of the market, you are left with another problem—deciding how the monopoly profit is to be divided among the member firms. This is a game similar to bilateral monopoly but with more players. If all firms agree on a division, there is a monopoly profit to be divided; if they cannot agree, the cartel breaks up, output rises, prices fall, and most of the monopoly profit vanishes.

One weakness of a cartel is that it is better to be out than in. A firm that is not a member is free to produce all it likes, selling at or just below the cartel's price. A large firm such as yours may be kept in by the fear that its defection would destroy the cartel, driving price back down to its competitive level. But that argument is less persuasive for the smaller firms. They may try for the best of both worlds—selling all they want at the monopoly price while letting the larger firms hold output down and price up. If you want to keep them in the cartel, you will have to give them more than their fair share of the profits.

A recent example is the OPEC oil cartel. The reduction of output seems to have been mostly by the big producers—Saudi Arabia and the United Arab Emirates. One result is that when the cartel discusses prices, the Saudis are the moderates; they know that if prices are high, they will be the ones paying for it in reduced sales. Being sensible people they make a virtue of necessity, attributing their opposition to price increases to their responsible concern for the economic health of the industrial world—for which they deserve to be rewarded, by their customers, with military and political support.

Having reluctantly agreed to the demands of the small fry in your industry, you are left with another problem—how to monitor and enforce the agreement. The problem is brought home to you by an internal memo reporting that the most successful members of your sales staff have been earning their bonuses by chiseling on the cartel price—offering better terms to customers who can be lured away from other firms and trusted to keep their mouths shut about the deal they are getting. It occurs to you that if your competitors' salesmen are equally enterprising, it may explain why you are having such a hard time keeping price up to, and output down to, the agreed-upon levels.

If only you were in a civilized European country where the courts were properly sympathetic to the problems of would-be monopolists, you could solve this problem by having all of the firms agree to sell through a common marketing agency. Unfortunately for you, such an agreement is not merely unenforceable in the United

States, it is probably illegal—and you face the risk of paying triple damages for violating antitrust law.

An alternative possibility is a merger—converting all the big firms in the industry into one gigantic firm. But you, and your competitors, are already large enough so that diseconomies of scale in administration are beginning to outweigh economies of scale in production; that is why the industry is an oligopoly instead of a natural monopoly. Making big firms even bigger will make that problem worse. And you may have a hard time persuading the antitrust division of the Justice Department to approve your merger.

While considering this problem, you come across a report from your research director boasting of the success of his department in securing patents on the processes used to produce toothpaste. It occurs to you to wonder why you are not collecting licensing fees on those patents from other firms in the industry. A few telephone calls later you have the answer: Each firm produces by a slightly different process, and each owns the patents necessary for its production.

You have an idea. Shortly later, you have a conference—of all the CEOs and research directors in the industry. Next comes a press release, announcing that, in order to raise industry productivity, all of the firms have agreed to license each other's patents.

Licensing patents you don't need does very little for your productivity, but it may do quite a lot for your profits. In exchange for the right to use the other firms' patents, you pay each of them two cents for each tube of toothpaste you produce—and they agree to make similar payments to you. On average, the result is a wash—you get back about as much as you pay. But on the margin of how many tubes you produce and sell the result is to raise your cost, since producing an extra tube will increase what you must pay them but, by cutting into their sales, reduce what they must pay you.

Since marginal cost is now higher, each firm finds it in its interest to charge more and produce less. If the combined output is still too high, you all agree to raise the licensing fees—and continue doing so until price reaches the profit-maximizing level. You have just discovered an elegant way of signing an enforceable cartel agreement in a country where cartel agreements are not merely unenforceable but illegal. In order to reduce the chance of getting caught, it would be prudent to start using some of your competitors' patented processes in your production—whether or not they represent any improvement on your patented processes.

There Oughta Be a Law

Cheating on a cartel agreement is a bad thing from the standpoint of the cartel's members, but a good thing from the standpoint of the rest of us—their customers. This raises the question of why devices that can be used to enforce cartel agreements are not illegal.

One reason is that they may also be used for other purposes. It is easy enough for me to assume that two imaginary toothpaste firms can each produce just as well using only its own patents, but there may be no easy way for a court to determine whether that is true of real firms in a real industry. Similarly, when firms merge, the reason might be to create a new firm with substantial monopoly power, but it might also be to lower production costs by combining the different strengths of several different firms.

This does not mean that the government makes no attempt to regulate such behavior. Mergers between large firms have often been the target of antitrust actions. One problem is that while such intervention may make it more difficult for oligopolies to charge monopoly prices, it may also make it more difficult for new firms to form that would compete with existing monopolies.

An economist of my acquaintance has proposed a simple rule for distinguishing procompetitive mergers from anticompetitive mergers: see who complains. If firms are merging in order to increase their monopoly power, the next step will be to cut output and raise prices— so the remaining firms in the industry should be in favor of the merger. If firms merge to make them more efficient producers, on the other hand, the result will be to drive prices down and make competitors worse off. So mergers should be permitted if competitors object to them and banned if competitors do not object. Obviously, in order for the rule to work, the antitrust division must be careful to keep it secret.

There Is a Law: Government to the Rescue

> . . . the high price for the crude oil resulted, as it had always done before and will always do so long as oil comes out of the ground, in increasing the production, and they got too much oil. We could not find a market for it . . . of course, any who were not in the association were undertaking to produce all they possibly could; and as to those who were in the association, many of them men of honor and

high standing, the temptation was very great to get a little more oil than they had promised their associates or us would come. It seemed very difficult to prevent the oil coming at that price.

> —John D. Rockefeller, discussing an unsuccessful attempt to cartelize the production of crude oil. Quoted by John McGee, "Predatory Price Cutting: The Standard Oil (NJ) Case," *Journal of Law and Economics,* vol. 2 (October 1958).

Rockefeller was too pessimistic; there is a way of keeping a high price from drawing more oil out of the ground. The solution is a monopoly in the original sense of the term—a grant by government of the exclusive right to produce.

Consider the airline industry. Prior to deregulation, no airline could fly a route unless it had permission from the Civil Aeronautics Board. From the formation of the CAB (originally as the Civil Aeronautics Administration) in 1938 until deregulation in the late 1970s, no major scheduled interstate airline came into existence.

Even if the airlines, with the help of the government, were able to keep out new firms, what prevented one airline from cutting its fares to attract business from another? Again the answer was the CAB; it was illegal for an airline to change fares without permission. The airline industry was a cartel created and enforced by the federal government, at considerable cost to the airlines' customers.

Private cartels are practical only in an oligopoly, an industry where most of the output is produced by a small number of firms. But with help from the government, it is possible to provide similar benefits in a naturally competitive industry, such as trucking under the ICC. By preventing the entry of new firms, the government eliminates the constraint that makes economic profit zero in a competitive industry—an improvement that should be appreciated, and rewarded, by those in the industry.

One form such arrangements often take is professional licensing. The government announces that in order to protect the public from incompetent physicians (morticians, beauticians, poodle groomers, egg graders, barbers, . . .), only those with a government-granted license may enter the profession. Present members of the profession receive licenses more or less automatically. The political support for the introduction of such arrangements comes, almost invariably, not from customers but from the profession. That is not surprising; the licensing requirement makes entry to the profession more difficult, increasing the price for which those already in the profession can sell their services.

EQUILIBRIUM IN OLIGOPOLY: TOO MANY ANSWERS

Oligopoly is a problem to which a cartel is one solution. Suppose that solution is not available: The inability to control entry, or unreasonable demands by some members of the cartel, or covert chiseling, or the vigilant eye of the antitrust division of the Justice Department prevents firms from getting together to promote their mutual interest in high prices. What happens instead?

One possible answer is a Nash equilibrium—each firm setting price and quantity to maximize profit, given what all the other firms are doing. Trying to work through the logic of that answer reveals an interesting problem—one of the reasons why Nash equilibrium is a less than satisfactory solution to the puzzle posed by many-player games.

The definition of Nash equilibrium requires each player to pick his optimal strategy while taking the other players' strategies as given—but it is not always clear what that means. If one firm increases its output and the others continue to charge the same price, they will find that they are selling less. If they want to sell the same amount as before, they will have to lower their price. When one firm changes its behavior, the behavior of the other firms must change—and a rational firm must take that fact into account. Interdependence is a fact of the problem, and there is no consistent way of assuming it out of existence.

This makes it important how we define a strategy. Two obvious alternatives are quantity or price. In the former case, each firm decides how much to sell and lets the market determine what price it can sell it at; in the latter, the firm chooses its price and lets the market determine the quantity it can sell at that price.

Following out each alternative gives us a formal mathematical problem that can be solved, provided we know the relevant cost curves and demand curves. The solutions are different. Nothing in either economic theory or game theory tells us which we should prefer.

We could, if we wished, continue the process using more complicated strategies. Perhaps we could find a third solution to oligopoly, and a fourth, and a fifth. But there is not much point in doing so. Two answers to one question are enough. More than enough.

FINAL WORDS

I hope I have convinced you that game theory is a fascinating maze. It is also, in my judgment, one that sensible people avoid when possible. There are too many ways to go, too many problems that have either no solution or an infinite number of them. Game theory is a great deal of fun, and it is often useful for thinking through the logic of strategic behavior, but as a way of actually doing economics it is a desperation measure, to be employed only when all easier alternatives fail.

Many mathematical economists would disagree with that conclusion. If one of them were writing this book, he would assure you that only game theory holds any real hope of introducing adequate mathematical rigor to economics, that everything else is a tangle of approximations and hand waving. He might concede that game theory has not produced much useful economics yet, but he will assure you that if you only give him enough time wonderful things will happen.

He may be right. As you have probably gathered by now, I have a high opinion of John von Neumann. When picking problems to work on, ones that defeated him go at the bottom of my list.

For Further Reading

For those interested in game theory, the original and still readable source is John von Neumann and Oskar Morgenstern, *Theory of Games and Economic Behavior* (Princeton: Princeton University Press, 1944). Two easier introductions are R. Duncan Luce and Howard Raiffa, *Games and Decisions: Introduction and Critical Survey* (New York: John Wiley & Sons, 1957), and Douglas G. Baird, Robert H. Gertner, and Randal C. Picker, *Game Theory and the Law* (Cambridge: Harvard University Press, 1994). An original set of essays on strategic problems is Thomas Schelling, *The Strategy of Conflict* (Cambridge: Harvard University Press, 1960). Readers interested in exploring the economics of virtue will find a much longer account of it in Robert Frank, *Passions Within Reason: The Strategic Role of the Emotions* (New York: Norton, 1988).

12

TIME . . .

So far we have been doing economics in an unchanging world in which each day is like the day before. We are about to migrate to a world with change but without uncertainty. In the next chapter we take the final jolting step into the changing and uncertain world in which we live.

TIME TRADERS

Markets exist across time as well as space. A good is *when* as well as *what*. An apple today and an apple tomorrow are two different goods, as any hungry child will tell you. Not only is there a price for apples today in terms of oranges today, there is also a price for apples today in terms of apples next year. If I trade 100 apples today for 104 next year, I am receiving an apple interest rate of 4 percent; giving you goods now in exchange for goods in the future is the same thing as loaning you goods in exchange for the goods plus interest in the future.

The price of goods this year measured in goods next year gives us the *real* interest rate. The price of dollars this year in dollars next year gives us the *nominal interest rate*—the rate you see in the paper. If prices are rising at 10 percent a year, buying 4 percent more goods next year costs about 14 percent more dollars. A real interest rate of 4 percent then corresponds to a nominal interest rate of about 14 percent.

We consume apples and automobiles and housing, not dollars, so it is the real, not the nominal, interest rate that is relevant to most of the decisions we make. In times of high inflation, that is an important thing to remember. Twenty percent a year sounds like a high interest rate—but if the inflation rate is 30 percent, the bank is, in real terms, paying you to borrow their money.

Pricing a Future

You have six oranges, three apples, and a watch. If markets exist for oranges, apples, and watches, you can transform that bundle of goods into any other bundle with the same total price—by selling what you have and buying what you want. So one useful way of summing up what you have is by what it is worth. This makes it possible to compare (for purposes of buying and selling but not of consuming) very disparate bundles. I do not like diamonds and do like ice cream cones, but as long as I have access to markets, I would rather have a one-carat diamond than an ice cream cone—even Baskin-Robbins's Pralines and Cream.

The same method can be used to price bundles across time. Suppose I am offered two employment contracts: Harvard wants to hire me for $80,000 a year for ten years, Yale offers $62,000 the first year but guarantees a $4,000 raise for each of the next nine. Each school is offering, in exchange for ten years of my working life, a bundle containing ten different goods: "money this year," "money next year," and so on. Which is a better offer?

I can compare the two bundles by converting each to a single good—money today. By borrowing a thousand dollars at 10 percent, I can convert $1,100 next year into $1,000 this year. If I convert all payments back to the first year and add, I will have the *present value* of what each school is offering me.

Consider Harvard's offer. Eighty thousand dollars at the beginning of year 1 is worth $80,000 in year 1, so the present value of the first term is easy. Eighty thousand dollars in year 2 can be converted into $80,000/1.1 in year 1; if I borrowed that sum in year 1, I could exactly pay it off with my year 2 income. Eighty thousand dollars in year 3 is equivalent to $80,000/(1.1 × 1.1) in year 1, and so on. Adding up the third column of Table 12–1 we find that the present value of Harvard's offer is $540,724. That is the sum I could borrow in year 1 and exactly pay off with the entire ten-year stream of payments.

Table 12-1   Comparing two job offers. Each is a stream of payments over time. I take the present value of each payment and sum for each offer. Harvard wins.

YEAR	HARVARD WAGE	PRESENT VALUE OF OF HARVARD WAGE	YALE WAGE	PRESENT VALUE OF YALE WAGE
1	$80,000	$80,000	$62,000	$62,000
2	$80,000	$72,727	$66,000	$60,000
3	$80,000	$66,116	$70,000	$57,851
4	$80,000	$60,105	$74,000	$55,597
5	$80,000	$54,641	$78,000	$53,275
6	$80,000	$49,674	$82,000	$50,916
7	$80,000	$45,158	$86,000	$48,545
8	$80,000	$41,053	$90,000	$46,184
9	$80,000	$37,321	$94,000	$43,852
10	$80,000	$33,928	$98,000	$41,562
Total		$540,722		$519,781

I can calculate the value of Yale's offer in the same way. It is smaller. The stream of income Harvard is offering could, by appropriate borrowing and lending, be converted into the stream Yale offers with something left over. So Harvard's offer is unambiguously better than Yale's, just as a bundle of goods worth $100 is unambiguously superior to a bundle worth $90, since one can sell the former, buy the latter, and have money left over.

Present value calculations can be used to evaluate any project, employment contract, or the like that can be described as a stream of payments, positive (revenue) or negative (cost), through time. If you must choose between two streams of payment, take the one with the higher present value.

What is the present value of $1 per year forever? It is $1 divided by the interest rate. To see why, imagine lending out $10 at 10 percent, collecting the interest, and reinvesting the $10. There is actually a security that works this way. It is called a British consol, and it pays one pound a year forever. Its market value is one over the interest rate.

ECONOMICS IN A CHANGING WORLD

In the previous eleven chapters we analyzed the economics of a world where every year is the same. Every decision could be evaluated by its current effect; if producing widgets is profitable this year, it will be profitable every year. In the real world, things are not so simple; firms must often weigh current losses against future gains.

Present values let us convert the problem of choice in a changing world to the simpler problem that we have already solved. A firm trying to decide whether to produce widgets converts all future gains and losses into present values and adds them. If the sum is positive (a net profit), it ought to produce; if the sum is negative (a net loss), it ought not to. Similar calculations can be made by a firm deciding how much to produce, what mix of inputs to use, and so forth. It compares the alternatives in terms of the present value of all gains and losses and chooses the one for which it is highest.

Suppose a firm is considering an investment (a factory, a piece of land, a research project) that lasts forever and produces a million dollars each year. The present value of a permanent income stream of a million dollars a year is $1,000,000/r$, where r is the market interest rate. So if the cost of the investment is less than that, it is worth making in present value terms. That makes sense; if

$$\frac{\text{Income}}{r} > \text{Investment}$$

then

   Income > r × investment,

which means that the investment is paying more than the market rate of return.

   The calculation is more complicated if you are investing in something that will eventually wear out; in that case, the investment must pay at least the interest rate plus its own replacement cost to be worth making. The corresponding present value calculation is to compare the present value of the stream of income generated by the investment with the initial expense plus the present value of any future expenses (maintenance, for example); if the present value of the payments is larger than the expense (the *net present value* is positive), the investment is worth making.

   Redoing the previous eleven chapters in these terms would make this a very long chapter indeed, so I will restrict myself to working out the logic of one particularly interesting case.

DEPLETABLE RESOURCES

Consider a depletable resource, say petroleum. There is a certain amount of it in the ground; when it has all been pumped up, there will never be any more. Firms that own oil wells must decide how to allocate their production over time in order to maximize profits. What will be the result?

   Assume, for simplicity, that it costs nothing to pump oil out of the ground; if you own an oil well containing 1,000,000 barrels of oil, your problem is simply to decide when to sell how much. Further assume that there are many oil firms, each with only a few wells, so each firm is a price taker. The market interest rate is 10 percent.

   Suppose this year's price is $10 a barrel and next year's price is going to be $12 a barrel. Under those circumstances, all firms would prefer to sell their oil in the second year. If they hold money for a year, they get 10 percent; if they hold oil for a year, they get 20 percent.

   But with no oil offered for sale in the first year, the price will be much more than $10 a barrel. The price structure I have just described—$10 this year, $12 next—is inconsistent with rational behavior. If it existed, it would make people behave in a way such that it could not exist. The only way to avoid such inconsistencies is a pattern of prices such that the price of oil is 10 percent higher in the second year, so that the present value a firm gets from a barrel of oil is the same whether it sells in the first year or the second.

The same argument applies to all future years. The price of oil must go up, year by year, at the interest rate. Any other pattern means that some of the firms are making a mistake—selling oil now when they would be better off holding it, or holding oil when they would be better off selling it.

Oil Prices and Insecure Property Rights

So far I have assumed that the owners of the depletable resource have secure property rights—that petroleum they do not sell this year will still be theirs to sell next year.

Suppose, instead, that anyone who owns an oil well this year has a 10 percent chance of being expropriated next year. Owners of oil wells will sell petroleum next year instead of this year only if the price is enough higher to compensate them both for the interest they lose by not selling the oil until next year and for the chance that when next year arrives, the oil will no longer belong to them. The same analysis implies that the price of petroleum will increase each year by a factor of $1.1 \times (1 + r)$.

Most oil, at present, belongs to governments. The rulers of Saudi Arabia would be foolish to base their production plans on the assumption that they will still rule Saudi Arabia ten years from now—especially with the fate of the shah of Iran and the invasion of Kuwait still recent history. They should be, and doubtless are, aware that money in Switzerland is a more secure form of property than oil under Saudi Arabia.

The effects of insecure property rights are not limited to distant sheiks. The American government may be stable, but its economic policies are not; the imposition of special taxes, such as the windfall profits tax, on oil companies amounts to a partial expropriation. If oil companies expect such taxes to increase, it is in their interest to produce oil now instead of saving it for the future—or, to put the conclusion more precisely, it is in their interest to produce more now and less in the future than they would if they did not expect such taxes to increase. The result is lower prices now, higher prices later.

Is Oil a Depletable Resource?

It may occur to some readers to ask whether the price of oil *has* been increasing at the interest rate (or perhaps faster, to cover the risk of expropriation) over, say, the last fifty or a hundred years. The answer is no. From about 1930 to about 1970, the *real* price of oil—the price allowing for inflation—fell substantially. The OPEC boycott brought the real price most of the way back up to where it had been in 1930, but events since have brought it back down to about what it was before the boycott—far below where it would be if it had been rising at the interest rate from 1930 to the present.

There are at least three possible explanations for the apparent divergence between theory and fact. The first is that the economic theory of depletable resources is wrong. The second is that the theory is logically correct but that one of its assumptions—a predictable world—does not apply. If, for example, each year people overestimated future demands and/or underestimated future supplies, future prices would consistently turn out lower than expected and price would fail to rise over time at the interest rate. Economists are generally skeptical of such an explanation because it requires not merely mistakes but consistent mistakes; one would expect that after a decade or two of overestimating future oil prices, people would learn to do better—especially people who own oil wells.

The third and most interesting explanation of the observed pattern of prices is that oil is not a depletable resource! If this seems like an odd idea, consider that the world has been "about to run out of oil" for a very long time; for most of the past century, proven reserves have been equal to between ten and twenty years of production. I started my analysis of a depletable resource by assuming that there were no production costs, so that the price of the resource was entirely due to the limited quantity. Suppose I had not made that assumption. How would the existence of production costs affect the conclusion?

If production costs can be predicted with certainty, we can repeat our previous analysis, simply substituting "price minus production cost" for price. Price minus production cost is what the owner of an oil well gets by selling his oil. If it rises faster than the interest rate, producers are better off holding their oil for future production; if it rises more slowly than the interest rate, producers are better off selling now. In equilibrium, price minus production cost rises at the interest rate.

So one explanation of the history of oil prices is that most of the price is production cost—including both the cost of pumping the oil and the cost of finding it. If production cost has been falling over time, price could be falling as well—even if price net of production cost was rising.

In the previous discussion, we were considering a *pure depletable resource*—a resource whose price was entirely determined by its limited supply. Consider, at the other extreme, a resource of which only a finite amount exists but for which production costs are substantial and for which that finite amount is very large compared to the quantity demanded at a price sufficient to cover the cost of production— so large that technology, law, and political institutions will have changed beyond recognition long before the supply is exhausted.

Under those circumstances, saving the good now in order to sell it when supplies run short is not a very attractive idea—before that happens we may have stopped using it, the owner may have been expropriated, or the human race may have wiped itself out. Changes in its price over time will be almost entirely determined by changes in production cost. The good is, strictly speaking, depletable, but that fact has no significant effect on its price. The pattern of oil prices over the past ninety years or so suggests that that may well be how the market views petroleum.

If the price of oil is determined by the cost of finding and producing it, then insecure property rights make the price of oil higher, not lower, than it would otherwise be. If someone who invests in finding and drilling an oil well has a 50 percent chance of having his well expropriated as soon as it starts producing, his return if he does keep the well must be at least twice his costs in order for him to be willing to make the investment. So the price of oil will be higher in a world of insecure property rights. The same condition that makes the present price of a depletable resource (more precisely, a resource whose price is mostly due to its limited total quantity rather than to its cost of production) lower makes the present price of a resource whose price is mostly due to cost of production higher!

What's the Difference Between a Tree and an Elephant?

Recycling paper is widely viewed as virtuous, even obligatory. One reason is the belief that it saves trees. That belief is not merely wrong but backwards. There may be good arguments for recycling paper, but, in the United States at present, one consequence is to reduce the number of trees.

Most wood used for paper production in this country is from trees grown for the purpose. Recycling lowers the demand for pulpwood. If you shift a demand curve down, both price and quantity fall. Land that was just worth using to grow trees on at the old price is no longer worth using for that purpose at the new price. Marginal land shifts to other purposes. The number of trees decreases as a result of recycling, just as the number of cattle decreases if more people become vegetarians.

One could imagine a world—many supporters of recycling do imagine a world—in which recycling saved trees, at least for a while. It would be a world with lots of trees that nobody had planted but that were not worth the cost of cutting down unless you could sell them. The higher the demand for pulpwood in that world, the more trees would get cut. Trees would be cut but not planted, so the total acreage of forest would decline with or without recycling, but more slowly with. That does not, popular conceptions to the contrary, describe the United States in this century.

Another fashionable cause is preventing the sale of elephant ivory. On the face of it, the same argument seems to apply. Part of the return from raising elephants comes from selling their tusks. By making that illegal, current law makes it less profitable to raise elephants, which should reduce the world elephant population—precisely the opposite of the ban's intended purpose.

In this case, however, the conclusion is less clear. The reason is insecure property rights: It is easier to steal a tusk than to steal a tree. The ivory ban makes poaching by people who do not own elephants, do not pay the cost of maintaining them, but would like to shoot them in order to cut off the tusks and sell them less profitable. So the overall effect of the ivory ban is unclear; it might save owners of elephants more money, by reducing the cost of protecting the elephants from poachers, than it costs them in lost ivory sales.

So far I have been offering theory. *At the Hand of Man* by Raymond Bonner discusses the facts; the book supports the goal of preserving African wildlife but is highly critical of the means. By his account, the ivory ban was opposed by southern African countries, where property rights in wildlife were relatively secure and poaching a minor problem, and by many wildlife experts. It was supported by wildlife organizations eager for a good fund-raising issue and by East African countries where property rights were poorly protected and poaching and political corruption common. In the 1989 vote that established the ban, seven of the twelve African countries with more than seven thousand elephants voted against it. The no votes were a minority of the countries of Africa but contained a majority of the elephants. That makes sense; countries that protect property rights in elephants are likely to have more elephants than countries that don't.

PRICE = VALUE THROUGH TIME AND SPACE

> "On a list of the differences between Lily and me it would be
> near the top that I park so I won't have to back out when I leave
> and she doesn't."
>
> —Archie Goodwin

Most of us, given the choice between an apple now or an apple
in the future, prefer to have it now. In choosing among alternative
patterns of pleasure over time—alternative utility streams—we discount utility just as we discount income. Income is measured in
dollars, pleasure in utiles. If I am indifferent between a 100-utile
pleasure now or a 105-utile pleasure next year, I may be said to
have an *internal discount rate* (for utility) of 5 percent. My internal
discount rate—my impatience—is a characteristic of my tastes; it
describes my preferences between pleasures now and pleasures in
the future.

The more impatient I am, the more willing I am to give up future
consumption in exchange for present consumption. As I shift consumption from the future to the present, I drive down the marginal
utility to me of present dollars (used to buy me caviar when I am
young) and drive up the marginal utility to me of future dollars
(needed to buy me bread when I am old). The process stops at the
point where the loss in utility due to transferring money from me
when I am old and poor to me when I am young and rich just balances the gain from getting my utility sooner.

My discount rate on a dollar is the rate at which I am just willing
to trade present dollars for future dollars (the combined effect of
impatience and changes in the marginal utility of income over time).
The interest rate is the rate at which I can trade present dollars for
future dollars. I will trade present dollars for future dollars (or future
for present) until they are equal. The argument is the same one that
gave us $MV = P$ back in chapter 4, applied across time instead of
between goods.

Efficient Allocation Across Time

Many discussions of depletable resources take it for granted that
we are exploiting them "too fast." What does that mean? How, in

principle, should one decide how to allocate a limited quantity of oil over time?

If oil sells for $10 a barrel this year, the marginal barrel goes to someone to whom it is worth exactly $10. If it sells for $12 next year, the marginal barrel goes to someone to whom it is worth $12. If we pumped one fewer barrel this year and one more next year, we would be trading $10 of value this year for $12 next year.

If the interest rate is 10 percent, then anyone who has $10 dollars this year can trade it for $11 next year, or vice versa. If $10 now is worth less to me than $11 then, I will lend out some of my income, transferring consumption from present to future. If $10 now is worth more to me than $11 then, I will borrow now against next year's income. In equilibrium, $10 today must be worth as much to me as $11 next year—just as a dollar's worth of one good I consume today must be worth as much to me as a dollar's worth of another. Price equals marginal value—across time as well as across goods.

If I am indifferent between $10 now and $11 next year, then trading $10 worth of oil today for $12 worth next year is a net gain. It continues to be a gain as long as the price of oil next year—and thus the value to the consumer of a marginal gallon next year—is more than 10 percent above the price this year. So we should keep transferring consumption from this year to next year until next year's price is down to this year's price plus 10 percent. Following out this argument, a benevolent energy czar would allocate oil in such a way that its price rose at the interest rate—exactly as the market does.

This is only a sketch of an argument that cannot be made precisely until after the discussion of economic efficiency in chapters 15 and 16. You may want to come back to it after reading those chapters.

Savings, Investment, and the Interest Rate

The individual consumer has a flow of income, an internal discount rate, a utility function, and an interest rate at which he can borrow or lend. His objective is a pattern of consumption over his lifetime that maximizes the present value of his utility. He gets it by rearranging his consumption wherever doing so gets him more utility, discounted at his internal discount rate back to time zero, than it costs. Someone who expects a high income early in his career and a low income later (a professional athlete, for example) saves money in the early years, lends it out at interest, and collects and consumes it later. Someone in the opposite situation (a medical student) borrows money when he is young and pays it back, with interest, when he is older.

So one of the things determining the net demand for loans is the pattern of lifetime earnings and expenditure opportunities. If the number of careers that, like medicine, require lengthy training increases, so will the demand for loans; interest rates will rise. If new medical technology gives old people new and very valuable ways of spending their money, individuals will choose to spend less of their income when young in order to save it to pay medical bills when they are old; the supply of loans will increase and interest rates fall.

A second factor is the internal discount rate. If some cultural change makes people more concerned about their own (or their children's) future, their savings will go up and their borrowing down. If everyone decides to enjoy life today whatever the consequences, savings will go down and borrowing up.

If all lending and borrowing were of this sort, total borrowing and total saving would have to be equal; you cannot borrow a dollar unless someone else saves it and lends it to you, so net demand for loans (at the equilibrium interest rate) would be zero. If demand for loans rises and supply falls, the interest rate goes up until quantity demanded and quantity supplied are again equal.

All lending and borrowing are not of this sort. In addition to individuals borrowing or lending in order to adjust their consumption patterns over time, there are also firms borrowing in order to invest. If interest rates are high, firms invest only in projects that have a high return. The lower the interest rate, the larger the number of projects that yield a positive net present value. So the lower the interest rate—the price of loans—the more firms wish to borrow.

Individuals and firms are not the only participants in the capital market. Governments borrow, both from their citizens and from foreigners, financing present expenditures with claims against future taxes. And capital may flow into (or out of) the country. Individuals, firms, and governments both here and abroad all contribute to the supply and demand curves that determine the U.S. interest rate.

One way of producing future goods from present goods is by building factories; another way is to put the present goods somewhere safe and wait. For goods without significant storage costs (gold bars—provided nobody knows you have them), one unit of the present good produces one unit of the future good, so the interest rate for such goods cannot be less than zero. You would never give ten ounces of gold in exchange for nine a year from now, since you could always hide your ten ounces and have ten ounces a year from now. That is not true for perishable goods (tomatoes) or for goods that are expensive to store (gold bars—if everyone knows you have them). For such goods, negative interest rates are possible.

Impatience and the Balance of Payments

In chapter 6, I showed that a trade deficit is equivalent to a net inflow of capital and argued that whether it is a good or a bad thing depends on why that inflow is occurring. We are now in a position to state the argument a little more clearly.

A capital inflow occurs because foreign investors can get a higher real interest rate here than at home. If the reason the interest rate is high is, as sometimes asserted, that Americans have become increasingly impatient, unwilling to give up present utility for future utility, then it is a symptom of a change that will ultimately make us poorer—we are living on future income and some day the bill will come due. If the reason is that American firms have lots of good investment opportunities and are therefore happy to offer higher rates than Japanese firms, the bill will still come due, but we will have the returns from those investments to pay it with.

TO THINK ABOUT

Some years ago, *Consumer Reports* ran an article on how to choose a mortgage. Different ways of borrowing a given amount of money (with or without down payment, short term or long term, etc.) were compared according to the total number of dollars paid out during the term of the mortgage—the fewer dollars the better.

What conclusion do you think they reached? By their criterion, what is the best way to buy a house? Were they right?

For Further Reading

The analysis of depletable resources in this chapter is not a product of recent concerns with the problem, summarized in phrases (and book titles) such as "limits to growth" and "spaceship earth." It was produced more than sixty years ago by Harold Hotelling in "The Economics of Exhaustible Resources," *Journal of Political Economy*, 39, pp. 137–75 (1931).

13

. . . AND CHANCE

I returned and saw under the sun, that the race is not to the swift, nor the battle to the strong, neither bread to the wise, nor yet riches to men of understanding, nor yet favour to men of skill; but time and chance happeneth to them all.
—Ecclesiastes 9:11

SUNK COSTS

You see an advertisement for a shirt sale at a store twenty miles from your home. When you arrive at the store, you discover that none of the shirts on sale are your size; shirts your size cost only slightly less than in your local store. What should you do?

Buy the shirts. The cost of driving to the store is a *sunk cost*—once incurred, it cannot be recovered. If you had known the situation before you left home, you would not have made the trip—but now that you have made it, you must pay for it whether or not you buy the shirts. Sunk costs are sunk costs.

There are two opposite mistakes with regard to sunk costs. The first is to treat them as if they were not sunk—to refuse to buy the shirts because their price is not low enough to justify the trip even though the trip has already been made. The second is to buy the shirts even when they are more expensive than in your local store, on the theory that you might as well get something for your trip. The something you are getting in this case is less than nothing. This is known as throwing good money after bad.

When, as a very small child, I quarreled with my sister and then locked myself in my room, my father would come to the door and say, "Making a mistake and not admitting it is only hurting yourself twice." When I got a little older, he changed it to "Sunk costs are sunk costs."

The idea of sunk costs is an essential tool to understanding the behavior of firms in an uncertain world. Once a factory is built, the cost of building it is a sunk cost. A rational firm will not build a factory unless it expects the resulting income to at least cover the cost of doing so, just as a rational shopper will not drive twenty miles to a shirt sale unless he expects the savings to be enough to pay for his gas and time. But once the factory is built, it is worth using it as long as the resulting income at least covers costs—including both operating costs and the opportunity cost of not selling the factory to someone else.

A firm will enter an industry only if the price it expects to receive is enough to cover all costs, including constructing a factory or designing a new product—costs are not sunk until they are incurred. Once a firm is in the industry, it will leave only if price is insufficient to cover recoverable costs—since that is all it can get back by leaving. So if an unexpected increase in demand pushes prices up, firms enter only until price is driven down to average cost including sunk cost. If an unexpected decrease in demand pushes prices down, firms leave until price is down to average cost not including sunk cost.

If price is insufficient to cover sunk costs, it is not worth replacing old factories when they wear out, so the number of factories will gradually decline and the price will gradually rise. Eventually price will be equal to average total cost, just as when we reached the equilibrium from above, but it may take a while; it takes longer to wear out a factory than to build one.

In an uncertain world, a firm deciding whether to enter an industry, or an entrepreneur deciding whether to create a firm, does not know what future prices will be, so he must make his decision in terms of his best estimate of the average return he can expect. The zero-profit condition continues to apply, but only in an average sense—if firms are lucky, they make money; if they are unlucky, they lose it. On average they break even.

How to Lie While Telling the Truth: A True Story

Many years ago, while spending a summer in Washington, I came across an interesting piece of economics involving these principles. The congressman I was working for had introduced a bill that would have abolished a large part of the farm program, including price supports for feed grains (crops used to feed animals). Shortly thereafter the Agriculture Department released a "study" of the effects of abolishing those particular parts of the farm program. Their conclusion, as I remember, was that farm income would fall by $5 billion while the government would save only $3 billion in reduced expenditure, for a net loss of $2 billion.

The Agriculture Department's calculations did not include the effect of the proposed changes on consumers—although the whole point of the price support program was (and is) to raise the price of farm products and thus of food. Using the Agriculture Department's figures, I calculated that the proposed abolition would have saved consumers about $7 billion, converting a net loss of $2 billion into a net gain of $5 billion. The Agriculture Department, which opposed the proposed changes, failed to mention that implication of its analysis.

Another part of the report asserted that the abolition of price supports on feed grains would drive down the prices of the animals that consumed them. It went on to say that the price drop would first hit poultry producers, then producers of pork and lamb, and finally beef producers. All of this, to the best of my knowledge, is correct. The conclusion that the authors obviously intended the readers to draw was that poultry producers would be injured a great deal by the change, lamb and pork producers somewhat less, and beef producers injured least of all. This is almost the precise opposite of the truth.

Removing price supports on feed grains lowers their price, reducing the cost of production for poultry, pork, lamb, and beef. In the case of poultry, the flocks can be rapidly increased, so the poultry producers will receive an above-normal profit (cost of production has fallen, price of poultry has not) for only a short time. Once the flocks have increased, the price of chickens falls and the return to their producers goes back to normal. The herds of pigs and sheep take longer to increase, so their producers get above-normal returns for a longer period, and the beef producers get them for longer still. The Agriculture Department appeared to be saying that the beef producers would receive the least injury and the poultry producers the greatest injury from the proposed change. What their analysis actually implied was that the beef producers would receive the largest benefit and the poultry producers the smallest benefit.

SPECULATION

It is difficult to read either newspapers or history books without occasionally coming across the villainous speculators. Speculators, it sometimes seems, are responsible for all the problems of the world—famines, currency crises, high prices.

How Speculation Works

A speculator buys things when he thinks they are cheap and sells them when he thinks they are expensive. Imagine, for example, that you decide there is going to be a bad harvest this year. You buy grain now, while it is still cheap. If you are right, the harvest is bad, the price of grain goes up, and you sell at a large profit.

There are several reasons why this way of making a profit gets so much bad press. For one thing, the speculator is profiting by other people's bad fortune, making money from, in Kipling's phrase, "Man's belly pinch and need." Of course, the same might be said of farmers, who are usually considered good guys. For another, the speculator's purchase of grain tends to drive up the price, making it look as though he is responsible for the scarcity.

But in order to make money, the speculator must sell as well as buy. If he buys when grain is plentiful, he does indeed tend to increase the price then; but if he sells when it is scarce (which is what he wants to do in order to make money), he increases the supply and decreases the price just when the additional grain is most useful.

The speculator, acting for his own selfish motives, does almost exactly what a benevolent ruler would do. When he foresees a future famine he drives up the current price, encouraging consumers to economize on food (by slaughtering meat animals early, for example, to save their feed for human consumption), to import food from abroad, to produce other kinds of food (go fishing, dry fruit, ...), and in other ways to prepare for the anticipated shortage. He then stores the wheat and distributes it (for a price) at the peak of the famine. Not only does he not cause famines, he prevents them.

Speculators, if successful, smooth out price movements, buying goods when they are below their long-run price and selling them when they are above it, raising the price toward equilibrium in the one case and lowering it toward equilibrium in the other. They do what governmental "price-stabilization" schemes claim to do—reduce short-run fluctuations in prices. In the process, they frequently interfere with such price-stabilization schemes, most of which are run by producing countries and designed to "stabilize" prices as high as possible.

Cui Bono?

> "Why indeed should we welcome you, Master Stormcrow?
> *Lathspell* I name you, ill-news; and ill news is an ill guest they say."
>
> —Grima to Gandalf in *The Two Towers* by
> J. R. R. Tolkien

Part of the unpopularity of speculators and speculation may reflect the traditional hostility to bearers of bad news—in this case, news of approaching shortages. Part also may be due to the difficulty of understanding just how speculation works. Whatever the reason, ideas kill, and the idea that speculators cause shortages must be one of the most lethal errors in history. If speculation is unpopular it is also unprofitable, since the speculator is at risk of having his stocks of grain seized by mob or government. In poor countries, which means almost everywhere through almost all of history, the alternative to speculation in food crops is periodic famine.

One reason people suspect speculators of causing price fluctuations is summarized in the Latin phrase *Cui bono?* A loose translation would be "Who benefits?" If the newspapers discover that a gubernatorial candidate has been receiving large campaign donations from a firm that made $10 million off state contracts last year, it is a fair guess that the information was fed to them by his opponent. When, after a third-world coup, the winners immediately allied themselves with the Soviet Union (or the United States), we did not have to look at the new ruler's bank records to suspect that the takeover was subsidized by Moscow (or Washington).

While *Cui bono?* is a useful rule for many things, it is not merely useless but positively deceptive for understanding price movements. The people who benefit from an increase in the price of something are those who produce it, but by producing they drive the price not up but down. The manufacturer of widgets may spend his evenings on his knees praying for the price of widgets to go up, but he spends his days behind a desk making it go down. The belief that price changes are the work of those who benefit by them is usually an error and sometimes a dangerous one.

Buying when prices are low raises low prices; selling when prices are high lowers high prices. Successful speculators decrease price fluctuations, just as successful widget makers decrease the price of widgets. Destabilizing speculators are, of course, a logical possibility; they can be recognized by the red ink in their ledgers. The Hunt brothers of Texas are a notable example. Some years ago, they lost several billion dollars in the process of driving the price of silver up to what turned out to be several times its long-run equilibrium level.

I once heard a talk by an economist who had applied the relationship between stabilization and profitable speculation in reverse. Central banks buy and sell currencies, supposedly to stabilize exchange rates. If profitable speculation is stabilizing, one might expect successful stabilization to be profitable. If the banks are buying dollars when they are temporarily cheap and selling them when they are temporarily expensive, they should be both stabilizing the value of the dollar and making a profit.

One implication of this argument is that the central banks are superfluous—if there are profits to be made by stabilizing currencies, speculators will be glad to volunteer for the job. A second implication is that we can judge the success of central banks by seeing whether they make or lose money on their speculations. The conclusion of the speaker, who had studied precisely that question, was that they generally lost money.

THE UTILITY LOTTERY: RATIONAL CHOICE IN AN UNCERTAIN WORLD

In chapters 1 through 11, we saw how markets determine prices and quantities in a certain and unchanging world. In chapter 12, we generalized the argument to a world that was changing but certain. In such a world, any decision involves a predictable stream of costs and benefits. One simply converts each stream into its present value and compares them.

The next step is to analyze individual choice in an uncertain world. Again our objective is to convert the problem we are dealing with into the easier problem we have already solved. To describe an uncertain world, we assume that each individual has a *probability distribution* over possible outcomes. He does not know what *will* happen, but he knows, or believes he knows, what *might* happen and *how likely* it is to happen.

The Rational Gambler

You are betting on whether a coin will come up heads or tails. Your problem is to decide what bets you should be willing to take. If the coin is a fair one, the answer seems obvious—take bets that offer a payoff of more than $1 for each $1 bet; refuse bets that offer less. More generally, take all bets that, on average, make money; decline all bets that, on average, lose money.

This is a sensible policy if you expect to make many such bets, since you can expect to end up with something close to the average outcome. Suppose, however, that you are only playing the game once—and the bet is not $1 but $50,000. If you lose, you are destitute—$50,000 is all you have. If you win, you gain $100,000. That is an attractive gamble, measured in dollars, but not necessarily one you should accept. A decline in your wealth from $50,000 to zero may hurt you more than an increase from $50,000 to $150,000 helps you. One could easily enough imagine situations in which losing $50,000 resulted in your starving to death while gaining $100,000 produced only a modest increase in your welfare.

This is an example of what economists call *declining marginal utility*. The dollars that raise you from zero to $50,000 are worth more to you per dollar than the additional dollars beyond $50,000. Dollars are used to buy goods, and we expect goods to be worth less to you the more of them you have.

When you choose a profession, start a business, buy a house, or stake your life savings playing the commodity market, you are betting a large sum, and the bet is not one you will repeat very many times. How will a rational individual decide whether or not to take such gambles?

The answer to this question was provided by John von Neumann, the same mathematician who invented game theory. He demonstrated that by combining the idea of expected return with the idea of utility, it was possible to describe the behavior of individuals dealing with uncertain situations—whether or not they were repeated many times. The fundamental idea is that a rational individual maximizes expected return in utiles, not in dollars—average utility, not average income. If the additional utility from each additional dollar becomes less as your wealth becomes greater, you will be risk averse, willing to accept an even bet only if the dollar gain if you win is more than the dollar loss if you lose—enough more to make up for the fact that the dollars you risk losing are more valuable to you than the dollars you hope to win.

Figure 13–1a shows the utility function of someone who is risk averse. His utility increases with income, but it increases more and more slowly the more income he has. Someone whose utility function curved the other way, as shown in Figure 13–1b, would be *risk preferring*. He would be willing to accept some bets that, on average, lost him money—as almost all of the bets offered by casinos and lotteries do.

These terms sound as though they describe attitudes toward uncertainty, with a risk preferrer liking and a risk averter disliking the thrill of a gamble, but that is wrong. Utility (or disutility) from the act of gambling may exist in some people, but they have not appeared anywhere in our analysis—we are concerned with people who judge gambles by their results. A risk averter is simply someone who has declining marginal utility of income, and as a result will accept only gambles that provide a gain in dollars large enough to outweigh the fact that the dollars he might win will be worth less to him than the dollars he might lose. A risk preferrer is simply someone with an increasing marginal utility of income.

Strictly speaking, what we call a "risk averter" is a "money risk averter." The same person might have declining marginal utility for money and increasing marginal utility for some other good—say life expectancy or number of children. There is nothing irrational about refusing to gamble, at even odds, a loss of $100,000 against a gain of $100,000, but being willing to gamble, at even odds, a ten-year reduction in life expectancy against a ten-year increase.

Suppose someone requires a certain amount of money in order to buy enough food to stay alive. Increases in income below that point extend his life a little, but he still ends up starving to death. An

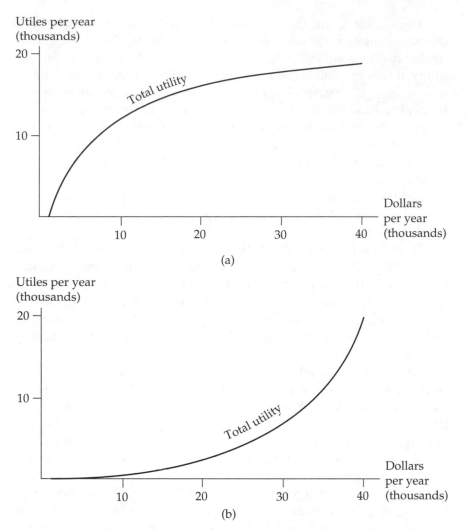

Figures 13-1a & b   Total utility of income for risk-averse (a) and risk-preferring (b) individuals.

increase in income that gives him enough to survive is worth a great deal to him. Once he is well past that point, additional income buys less important things, so marginal utility of income falls. The corresponding utility function is shown as Figure 13–2a; marginal utility first rises with increasing income, then falls.

Such an individual would be a risk preferrer if his initial income were at point *A*, below subsistence. He would be a risk averter if he were starting at point *B*. In the former case, he would, if necessary,

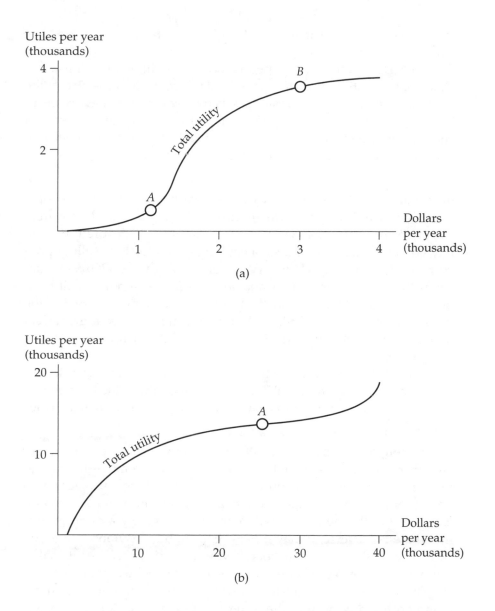

Figures 13-2a & b   Individuals who are risk averters for some incomes and risk preferrers for others. Figure 13–2a shows someone whose marginal utility of income increases as his income approaches what he needs to survive, then decreases beyond that. Figure 13–2b shows the opposite pattern—someone who is risk averse at low incomes but risk preferring at high. Starting at point A he could increase his expected utility by buying both insurance and lottery tickets.

risk $1,000 to get $500 at even odds. If he loses, he only starves a little faster; if he wins, he lives.

Your risk preference depends on three different things—the shape of your utility function, your initial income, and the size of the bet you are considering. For small bets, we would expect everyone to be roughly risk neutral; the marginal utility of a dollar does not change very much between $19,999 and $20,001. For larger bets, risk aversion and risk preference become more important.

Insurance. Risk aversion provides one explanation for why people buy insurance. On average, insurance is a losing bet for the insured, since the insurance company must make enough on premiums to pay not only what customers collect but also the costs of selling policies and investigating claims. A customer who pays $300 to insure against one chance in a thousand that his $200,000 house will burn down is losing $100 on the deal—measured in money. But if the house burns down, the utility of money to him will be a great deal higher than if it does not. Measured in utility, the insurance may well be worth its price.

One implication of this is that, since people are (almost) risk neutral with regard to small risks, they are much more likely to insure against large risks than against small. That seems generally to be true.

The Lottery-Insurance Puzzle. When you buy insurance, you accept an unfair gamble—a gamble that loses money on average—in order to reduce uncertainty. When you buy a lottery ticket, you also accept an unfair gamble—on average, the lottery pays out in prizes less than it takes in—but this time you do it in order to increase your uncertainty. If you are risk averse, it may makes sense to buy insurance—but you should never buy lottery tickets. If you are a risk preferrer it makes sense to buy a lottery ticket—but you should never buy insurance.

This brings us to a puzzle that has bothered economists for more than two hundred years—the lottery-insurance paradox. In the real world, the same people sometimes buy both insurance and lottery tickets. Can this be consistent with rational behavior?

There are at least two possible ways in which it can. One is illustrated in Figure 13–2b. The individual with the utility function shown there is risk averse at low incomes and risk preferring at high incomes. If he starts at point A, in between the two regions, he may be interested in buying both insurance and lottery tickets. Insurance protects against risks that might move his income below *A*—where he is risk averse. Lottery tickets offer the possibility of an income above *A*—where he is risk preferring.

This solution is logically possible, but not very plausible. Why should people have such peculiarly shaped utility functions, with the value to them of an additional dollar first falling with increasing income then rising again? And if they do, why should their incomes just happen to be near the border between the two regions?

Another explanation is that in the real-world situation we observe, one of our assumptions does not hold. We have been considering situations where the only difference among the outcomes is money; the utility of each depends only on the amount of money it leaves you with. It is not clear that this is true for the individuals who actually buy lottery tickets.

Consider the lotteries you have yourself been offered—by *Reader's Digest*, Publisher's Clearinghouse, and similar enterprises. The price is the price of a stamp, the payoff—lavishly illustrated with glossy photographs—a (very small) chance of a new Cadillac, a Caribbean vacation, an income of $20,000 a year for life. My rough calculations—based on a guess of how many people respond to the lottery—suggest that the value of the prize multiplied by the chance of getting it comes to less than the cost of the stamp. The expected return is negative.

Why, then, do so many people enter? The explanation I find most plausible is that what they are getting for their stamp is not merely one chance in a million at a $40,000 car. They are also getting a certainty of being able to daydream about getting the car— or the vacation or the income—from the time they send in the envelope until the winners are announced. The daydream is made more real, and so more satisfying, by the knowledge that there is a chance, even if a slim one, that they will actually win the prize. The lottery is not only selling a gamble. It is also selling a dream—and at a very low price.

This explanation has the disadvantage of pushing such lotteries out of the area where economics can say much about them; we know a good deal about rational gambling but very little about the market for dreams. It has the advantage of explaining not only the existence of lotteries but some of their characteristics. If lotteries exist to provide people a chance for money, why do the prizes often take other forms? Why not give the winner $40,000 and let him decide whether to buy a Cadillac with it? That would not only improve the prize from the standpoint of the winner but would also save the sponsors the cost of all those glossy photographs.

But people may find it easier to daydream about their winnings if the winnings take a concrete form. So the sponsors offer goods instead of money—and provide a variety of prizes to suit different tastes in daydreams. This seems especially common with "free" lotteries—ones where the price is a stamp and the sponsor pays for the prizes out of someone's advertising budget. Lotteries that sell tickets seem more inclined to pay off in money—why, I do not know.

In chapter 1, I included in my definition of economics the assumption that individuals have reasonably simple objectives. You will have to decide for yourself whether a taste for daydreams is consistent with that assumption.

Buying Information

You are trying to decide between a Honda Accord and a Nissan Altima. You expect that you will like one of the cars better than the other, but unfortunately do not know which. One solution is to flip a coin and buy one of the cars tomorrow. A more expensive alternative is to rent an Accord for your next long trip and an Altima for the trip after that; the additional information will raise the chance of choosing the right car from 50 percent to a near certainty. You should rent if and only if the benefit of being sure to get the right car is more than the extra cost of using a rented car for the next two trips.

This simple example illustrates the logic of buying information. By paying some *search cost* you reduce uncertainty, improving the average outcome of your decisions. To decide whether the search cost is worth paying, you compare expected utility without search to expected utility with search, remembering to include the cost of the search in your calculation.

One example that has received a great deal of attention is job search. Many people who consider themselves unemployed could find a job almost instantly—if they were willing to wait tables, wash dishes, or drive a cab. What they are looking for is not a job but a good job. The longer they look, the better, on average, will be the best job opportunity they find. Their rational strategy is to keep looking as long as they expect to gain more from additional search than it costs them. Such *search unemployment* makes up a substantial fraction of the measured unemployment rate.

One implication is that increases in unemployment compensation tend to increase the unemployment rate. The reason is not that the unemployed are lazy bums who prefer collecting unemployment to working but that they are rational searchers. The higher the level of unemployment compensation, the lower the cost of being unemployed while searching for a job. The less it costs to search, the more searching it pays to do.

WHERE WE ARE NOW

In the first eleven chapters of this book, we used economics to understand how markets work in a certain and unchanging world. In chapter 12, we showed that the same tools could be applied to a changing but certain world—by measuring costs and benefits in present values instead of annual flows. We have now seen how to apply the same analysis to an uncertain world: by measuring costs and benefits as expected utilities of probabilistic outcomes instead of utilities of certain outcomes. Combining the lessons of the two chapters to analyze choice in a world that is both changing and uncertain would be straightforward: Measure costs and benefits in present value of expected utility.

Introducing time and change creates some new problems, such as those associated with sunk costs. Yet it is still true that in learning to deal with the simple world of chapters 1 through 11 we learned most of the basic ideas of economics, and that in chapters 12 and 13 we have taken a large step toward making those ideas applicable to the world we live in.

TO THINK ABOUT

In one episode of *Star Trek,* Spock is in an orbiting landing craft that is running out of fuel and will shortly crash. Captain Kirk and the *Enterprise* are about to leave the planet, having somehow misplaced one landing craft and science officer. Spock fires his rockets, burning up all the remaining fuel, in the hope that the *Enterprise* will notice the flare and come rescue him. Later Kirk twits the supremely logical Spock with irrationality for having traded his last few hours of fuel for a one-in-a-hundred chance of rescue. Was Spock's behavior irrational?

For Further Reading

The original discussion of von Neumann utility is in John von Neumann and Oskar Morgenstern, *Theory of Games and Economic*

Behavior (Princeton: Princeton University Press, 1944), chapter 1.

A classic discussion of the lottery-insurance paradox is Milton Friedman and Leonard J. Savage, "The Utility Analysis of Choices Involving Risk," *Journal of Political Economy*, vol. 56, no. 4 (August 1948), pp. 279–304.

14

WHO GETS
HOW MUCH WHY?

When a psychiatrist wants to get his audience's attention, he talks about sex. Economists talk about the income distribution. In both cases the audience's interest is prurient (what are other people doing?), puritanical (that they shouldn't be?) and personal (how am I doing?). In both, there is the thrill of violating taboo; although sex is gradually becoming an accepted topic of conversation, asking how much money someone makes is still beyond the pale.

In this chapter, I approach the forbidden question from three different angles. First, and most briefly, I discuss why most "facts" about the U.S. income distribution contain less information than meets the eye. Second, I discuss two questions that lie at the heart of many political disagreements—"What determines the distribution of income?" and "Is it just?" Finally, I consider the matter from the perspective of a more personal and self-interested question: How can I figure out whether some particular change will make me better or worse off?

LIES, DAMN LIES, AND STATISTICS

You read in the paper that the bottom 20 percent of households receives less than 5 percent of all income, while the top 20 percent receives more than 40 percent. That sounds like a world of radical inequality.

There are at least two things wrong with such figures. The first is that they do not distinguish between differences in people's lives and differences in where in their lives people are. Some of those in the bottom 20 percent are retired people living comfortably on their savings in a home they own, or college students with part-time jobs. The second is that it does not distinguish temporary random differences, people having good or bad years, from permanent differences. Correcting those problems by comparing individuals on the basis of the present value of their lifetime stream of income eliminates about half the measured inequality.

A more subtle problem arises with attempts to measure changes over time. Suppose you take a random sample from the bottom 10 percent of this year's income distribution and ask them how much money they made last year. You discover that they did better last year than this year and conclude that the poor are getting poorer.

You then encounter another researcher, who did almost but not quite the same experiment. His sample was from last year's bottom 10 percent. This year, they are doing better than last year. He concluded that the poor are getting richer.

You have just discovered what statisticians call the *regression fallacy*. At any given instant, the bottom 10 percent consists in part of people who are permanently poor and in part of people who happen to be having a bad year. If this happens to be an unusually bad year, the odds are that last year was and next year will be better.

The title of this section is from a famous wisecrack. "There are three kinds of lies: lies, damn lies, and statistics." Applied to the work of professional statisticians it is a wholly unjustified slander; one of their professional skills is avoiding such errors. But applied to the "statistics" in the daily paper or on TV news shows, it is a fair comment.

Economics, Justice, and Inequality

One thing about which everyone agrees is that he is paid less than he should be. Most of us are willing to agree that our friends, too, are paid less than they should be. Being paid too little means receiving less than your fair share of the world's goods—and if I am getting less than my fair share, someone else must be getting more than his. Most of us are willing to suggest candidates.

This raises two obvious questions: What determines how much each of us gets? And what determines how much each of us ought to get?

To Each According to His Value. An employer is deciding whether to hire another worker. He calculates how much more output he could produce as a result. As long as the market value of the increased output, net of any associated costs, is larger than what he must pay the worker, he hires—and profit goes up. He stops hiring at the point where one more worker is worth exactly what he costs. So the individual worker receives a wage just equal to his marginal revenue product—the value of the increased production due to his presence.

The argument applies to the other inputs to production as well, as we saw back in chapter 9. So the prices received by the owners of all inputs—the wages of labor, the rent of land, the interest on capital—are equal to the marginal revenue products of those inputs.

To Each According to His Cost. Next consider the situation from the standpoint of the worker. A worker free to choose how many hours he wants to work will work up to the point where his wage equals the marginal value of his leisure—the cost, to him, of working an additional hour. So his wage is equal to what it costs him to work. Similarly, individuals will save up to the point at which the cost of giving up a little more present consumption in exchange for future consumption just balances what they gain by doing so—the interest on the money saved. So the interest on capital is equal to the marginal cost of producing it.

One Explanation Too Many? We appear to have two explanations of the distribution of income—which some might consider one explanation too many. But neither is complete by itself. Labor receives its marginal product—but the marginal product of labor is determined in part by how much labor (and capital and land and . . .) is being used; the law of diminishing returns tells us that as we increase the amount of one input while holding the others constant, the marginal product of that input eventually starts to go down. Labor is paid its marginal cost—but that cost depends in part on how much labor is being sold; the cost to you of working one more hour depends in part on how many hours you are working.

What we have is a description of equilibrium on the market for inputs. The full explanation of the income distribution is that the price of an input is equal to both its marginal cost of production and its marginal revenue product, and the quantity of the input sold and used is that quantity for which the marginal cost of production and the marginal revenue product are equal. (Marginal) cost equals price equals (marginal) value.

Is It Just?

Supporters of the market system sometimes defend it by arguing that everyone gets what he produces, which seems fair. The wages of the laborer equal the value of the additional output he produces, the interest received by the capitalist equals the value of the additional output his capital produces, and so on.

Even if you argue, as many would, that some inputs belong to the wrong people—for instance, that much of the land in the United States was unjustly stolen from the American Indians and should be given back—the argument still seems to justify a large part of the existing division of income. In the United States at present, income to human inputs adds up to about 80 percent of the total, with the rest made up of interest, land rent, and corporate profits—and most people would agree that we own ourselves.

One might also try to justify the distribution of income by appealing to the second half of the market equality—price equals cost of production. The capitalist deserves the interest he receives because it compensates him for the cost to him of postponing his consumption—giving up consumption now in exchange for more consumption later. The worker deserves his wage because it compensates him for the leisure he had to give up in order to work.

The problem with these arguments is that the product and the cost that equal price are marginal product and marginal cost, and both depend on the quantity of other inputs. The worker's salary just compensates him for the last hour he works—but he gets the same salary for all the other hours. The interest collected by the capitalist equals the value of the additional production made possible by the addition of his capital—but that depends, in part, on how much labor, land, and other inputs are being used. Pure capital, all by itself, cannot produce much.

Fortunately, determining what is just is one of the problems that is not part of economics. Yet.

Getting Personal: What's in It for Me?

Let us now abandon moral philosophy to the philosophers and turn to a more practical question. What does economic theory tell me about what changes in the economy make me better or worse off? When should I boo, when should I cheer, and what should I vote for?

One simple answer is that an increase in the supply of an input I own drives down its price and my income. So does an increase in the supply of an input that is a close substitute for an input I own. If I happen to own an oil well, I will regard someone else's discovery of a new field of natural gas—or a process for producing power by thermonuclear fusion—as bad news.

An increase in the supply of an input used with the input I own (a *complement in production*) has the opposite effect. As the relative amount of my input used in production declines, its marginal product increases (the principle of diminishing returns, applied in reverse). If I own an oil well, it makes sense to lobby for more highways.

Economic changes affect what I buy as well as what I sell. Increases in the supply of goods I buy, or of inputs used to produce goods I buy, lower the price of those goods and so tend to benefit me. Decreases in their supply tend to make me worse off, for the same reason. As an avid user of computers—I own six working ones, not counting my old LNW, obsolete but not forgotten, in a box in the basement—I regard restrictions on the import of RAM chips with horror.

This simple answer, however, will not help me very often. It is clear enough that if I am a (selfish) physician, I should be in favor of restrictive licensing laws that keep down the number of physicians, and that if I am a (selfish) patient, I should be against them. It is much less clear how I should view the effect on my welfare of government deficits, restrictions on immigration, laws controlling the use of land, or any of a myriad of other things that do not directly affect the particular things I sell or buy.

And for Our Next Act

You may by now have realized that economics involves a continual balancing act between unrealistic simplification and unworkable complication. For the last seven chapters we have been making our picture increasingly complicated in the process of fitting it more closely to the real world. It is time to swing back in the other direction. In the next section, we will see how, even in a complicated economy such as ours, we can simplify production down to three inputs. By doing so, we make it possible to predict the effect on your welfare of economic changes involving goods that you neither buy nor sell.

PART 2: THE FACTORS OF PRODUCTION

A Golden Delicious apple, a Jonathan apple, and a Granny Smith apple are three different things. Indeed, two Jonathan apples are different things; one is a little redder than the other. Even if we considered two identical apples, they would still be in different places, and the location of a good is one of its important characteristics; oil companies spend large sums converting crude petroleum two miles down into crude petroleum in a tank above ground.

One cost of fine distinctions is that they make analysis more complicated. It is more precise to treat Golden Delicious apples and Red Delicious apples as two different goods that happen to be close substitutes; it is simpler to treat them as the same good. One could make a simple picture complicated by viewing every apple as a different good. I am instead going to make a complicated picture simple by viewing many different things as one good. This is how it works.

If you've Seen One Acre, You've Seen Them All

There are three kinds of land—meadow, hillside, and highland. Meadow is especially good for growing wheat, hillside for grapes. Highland can grow either—wheat as well as meadowland, grapes as well as hillside. Currently all of the meadows are used for wheat, all the hillsides for grapes, and the highlands are divided between the two crops.

Suppose a flood wipes out a hundred acres of meadow. The initial effect is to raise the market price of wheat and of land growing wheat. Some highland is now shifted from grapes to the (more profitable) wheat. The quantity of wheat supplied increases, driving the price of wheat part of the way back down toward what it was before the flood. The quantity of grapes supplied decreases, since some land that had been producing grapes is now producing wheat; the price of grapes rises. When equilibrium is reestablished, the prices of all three kinds of land are again the same. The final effect on the prices of wheat, grapes, and land is the same as if the flood had wiped out a hundred acres of highland or of hillside.

As long as we consider only changes in supply and demand (of land, wheat, and grapes) that leave some highland growing grapes and some growing wheat, the situation is the same as if all the land were identical! We cannot directly replace meadow with hillside (or vice versa), but we can do so indirectly by replacing meadow with highland and highland with hillside. In analyzing this particular economy, we can reduce three different inputs—three kinds of land—into one.

Land in the real world does not fall into such tidy categories, but the qualitative result still holds. For many purposes, we can think of land as a single good with a single price and quantity—not because all land is the same but because there are always some pieces of land that are on the margin between being used for one purpose or another.

Land is not the only thing that can be treated in this way. There are three traditional *factors of production*—land, labor, and capital. Each is a group of goods that substitute for each other sufficiently well to be treated, for some purposes, as a single good.

Most inputs to production can be classified as either land, labor, or capital, although not always in the way a noneconomist might expect—a surgeon, for example, is largely capital! So this approach allows us to view even a very complicated economy as if it used only three inputs. For analyzing short-run changes, the approach is not very useful—an increased demand for economists is unlikely to have much immediate effect on either the wages of ditchdiggers or the interest on bonds, although economists are a mixture of labor and capital, the wages of ditchdiggers are a measure of the price of labor, and the interest on bonds is a measure of the price of capital.

In the longer run, it is easier to transform one form of land, labor, or capital into another. If the demand for economists increases, more people become economists, leaving fewer for other jobs. Training those additional economists requires someone—the student, his parents, investors funding student loans, or the government—to spend money now for a return in the future. So less money will be available to be spent now for a future return in other ways—to build factories, do research, or train people in other professions. Labor and capital are being shifted into producing economics and out of producing ditches, cars, and many other things.

Zap—You're a Ditchdigger

People are not identical; a big man can probably dig more ditches per day than a small woman. If the person who could dig twice as many ditches could also type twice as many pages and treat twice as many patients, we could simply describe one person as two units of labor and the other as one. In a more complicated world, we have to take account of differing skills and indirect transformations.

One way of transforming secretaries into ditchdiggers is by having the biggest and strongest secretaries switch jobs. That will not produce many ditchdiggers. A better way may be to convert secretaries into truck drivers and (other) truck drivers into ditchdiggers. Truck driving, despite its macho image, is a job that does not require a great deal of physical strength; it can be and often is done by women. If one secretary can be transformed, through this indirect route, into one ditchdigger, secretaries and ditchdiggers each contain the same amount of labor. If one secretary can be transformed into two ditchdiggers (perhaps ex-secretaries make unusually good truck drivers, and ex-truck drivers unusually good ditchdiggers), then a secretary contains twice as much labor as a ditchdigger—even if she can't lift a shovel.

Land

In my earlier discussion, I set my assumptions up so that an acre of each kind of land was equivalent to an acre of each other kind. I could as easily have assumed that one acre of meadow produced the same return as two acres of highland used for wheat, and that one acre of highland used for growing grapes produced as much as two acres of hillside. In that case, the price of an acre of meadow would have been twice the price of an acre of highland and four times the price of an acre of hillside. Meadow contains four units of land per acre, highland two, hillside one—just as a secretary contained two units of labor and a ditchdigger one in the previous example. We could still analyze land as if it were all the same—with the total quantity equal to the amount of hillside plus twice the amount of highland plus four times the amount of meadow.

There are a certain number of square miles on the surface of the earth; the number has not changed significantly in the past hundred thousand years, and, short of some massive redesign of the planet, will not change significantly in the next hundred thousand. So if we consider only *raw land* and classify investments that increase its productivity (fertilizing, draining, clearing) as capital, the supply of land, unlike the supply of most other things we have discussed, is almost perfectly inelastic.

If the supply of land is perfectly inelastic, the supply curve for land is vertical, so a tax on land is borne entirely by the owner, with none of it passed on to the renter. Such a tax generates no excess burden; you cannot distort the production of something that is not being produced. These facts have sometimes been used to argue that land is the ideal thing to tax—there is no excess burden, and all of the tax is borne by the landowners.

Raw land may be in perfectly inelastic supply, but the land we actually use—to live on, grow our food on, build our roads on—is not. It is a combination of raw land and other resources—labor used to clear the land, capital invested in improving it. One measure of the difference between land in use and raw land is the fact that only about one-tenth of the land area of the earth is under cultivation—and the amount used for houses, roads, and the like is even less.

If you tax the market value of land, you discourage improvements; the supply curve for improved land is by no means perfectly inelastic. In order to tax only raw land, you first have to find some way of measuring it.

Rent and Quasi-Rent

Because land is the standard example of a good in perfectly inelastic supply and because payment for the use of land is called rent, the term *rent* has come to be used in economics in two different ways. One is to mean payment for the use of something, as distinguished from payment for ownership (price). You buy cars from GM but rent them from Avis. The other is to mean payment for the use of something in fixed (i.e., perfectly inelastic) supply—or, more generally, payments above what is needed to call something into existence.

In this second sense, rent is paid for many things other than land. Scarce human talents—the abilities of an inventive genius or the combination of good coordination and very long legs—can be thought of as valuable resources in fixed supply and without close substitutes; the wages of Thomas Edison or Wilt Chamberlain may be analyzed as a sort of rent. Rent in this sense is a price that allocates the use of something among consumers but does not tell producers how much to produce, since the good is not being produced.

Just as one can argue for taxing away the rent on the site value of land, on the grounds that such a tax will result in no excess burden, so one can argue for taxing away the rent on scarce human talents. Here again, problems arise when you try to measure what you want to tax. It is not clear how the IRS can tell which athletes and which inventors will continue to exercise their abilities even if they are paid no more than the normal market wage, and which will decide to do something else.

In the very short run, practically everything is in fixed supply. In the longer run, many things are. In the very long run, practically nothing is. Perhaps if certain talents produce high incomes, the possessors of those talents will be rich and have lots of children, increasing the supply of those talents. Perhaps a sufficiently high rent on land will encourage the exploration and development of other planets. The economic analysis developed to explain the rent on land may be inapplicable to anything—even land—in the (very) long run. But it can be used to explain the behavior of many prices in the short run—which may be a day for fresh fish and thirty years for houses. The return on goods whose supply is inelastic in the short term, such as factories in a declining industry that are worth using but not worth replacing, is called a *quasi-rent*.

Capital

The third factor of production is capital. The meanings of labor and of land (more generally, unproduced natural resources) seem fairly obvious; the meaning of capital is not. Does producing capital mean saving? Building factories? Investing your savings? What is capital—what does it look like?

One (good) answer is that using capital means using inputs now to produce outputs later. The more dollar-years required (number of dollars of inputs times number of years until the outputs appear—a slight oversimplification, since it ignores the effect of compound interest, but good enough for our purposes), the more the amount of capital used. Capital is productive because it is (often) possible to produce more output if you are willing to wait than if you are not—to spend a week chipping out a flint ax and then use the ax to cut down lots of trees instead of spending two days scraping through a tree with a chunk of unshaped flint, or to make machines to make machines to make machines to make cars instead of simply making cars. Capital is expensive because people usually prefer consumption now to consumption in the future and must be paid to give up the former in exchange for the latter. *Capital goods* are the physical objects (factories, machines, apple trees, flint axes) produced by inputs now and used to produce outputs in the future.

Many capital goods, once built, have only a narrow range of uses. There is no way an automobile factory can produce steel or a milling machine grow grain. In the case of labor and land, one variety may substitute for another through a chain of intermediates—secretary to truck driver to ditchdigger. Finding a chain to connect a steel mill to a drainage canal, or an invention (capital in the form of valuable knowledge produced by research) to a tractor, would be hard.

A steel mill cannot be converted into a drainage canal—but an investor can decide whether he will use his savings to pay workers to build the one or the other. So the anticipated return on all investments—the interest rate—must be the same. If investors expected to make more by investing a dollar in building a steel mill than by investing a dollar in digging a drainage canal, capital would shift into steel; the increased supply of steel would drive down the price of steel and the return on investments in steel mills. The reduced supply of capital in canal building would, similarly, increase the return on investments in canals. Investors would continue to shift their capital out of the one use and into the other until the returns on the two were the same.

A reduction in the supply of steel mills—the destruction of a hundred mills by a war or an earthquake—will drive up the price of steel, increase the return on investments in steel mills, attract capital that would otherwise have gone elsewhere into the steel industry, and so drive up the interest rate. In the long run, there is a single quantity of capital and a single price for its use. All capital is the same—before it is invested.

After it is invested, capital takes many forms. One of the most important is human capital. A medical student who invests $90,000 and six years in becoming a surgeon is bearing costs now in return for benefits in the future, just as he would be if he had invested his time and money in building a factory. If the salary of surgeons were not high enough to make investing in himself at least as attractive as investing in something else, he would have invested in physical capital instead. So the salary of a surgeon is in part wages of labor, in part rent on scarce human talents, and in part interest on human capital.

There is one important respect in which human capital differs from other forms of capital. If you have an idea for building a profitable factory, you can raise money to pay for it either by making other investors part owners or by borrowing, using the factory itself as your security. Your ability to invest in human capital is much more limited. You cannot sell shares of yourself because that would violate the laws against slavery—you cannot put yourself up as collateral for the same reason. You can borrow money to pay for your training—but after the money is spent you may, if you wish, declare bankruptcy. Your creditors have no way of repossessing the training that you bought with their money.

So investments in human capital will be made only if the human in question (or his parents or someone else who values his future welfare or trusts him to pay back loans) can provide the necessary capital. In that respect, the market for human capital is an imperfect one.

The source of the imperfection was discussed in chapter 12—insecure property rights. In chapter 12, the property rights of owners of oil were insecure because of the possibility of expropriation—one consequence was to discourage investment in finding oil and drilling oil wells. Here the property rights of lenders are insecure because of the possibility of bankruptcy; the result is to discourage investment in (someone else's) human capital. The imperfection provides, on the one hand, an argument for government provision (or guarantees) of loans for education and, on the other hand, an argument for relaxing the prohibition against (self-chosen) slavery—to the extent of limiting the ability of people who borrow for their education to declare bankruptcy.

Another argument for relaxing the prohibition on voluntary slavery is the history of immigration to the United States. Many of the immigrants of the seventeenth and eighteenth centuries came as indentured servants. Since they did not have enough money to pay for their own transportation, they agreed to be auctioned off on arrival—with the winner the employer willing to accept the shortest number of years of labor in exchange for paying what they owed the ship captain. They would have been better off coming over without such an agreement—but without the agreement they would not have been able to come.

PART 3: APPLICATIONS

The factors of production are a powerful tool for figuring out how a change in one part of the economy affects others—including the part with your name on it. In this section we apply that tool to three public policy issues—immigration restrictions, limitations on foreign investment in poor countries, and controls on land use.

Immigration

Prior to the 1920s, the United States followed a policy of open immigration, save for some restrictions on immigration of Chinese and Japanese. The result was a flood of immigrants that at its peak exceeded a million a year. Suppose we went back to open immigration. Who would benefit and who would lose?

Immigrants have, on average, less human and physical capital than the present inhabitants of the United States; they are less skilled and poorer. So increased immigration would increase the ratio of labor to capital. Immigrants bring labor and some capital but no land, so another result would be to decrease the ratio of land to both labor and capital. The price of labor would fall and the price of land rise; the effect on the price of capital is ambiguous, since it becomes scarcer relative to labor and less scarce relative to land. My guess is that since the additional immigrants who would come in under a policy of unrestricted immigration would bring very little capital with them—rich immigrants can come in under present laws—the return on capital would increase.

The net result might well be to injure the most unskilled American workers. It would benefit many, perhaps most, other workers, since what they are selling is not pure labor but a mixture containing a large amount of human capital. People who were net buyers of land would be injured by the increased price of land; people who were net sellers of land would be benefited. Net lenders would be benefited if the return on capital (the interest rate) increased; net borrowers would be injured.

Can we say anything about the overall effect on those presently living in the United States? Yes—but to do so, we must bring in arguments from a previous chapter. One way of looking at immigration restrictions is as barriers to trade; they prevent an American consumer from buying the labor of a Mexican worker by preventing the worker from coming to where the labor is wanted. The comparative advantage arguments of chapter 6 apply here as well. The abolition of immigration restrictions would produce a net benefit for present Americans, although some would be worse off—just as the abolition of tariffs would produce a net benefit for Americans, although American autoworkers (and GM stockholders) might be injured. These net benefits are in addition to very large benefits to the new immigrants.

A more precise discussion of what we mean by net benefits would carry us into the next chapter—which is about just such questions. A more rigorous explanation of why open immigration produces net benefits would carry us beyond the limits of this book. There are, however, two more points worth making before we finish with the question of immigration.

So far in my discussion of immigration, I have assumed that the only way immigrants get income is by selling labor or other inputs. In fact there are at least two other ways—from government (in the form of welfare, unemployment payments, and the like) and by private violation of property rights (theft and robbery). To the extent that new immigrants support themselves in those ways, they impose costs on the present inhabitants without providing corresponding benefits; the demonstration that new immigrants provide net benefits no longer holds.

Is there a connection between that argument and the historical abandonment of open immigration? Perhaps immigration restrictions are simply one consequence of the welfare state. As long as it was clear that poor immigrants would have to support themselves, they were welcome; once they acquired the right to live off the taxes of those already here, they were not. The argument neatly links two of the major changes of the first half of this century—and does so in a way that fits nicely with my own ideological prejudices.

Unfortunately for the argument, immigration restrictions were imposed in the early 1920s, and the major increase in the size and responsibility of government occurred during the New Deal—about a decade later. At most one might conjecture that both resulted from the same changing view of the role of the state.

Whatever the history of immigration restrictions, current hostility to immigration is in part based on the fear that immigrants may come for welfare, not work. It is far from clear that that fear is justified; a good deal of evidence seems to suggest that new immigrants are more likely to start working their way up the income ladder—in response to the opportunity to earn what are, from the standpoint of many of them, phenomenally high wages.

Opponents of immigration sometimes argue that it hurts the poor and helps the rich, since the obvious losers are unskilled American workers. If we limit our discussion to those presently living here, they may be right—"may" because even unskilled American workers have some skills, such as fluency in English and familiarity with America, that immigrants lack, and because the recent experience of Miami suggests that even poor Americans may benefit from a large influx of immigrants.

But whatever the effects on those already here, the big gainers from immigration are the immigrants—most of whom are much poorer than the American poor. From a national standpoint, free immigration may hurt the poor; from an international standpoint, it helps them. By world standards, the American poor are, if not rich, at least comfortably well off.

Economic Imperialism

The term *economic imperialism* has at least two meanings. One describes parts of this book—the application of the economic approach to what are traditionally considered noneconomic questions. We are imperialists reconquering the intellectual territory presently claimed by political scientists, sociologists, legal scholars, and the like.

The older and more common use of this term is as a way of condemning foreign investment in poor nations. The implication is that such investment is only a subtler equivalent of military imperialism—a way by which capitalists in rich and powerful countries control and exploit the inhabitants of poor and weak countries.

One interesting feature of such "economic imperialism" seems to have escaped the notice of most Marxists. Developing countries are labor rich and capital poor, so the wages of labor are low and the profits of capital high. That is what makes them attractive to foreign investors.

Foreign investment raises the amount of capital in the country, driving wages up and profits down—immigration, but this time of capital, not labor. People who attack economic imperialism regard themselves as champions of the poor and oppressed. To the extent that they succeed in preventing foreign investment in poor countries, they are benefiting the capitalists of those countries by holding up their profits and injuring the workers by holding down their wages. It would be interesting to know how much of the clamor against foreign investment in such countries is due to Marxist ideologues who do not understand this and how much is financed by local capitalists who do.

Land-Use Restrictions

Suppose the English government requires (as it does) that green-belts be established around major cities. That reduces the amount of residential land—driving up rents. A law that is defended as a way of protecting urban beauty against greedy developers has as one of its effects raising the income of urban landlords at the expense of their tenants. It would be interesting to analyze the sources of support for imposing and maintaining greenbelt legislation to see how much comes from residents and how much from landlords.

HOW COME HE MAKES MORE THAN I DO?

> There's not a man among'em who could mend or could make
> If it wasna for the work of the weavers.
> —Scottish folk song

As we all know, the chief source of interest in other people's incomes is a disinterested concern with injustice—the injustice of other people making more money than we do. There may be a profession somewhere that does not believe it is essential, underappreciated, and badly underpaid, but I have not yet come across it. Even Bill Gates probably believes, in his heart of hearts, that the fortune with which his efforts have been rewarded badly understates their true worth—and, speaking as a stockholder enriched by those efforts, I am not sure he is wrong.

This raises an obvious question, and one we now have the tools to answer: What determines the differing wages of different professions? I have just been arguing that all sorts of labor are in some sense the same. So why don't they all, from dishwasher up (or down) to trial lawyer, get the same wage?

Wait a While

The first answer is that we may not be in long-run equilibrium. Time and money spent learning to be a lawyer are sunk costs; you will only retrain for another profession if the return is not only larger but enough larger to make you willing to scrap your investment in yourself and replace it with new training—tear up your law school diploma and go back for an MBA.

This is less of a problem for new workers coming onto the market, since they have not yet made the investment—but it may take a long time before a reduced inflow of new workers has much effect on the total number in the profession. If tort reform reduces the demand for lawyers, law school enrollments will fall immediately, but it may be years before the reduced inflow of new lawyers brings wages back up. Similarly, when the discovery of the class action, design-defect liability, and a host of other litigation gold mines drove up the demand for lawyers, those already in the field did very well for themselves—for a while. The logic of the situation is the same as in our earlier discussion of sunk costs, applied to people instead of factories. The lifestyles of the rich and famous of the plaintiff bar were paid for out of legal quasi-rents.

Differing Abilities

Differing wages may also reflect differing abilities—which explains why some people make less than we do, if not why others make more. If nuclear physicists are more intelligent than grocery store clerks, they will also have higher average wages. The individual nuclear physicist may earn no more than he would as a clerk—but an average physicist would be an above-average clerk.

If this were the whole story, there is no obvious reason why nuclear physicists would be more intelligent than clerks—the intelligent individual would get the same return in either profession. But many abilities, including intelligence, are more useful in some fields than in others. Being seven feet tall is very useful if you are a basketball player; if you are a college professor, it merely means that you bump your head a lot.

If 10 percent of the population consisted of men who were seven feet tall and well coordinated, basketball players would not get unusually high salaries—there would be too many tall clerks, tall professors, and tall ditchdiggers willing to enter the profession if they did. On the other hand, if there were only ten such people in the country, their salaries would be bid up to a level reflecting the difference between their value to a team and the value of the ordinary recruit who would be the only alternative, once all ten of them were taken. The ten tall athletes would be earning rents on their scarce abilities.

Of course, the world does not divide itself neatly into potential superstars and everyone else. In equilibrium the wage is such that the marginal basketball player—the individual just balanced between choosing to play basketball and choosing to do something else—finds both alternatives equally attractive. If the average player is considerably better than the marginal one, he will also receive a higher salary. Michael Jordan is, and Wilt Chamberlain was, a long way from the margin.

All Things Considered

Consider a group of professions, none of which requires any rare abilities. There have been no unexpected changes in the demand for different sorts of labor recently, so everyone is getting about the wage he expected to get when he chose his field. Nonetheless, we observe wide variations in wages.

What is equal in equilibrium is the net advantage in each field, not the wage. If a particular profession, such as economics, is much more fun than other professions, it will also pay less. If it did not—if its wages were the same as those in less exciting fields—then on net it would be more attractive. People who were leading dull lives as ditchdiggers, sociologists, or lawyers would pour into economics, driving down the wage.

The argument applies to professions with other nonpecuniary advantages as well. If many people very much want to be watched by adoring multitudes, that will drive down the wages of rock and film stars. It works in reverse for professions with nonpecuniary disadvantages. That is why it costs more to hire people to drive trucks loaded with dynamite than trucks loaded with dirt.

Professions also differ in the cost of admission. Becoming a checkout clerk requires almost no training; becoming an actuary requires years of study. If both earned the same wages, few people would become actuaries. In equilibrium the wage of the actuary must be enough higher to repay the time and expense invested in learning the job. The wages of actuaries buy human capital as well as raw labor.

In some professions, the wage is predictable; in others it is not. Movie stars make large incomes, but the only actress I ever knew personally supported herself mostly by temporary secretarial work. In a profession where most people are failures, at least from a financial standpoint, it is not surprising that the few successes do very well. The apprentice actor has bought a ticket in a lottery—a tiny chance of making several hundred thousand dollars a year, a near certainty of barely scraping by on an occasional acting job supplemented by part-time work and unemployment compensation, and a small chance of something between the two extremes. My impression is that the average wage is quite low—perhaps because actors are optimists, perhaps because they would rather starve on stage than eat well anywhere else.

TO THINK ABOUT

When I married my wife, she was a geologist employed by an oil company. We spent less than 1 percent of our joint income for gasoline and several percent more for heating (gas) and power. Were we better or worse off when the price of oil rose? Would the answer be very much different if we had oil heat? If she was a geologist employed by a university?

The government decides there are too many buildings in America and proposes a 50 percent tax on constructing new buildings. What groups will support or oppose the tax?

For Further Reading

The final section of this book is my rewrite of something first published in 1776. It can be found in Chapter X, Book I, of Adam Smith, *An Inquiry into the Nature and Causes of the Wealth of Nations* (New York: Oxford University Press, 1976). The book is still well worth reading.

The most famous supporter of the idea of taxing the site value of land, Henry George, stated his argument in *Progress and Poverty* (New York: Robert Schalkenbach Foundation, 1984).

STANDING IN FOR MORAL PHILOSOPHY: THE ECONOMIST AS JUDGE

15

SUMMING PEOPLE UP

They keep coming to us with questions: "Should we have a tariff?" "Should we have rent control?" We answer, "Should? Economists don't know anything about 'should'; go talk to a philosopher. If you have a tariff, such and such will happen; if you have rent control, . . . " "No, No," they say. "We don't want to know all that. Is it good or bad?" The economist finally answers as follows:

I have no expertise in good and bad. I can, however, define something called efficiency that has the following characteristics. First, it is an important part of what I suspect most of you mean by "good." Second, economics helps answer the question of whether a change leads to greater efficiency. Third, I cannot think of any alternative measure closer to what you want that also has the second characteristic.

The rest of this chapter will be spent explaining what economists mean by "efficiency." By the end, you should understand why our response to the question "What should we do?" is less than adequate, but substantially better than no answer at all—or the answers given without the use of economics.

MEASURING BETTER AND WORSE

Consider a change (the abolition of tariffs, a new tax, rent control, . . .) that affects many people, benefiting some and hurting others. Suppose we could find out from each person who was against the change how much money he would have to be given so that the money plus the change would leave him exactly as well off as before—the amount that would make him just willing to accept the change. Suppose we could ask each gainer what would be the largest amount he would pay to get the change—the sum that would just balance his gain. We could, assuming everyone was telling us the truth, sum all of the gains and losses, reduced in this way to a common measure. If the sum was a net gain, we would say that the change was an *economic improvement*.

This definition does not correspond perfectly to our intuition about when a change is desirable for at least two reasons. First, we are accepting each person's evaluation of how much something is worth to him; the value of heroin to the addict has the same status as the value of insulin to the diabetic. Second, by comparing values according to their money equivalent, we ignore differences in the utility of money to different people. If you were told that a certain change benefited a millionaire by an amount equivalent for him to $10 and injured a poor man by an amount equivalent for him to $9, you would suspect that in some meaningful sense $10 was worth less to the millionaire than $9 to the poor man. Economic improvement is intended as a workable approximation of our intuitions about what changes are on net good or bad. A definition that involved adding up happiness instead of dollars might be better—but until we have a way of measuring happiness, it is less useful.

How do we measure value in order to find out what changes are economic improvements? The answer is that we have been doing it, without saying so, through much of the book. Consumer (or producer) surplus is the benefit to a consumer (or producer) of a particular economic arrangement measured in dollars according to his own values. If we argue that some change in economic arrangements results in an increase in the sum of consumer and producer surplus, as we shall be doing repeatedly in the next few chapters, we are arguing that it is an economic improvement.

Our problem is how to add different people's utilities together in order to decide whether a gain to one person is enough to compensate for a loss to another. Our solution is to add utilities as if everyone got the same utility from a dollar. The advantage of that way of doing it is that it makes the question "Is that change an improvement?" into one that economics can often help us answer.

Alfred Marshall, the economist who originated this approach to defining economic improvement, was aware of the obvious argument against treating people as if they all had the same utility for a dollar: They don't. His view was that that was a serious problem for evaluating a change that benefited one rich man and injured one poor man. But the changes economists are usually asked to evaluate are ones that affect large and diverse groups of people: all consumers of shoes and all producers of shoes, all the inhabitants of London and all the inhabitants of Birmingham. In such cases, individual differences could be expected to cancel out, so that the change that improved matters in Marshall's terms probably also made things better in the vaguer and more important sense of increasing total human happiness.

There is another respect in which Marshall's definition of improvement is useful. If a situation is inefficient, that means that there is some possible change in it that produces net (dollar) benefits. If so, a sufficiently ingenious entrepreneur might be able to organize that change, paying those who lose by it for their cooperation, being paid by those who gain, and pocketing the difference. If you conclude that converting the empty lot on the corner into a McDonald's restaurant would be a Marshall improvement, one conclusion you may reach is that the present situation is inefficient. Another is that you could make money by buying the lot, buying a McDonald's franchise, and building a restaurant.

MARSHALL, MONEY, AND REVEALED PREFERENCE

There are several ways in which it is easy to misinterpret the idea of economic improvement. One is by concluding that since net benefits are in dollars, "Economics is only about money." Dollars are not what the improvement is but what it is measured in. Money is no more the only thing with value than yardsticks are the only things with length. Life, health, wisdom, all have value—provided someone is willing to give up money to get them. The definition of economic improvement does not even require that money exist; we could have used apples. As we saw in the discussion of arbitrage some chapters back, any tradable commodity can be used to define prices. As long as relative prices are consistent, any tradable commodity will give the same results for what changes are or are not improvements.

A second mistake is to take too literally the idea of asking every-one affected how much he has gained or lost. Basing our judgments on people's statements would violate the principle of revealed prefer-ence, which tells us that values are measured by actions, not words. That is how we measure them when analyzing what is or is not an improvement. Consumer surplus, for example, is calculated from a demand curve, which shows what consumers do, not what they say.

EFFICIENCY AND THE BUREAUCRAT-GOD

We now know what economists mean when they call a change an "improvement." A closely related term that you will often see is "effi-cient." A situation is *efficient* if all possible improvements have already been made, so that no more improvements are possible.

In describing some economic arrangement as efficient or ineffi-cient, we are comparing it to possible alternatives. This raises a diffi-cult question: What does "possible" mean? One could argue that only what exists is possible. In order to get anything else, some part of reality must be different from what it is. It follows that no outcome can be improved, hence all are efficient.

But one purpose of concepts such as efficiency is to help us make choices, and by doing so change reality. A change such as the inven-tion of cheap thermonuclear power or a medical treatment to prevent aging would be an economic improvement—and that observation would be relevant if this were a book on medicine or nuclear physics. A rain of manna from heaven might be an improvement, and that observation might be relevant if this were a book on the power of prayer. Since it is a book on economics, the changes we are concerned with involve using the present state of technological knowledge and the presently available inputs, but changing what is produced and consumed by whom.

I find it useful to embody this point in a construct that I call a *bureaucrat-god*. A bureaucrat-god has all of the knowledge and power that anyone in the society has. He knows everyone's preferences and production functions and has unlimited power to tell people what to do. He does not have the power to make gold out of lead or produce new inventions. He is benevolent; his sole aim is to maximize effi-ciency in Marshall's sense, to make all possible Marshall improve-ments. Think of him as a three-way cross between Joseph Stalin, Mother Teresa, and the latest Cray supercomputer.

An economic arrangement is efficient if it cannot be improved by a bureaucrat-god. The reason we care whether an arrangement is efficient is that if it is, there is no point in trying to use economics to improve it. If it is not efficient, there still may be no way we can improve it—since no bureaucrat-gods are available—but it is at least worth looking.

It may occur to you that while efficiency as I have defined it is an upper bound on how well an economy can be organized, it is not a very useful benchmark for evaluating real societies. Real societies are run not by omniscient and benevolent gods but by humans with limited knowledge and self-interested objectives. How can we hope, out of such components, to assemble a system that works as well as it would if it were run by a bureaucrat-god? Is it not as inappropriate to use "efficiency" in judging the performance of human institutions as it would be to judge the performance of race cars by comparing their speed to its theoretical upper bound—the speed of light?

The surprising answer is no. As we will see in the next chapter, it is possible for institutions that we have already described, institutions not too different from those around us in the real world, to produce an efficient outcome. That is one of the most surprising—and useful—implications of economic theory.

MARSHALL DISGUISED AS PARETO

Some of you probably took economics in college, and a few may remember enough to notice something odd about my explanation of efficiency. You are right. I am describing the idea as it is used by economists, but not as it is taught by economists.

While Alfred Marshall was in other respects a much more important figure in the history of economics than the Italian economist Vilfredo Pareto, it is Pareto's approach to defining "improvement" and "efficiency" that dominates the textbooks. Pareto defined an improvement as a change that benefits someone and injures nobody; a situation is Pareto-efficient if no further Pareto improvements are possible. This approach avoids the problem of trading off gains to one person against losses to another—at the cost of producing a criterion that is almost totally useless for judging real-world alternatives.

Consider the example of tariffs. The abolition of tariffs on automobiles would benefit Americans who buy cars or produce export goods, but it would make American autoworkers and stockholders in American car companies worse off. As we will see in chapter 19, there is good reason to believe that the gains to the first group are larger than the losses to the second, so the change is an economic improvement in Marshall's sense of the term. But there are some losers, so it is not a Pareto improvement. A similar situation would arise with almost any other policy issue one can imagine.

Suppose that some change, such as abolishing tariffs, would be a Pareto improvement if combined with a suitable set of transfers. If, for example, you gain $10 and I lose $8 when tariffs are abolished, then abolishing tariffs and simultaneously transferring $9 from you to me would leave us both better off than before the change. Abolishing tariffs is then a *potential Pareto improvement* (also called a *Hicks-Kaldor improvement* after the economists who thought up this approach), a change that would be a Pareto improvement if combined with the right transfers.

If we are willing to settle for potential Pareto improvements instead of real ones, we can answer real questions, such as whether to abolish tariffs. The answers are almost always the same ones we would get if we used Marshall's definition of improvement instead. That is hardly surprising. If a change produces net gains (is an economic improvement in Marshall's sense), that means that the gainers can compensate the losers and still have something left over. And if the gainers can compensate the losers while leaving something over, there must be net gains.

What is wrong with the potential-Pareto approach is that it is used to argue for changes that are not going to be combined with side payments (as in the tariff example), and are thus not going to be actual Pareto improvements. It thus presents the pretense of avoiding interpersonal comparisons while actually recommending policies that make some people better off and others worse off. I prefer the Marshallian approach, which makes the same recommendations without the pretense.

A more subtle version of the same mistake starts by arguing that since abolishing tariffs and making compensating payments would be a Pareto improvement, a world with tariffs is Pareto-inefficient. A world without tariffs cannot be Pareto improved (assuming there is nothing else wrong with it), so it is Pareto-efficient. Obviously, an efficient world is better than an inefficient world, so we should abolish tariffs.

There are two problems here. The first is that although we can abolish tariffs, we cannot make the transfers necessary to convert the abolition into a Pareto improvement; we don't know enough about who gains and who loses by how much. So the Pareto improvement is not possible, so the initial situation is not inefficient.

The second problem is that a Pareto-efficient situation is not necessarily better than a Pareto-inefficient one. The situation with the tariff is inefficient not because it is Pareto-inferior to the situation without the tariff but because it is Pareto-inferior to a third alternative: abolition of the tariff plus compensating payments.

Suppose we are dividing twenty cookies and twenty Cokes between us. A division that gives me everything is Pareto-efficient, since any change must leave me worse off and so cannot be a Pareto improvement. A division that gives each of us ten cookies and ten Cokes is inefficient since, given our different tastes, both of us prefer for you to have eleven cookies and me eleven Cokes.

The division that gives me everything is Pareto-efficient and the even division is not. Yet it would seem very odd for me to use that as grounds for claiming that the former is superior to the latter and should therefore be chosen, and odder still for me to expect you to agree.

Adopting a general policy of "Wherever possible, make Marshall improvements" may come very close to being a Pareto improvement, even though individual Marshall improvements are not. In one case, the Marshall improvement benefits me by $3 and hurts you by $2; in another it helps you by $6 and hurts me by $4; in another . . . Add up all the effects and, unless one individual or group is consistently on the losing side, everyone, or almost everyone, benefits. That is one more reason to be in favor of such a policy.

While the way in which this book presents economics is unconventional, the contents—what I present—are not very different from what many other economists believe and teach. This chapter is a major exception. Many of my colleagues share my discomfort with the Paretian approach, but most of them continue to teach it. I prefer to admit that we are trading off gains to one person against losses to another in an imperfect sort of way, instead of following the Paretian strategy of doing the same thing but pretending not to. In that respect, this part of the book is either "on the frontier" or "out of the mainstream," according to whether one does or does not agree with it.

It's Mine and I'm Keeping It: When the Starting Point Matters

Economic improvement usually provides a reasonably good way of judging changes, but not always. Imagine a society of two people, you and me. One of us has a life-extension pill that doubles the life expectancy of whoever takes it. Suppose we want to use Marshall's approach to decide which of us should end up with the pill.

If I had the pill, nothing you could offer me would make me willing to give it up, so the dollar value of the pill to me (the amount I would have to be paid to give it up) is greater than its dollar value to you (the amount you would pay to get it). Leaving me with the pill is, by Marshall's criterion, the preferred outcome.

But suppose you start with the pill. Following exactly the same argument, we find that leaving you with the pill is the preferred outcome! Since the pill is immensely valuable, whoever has it is much wealthier as a result—not in money but in something money cannot buy. Wealthier people value the same benefit—in this case the benefit of having the pill—at more dollars. So we get different results according to who starts off with the pill. More generally, whether a change is an economic improvement sometimes depends on what we assume about the initial allocation of goods, since that affects what people have and thus what they are willing to pay to get changes that benefit them.

Most applications of Marshall's definition of improvement do not involve this problem. If, for example, we consider the desirability of tariffs, it probably does not matter whether we start by assuming that tariffs exist and ask how people would be affected by abolishing them or start by assuming they do not exist and ask how people would be affected by imposing them. One reason it does not matter is that most of the gains and losses are monetary; the dollar value to you of a $1 increase in your income is the same however rich you are. Another reason is that even if some of the gains and losses were nonmonetary, the abolition (or institution) of tariffs would have only a small effect on most people's income, hence a small effect on the monetary equivalent to them of some nonmonetary value.

This problem is not limited to the Marshallian approach. Under the strict Pareto criterion, most alternatives are incomparable; not only is there no way of deciding who should get the life-extension pill, there is no way of deciding whether tariffs should be abolished. Under the potential-Pareto criterion, one gets exactly the same problems as with Marshall's approach.

Efficiency as the Least Bad Solution

It is easy for someone who understands the idea of economic efficiency to point out its defects. The economist's definition of improvement assumes away the difference between the value of money to a rich man and its value to a poor man and assumes away the possibility that people may not know what is in their own interest. And it is likely in practice, although not in principle, to ignore the value of goods that cannot be readily owned and traded, such as the value of living in a courteous and culturally rich society.

It is much harder to propose a better criterion. The most popular alternative seems to be intuition: One thinks about a change and decides whether it is, on the whole, good or bad. In order to do that right, one must take account of the consequences for everyone affected—hundreds, thousands, in some cases hundred of millions of people. But nobody I know is mentally equipped to intuit the lives of hundreds of different people, nor do we come equipped with knowledge of what effect a particular change will have on each of them.

What actually happens is that we think of the effect on a small number of people, either people like us and our friends (those being the ones we know about) or imaginary stereotypes ("the poor," "the workers") that we know very little about. We then add up the effect for the six people we are capable of simultaneously imagining and assume that the result is a good measure of the overall effect on everyone. One result is a tendency to believe that policies that benefit me and people like me are good for the nation, and policies that hurt me and people like me are bad for the nation.

Another result is a tendency to support policies that have obvious benefits and nonobvious costs. Consider a simple example: deciding whether a piece of land should be reserved as a city park. Almost anyone, imagining himself as living in that city, will answer "yes." He is considering the effect from the viewpoint of a potential user of the park—a beneficiary. He is not imagining himself as one of the people who would have lived on that land and must now live in some other and less desirable location. If you add up all the gains and none of the losses, you are guaranteed to get a positive sum— but that tells us nothing about whether the change is really an improvement. Intuition, especially biased intuition, is a poor substitute for analysis, even very imperfect analysis.

For Further Reading

For an original, interesting, and readable discussion of the idea of economic improvement, see Alfred Marshall, *Principles of Economics*, 8th. ed. (London: Macmillan, 1920), chapter VI.

Under most circumstances, the Marshallian and potential Paretian definitions of efficiency lead to the same conclusions. For circumstances under which they do not, see: David Friedman, "Does Altruism Produce Efficient Outcomes? Marshall vs. Kaldor," *Journal of Legal Studies*, vol. 17 (January 1988).

16

WHAT IS EFFICIENT?

The hat is loaded, the rabbit is awake. There is nothing up my sleeves. Out of the first nine chapters of this book I am about to produce a bureaucrat-god.

DECENTRALIZED PLANNING

Consider the competitive industry of chapter 9, selling its output to consumers, buying its inputs from their owners: workers, landlords, investors. Everyone—firms, consumers, owners—is a price taker. Is the result efficient? Could it be improved by a bureaucrat-god?

The bureaucrat-god could have the same quantity of the good produced in the same way while changing its *allocation*—who gets it. He could produce the same quantity and allocate it to the same people, while changing how it is produced. He could change the quantity produced. Is there any such change, or any combination of such changes, that would be an economic improvement?

Allocation

The good is sold at a price; everyone consumes the quantity for which the value to him of one more unit equals that price: $MV = P$. Suppose we now transfer some units from Uno to Duo. We are taking away from Uno units that were worth at least P to him, since at that price he chose to buy them. We are giving Duo units that are worth less than P to him, since at that price he chose not to buy them. Each unit transferred is worth more to the person who loses it (Uno) than to the person who gets it (Duo), so the change is a worsening, not an improvement.

The allocation produced by selling the good to all comers at the same price allocates units of the good to those who most value them; any reallocation must transfer from someone who values the units of the good he is losing at more than their price to someone who values the units he is gaining at less. So no reallocation can be an improvement. The argument applies to any quantity of output; however much is produced, selling it at the price at which that quantity is demanded is the efficient way to allocate it.

Production

Could the bureaucrat-god command a firm to produce the same output in some less expensive way—perhaps with a different mix of inputs? No. Each firm is already producing its output in the least costly way—any reduction in cost would have increased the firm's profits and so would already have been made. As we saw in chapter 9, a firm gets its total cost curve from its production function by finding, for each level of output, the least expensive way of producing it.

What about changing the number of firms: closing down one firm and having each of the others produce a little more or creating a new firm and having each produce a little less? In equilibrium, as you may remember from chapter 9, the firms in a price-taking industry are producing at the minimum of their average cost curves. Since the firms are producing at minimum average cost, any change in output per firm must raise average cost, not lower it.

No change in how output is produced or in how it is allocated can be an improvement. In at least these two dimensions, the competitive industry is efficient in the strong sense discussed in chapter 15; no change that a bureaucrat-god could impose can be an improvement. The one remaining possibility for improvement is a change in the quantity produced.

Quantity

A consumer buys a good up to the point where the value to him of one more unit is just equal to the price he must pay for it: $MV = P$. In competitive equilibrium, the price of a good is just equal to the cost of producing a little more of it: $P = MC$. So any increase in quantity means producing units that cost more to produce than they are worth to the consumers; any reduction means failing to produce units worth more to the consumers than they cost to produce. A change in either direction would be an economic worsening.

Could the bureaucrat-god improve the outcome by changing two or three variables at once? No. We proved that the market allocation rule (sell at the price at which consumers want to buy exactly the amount produced) is the efficient way to allocate any quantity of output and that the way in which a competitive industry produces is the efficient way to produce any quantity of output. Whatever the quantity produced, allocation and production should be done as they would be by a competitive industry. That leaves only one variable—quantity—and we have just proved that if output is produced and allocated in that way, the efficient quantity is the quantity a competitive industry chooses to produce.

We are done. We have shown that no change in the outcome produced by an industry of competitive, price-taking firms can be an economic improvement. A competitive market is efficient. The bureaucrat-god is alive, well, and ubiquitous—thinly spread through the economy.

Filling in Details

I have ignored some important points in order to show the overall logic of the argument. It is now time to go back and fill them in.

Dollar Cost, Value Cost. I showed that no change in how the industry produces its output can lower its cost of production. This is not quite the same thing as showing that no change can be an improvement. A change in cost of production, after all, is merely a change in the number of dollars paid by a firm to the owners of its inputs. What is the connection between showing that a change raises the number of dollars paid ("raises cost") and showing that it is an economic worsening ("net loss of value")?

That connection comes from chapter 5, where we saw that the price of an input (labor in that case) was equal to the cost to the individual of producing it. The marginal disvalue of labor (aka the marginal value of leisure) equals the wage rate. If a producer changes his production process by using an extra hour of labor, the price he must pay for that labor, its cost in dollars, equals the cost to the worker of working the extra hour, its cost in value. The worker is neither better nor worse off as a result of working the extra hour (and being paid for it), and the firm is worse off by the amount it has paid. The same analysis applies if the firm uses an hour less of labor—the money saved by the firm is just equal to the value to the worker of the extra leisure he gets. The analysis applies equally well to other inputs.

What about inputs that the firm bids away from individual consumers—apples that can either be turned into applesauce or eaten as is? Each consumer consumes a quantity of apples for which the marginal value of the last apple is just equal to its price, so if he eats one less apple (because the firm has bought it to make applesauce), the loss of value to him is the same as the dollar cost to the firm.

The cost to the firm of any method of production—any set of inputs—is equal to the sum of the cost to other people of producing (or not consuming) those inputs. So a change that lowers dollar cost also lowers the value cost of producing the goods, and a change that increases dollar cost also increases value cost.

What if firms get additional inputs by bidding them away from other firms? If the steel industry chooses to use more labor, that may mean not that workers have less leisure but that some workers move from producing autos to producing steel.

The cost to the auto industry of losing a worker is the worker's marginal revenue product: the increase in output, measured in dollars, from employing him. That, as we saw in chapter 9, is equal to his wage, which is what the steel industry must pay to get him. So the cost in dollars to the firm hiring the input is again the same as the cost in value elsewhere; this time, the loss of value takes the form of lost output in another industry rather than of lost leisure to the worker. The argument applies to other inputs as well. In order for a firm to get the use of land or capital, it must bid them away from other firms—and those firms will be willing, if necessary, to offer anything up to what they lose by not getting those inputs. So the price an industry must pay for its inputs equals the lost output elsewhere as a result of diverting those inputs to that industry.

I have now shown that cost of production as measured by a firm—the cost to it of its inputs—equals the loss of value as a result of its using them, whether in leisure or the value of other goods that those inputs could have been used to produce. Since a competitive industry produces its output at the minimum cost in dollars, it also produces it at the minimum cost in value. Any change in how it produces that quantity of output (everything else held fixed) must be an economic worsening.

Shuffling Money. In proving the efficiency of competitive equilibrium, I have ignored gains or losses of value due to the money payments associated with the transfer of inputs or outputs. A transfer of money from one person to another is neither an improvement nor a worsening: One person gains a dollar, another loses a dollar. In this case as in many others, one of the virtues of economic theory is that it lets you see through the veil of money transactions to the underlying reality—the production and consumption of goods.

If a firm decides to buy one more hour of labor, one effect is that a worker works an additional hour. Another is that the additional demand bids wages up a little. That small increase in wages can be ignored by the firm that causes it, since it is a price taker on the market for inputs as well as for outputs. But for the industry as a whole, or the economy as a whole, that small increase in the wage rate must be multiplied by all of the hours worked by all workers. Should I not take that into account in calculating the costs and benefits that result from increasing the firm's input of labor by one unit?

The answer is no. The increase in wages is a transfer between the sellers and the buyers of labor. Each dollar that one person loses, someone else gets. There is no net gain or loss, hence no effect on whether the change is or is not a net improvement.

One problem with a proof of this sort is that I am presenting mathematical arguments in verbal form. Strictly speaking, the analysis should be put in terms of infinitely small changes: working an extra millisecond rather than an extra hour. Since any large change can be broken up into an infinite number of infinitely small changes, proving that each small change makes things worse also proves that large changes do so. Putting things that way is harder in a verbal argument than in a mathematical one, but the failure to do so introduces some imprecision.

It would be possible to give a precise verbal statement of the proof that a competitive equilibrium is efficient, but it would make the proof considerably more difficult than it already is. The proof as given is, I think, sufficiently precise to give you a clear understanding of why the result is true.

Competitive Layer Cake. I have been describing an economy with only a single layer of firms between the ultimate producers and the ultimate consumers. Most real economies are more complicated than that. Many of the outputs of firms—steel ingots, typewriters, railroad transport—are inputs of other firms. While this makes the situation harder to describe, it does not change its essential logic.

To see why, start one layer up from the bottom. Consider an industry that buys its inputs from their original owners (workers, landowners, owners of capital) and uses them to produce typewriters, which it sells at a price equal to marginal cost. So the price that firms one layer further up pay for typewriters is an accurate signal of the real human cost of what they are using, just as the wage they must pay their workers is an accurate signal of the human cost of their labor. So our proof of the efficiency of competitive equilibrium applies to the second layer too. We can repeat the argument for as many layers as necessary. The whole competitive layer cake is efficient.

A number of other simplifications went into our argument. One is the assumption that each firm produces only one kind of good. Dropping that introduces an interesting set of puzzles involving *joint products* (things produced together, such as wool and mutton, or two metals refined from the same ore), quality variations among goods, and the like, but does not change the result.

What about the complications of time and uncertainty discussed in chapters 12 and 13? As we saw, we can incorporate time and change into our analysis by doing all calculations using present values of future flows of revenue, cost, and value. By redoing the argument in that form we could prove the efficiency of competitive equilibrium in a changing (but perfectly predictable) world.

Efficiency in an uncertain world is a more complicated issue. We must be careful to specify just what the bureaucrat-god is assumed to know—what sort of perfect economy we are using as our benchmark. If the bureaucrat-god knows the future and the real participants in the market do not, he can easily improve on their performance. But in defining the bureaucrat-god, we assumed that he had all of the information any person had and only that information.

That implies that he, like bureaucrats in the real world, has no better a crystal ball than the rest of us. The efficiency proof then holds in an uncertain world as well as in a certain one.

Competitive Efficiency: Summing Up

At the end of chapter 15, I asked whether efficiency was an unreasonably severe standard for judging real-world economies. You are now in a position to understand the answer. One can describe a set of institutions—competitive markets—that produce an efficient outcome, an outcome that cannot be improved by a bureaucrat-god. Real markets do not correspond perfectly to the model—they do not, for example, consist of industries all of which have an infinite number of firms producing identical goods—but they sometimes approximate it.

As you may suspect from the amount of attention devoted to this discussion and the number of different things that have fed into it, the efficiency of a competitive market is an important result. If you want to use economics to improve the well-being of mankind, it is probably the most important single result of economic theory. While we cannot expect a real-world economy to fit the assumptions of the proof precisely, many parts of many economies come close enough to make us suspect that they are close to efficient—closer than any alternative institutions are likely to be. Where the assumptions necessary to prove efficiency break down, understanding the reason for the inefficiency is the first step toward figuring out how to reduce it.

MONOPOLY

Words such as *efficient* or *competitive* are technical terms in economics, with meanings quite different from the same words in ordinary conversation. Consider the sentence "Monopoly is inefficient." The natural response is, "Of course; everybody knows that. Monopolists are rich and lazy; they have no competitors to put pressure on them, so they run their firms badly."

Rich and lazy monopolists running their firms badly are not what an economist means when he says that monopoly is inefficient. In the sense in which "efficient" is used in ordinary conversation, economic theory suggests that monopolies should be just as efficient as competitive firms. It is only in the very different sense discussed in the previous chapter that we have reasons to expect some kinds of monopolies to be inefficient—not because the monopolist runs his firm badly but because he runs it well.

Single-Price Monopoly

It costs $10 million to design a typewriter and build a factory to produce typewriters; once built, the factory can produce as many typewriters as anyone wants to buy at a cost of $100 apiece. The more units fixed cost is spread over, the lower the average cost, so the typewriter firm can afford to undersell any smaller producer; it is a natural monopoly.

We proved that a competitive industry was efficient in three ways: allocation, production, and quantity. As far as allocation and production are concerned, the proof applies to a (single-price) monopoly as well. Like a competitive firm, the typewriter company sells its typewriters at the same price to all comers—the efficient way of allocating its output. Like a competitive firm, it produces its product at the lowest possible cost, since reducing cost increases profits.

What about quantity? As we saw back in chapter 10, a single-

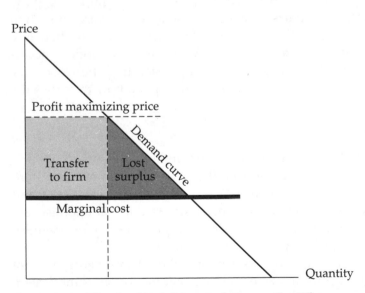

Figure 16-1   The deadweight cost of monopoly. When a monopoly charges a price above marginal cost in order to maximize its profit, the increased price of the goods still sold is a transfer to the firm but the reduction in consumer surplus due to the reduction in output is a net loss.

price monopoly, unlike a firm in a competitive industry, maximizes its profit at a price higher than marginal cost. If a typewriter costs $100 to produce but sells for $150, someone to whom it is worth $140 does not get one, which is inefficient. If the monopoly produced one extra typewriter and gave it to the customer, it would be worse off by $100 and he would be better off by $140—for a net gain of $40. The net gain would be the same if he bought the typewriter for $150—a $50 gain to the firm and a $10 loss to the customer adds up to a $40 gain. Of course, neither is going to happen—the firm will not sell at a price lower than $150, since that maximizes its profit, and the customer will not buy at any price higher than $140.

Figure 16–1 shows the inefficiency in graphical form. The shaded region is the difference between consumer surplus at the monopoly's profit-maximizing price and consumer surplus at a price equal to marginal cost. Part of that is a transfer—a higher price paid to the firm by its customers for the goods they buy. The rest is the lost consumer surplus on units consumers would buy at marginal cost but do not buy at the price that maximizes monopoly profit; consumers lose that surplus but nobody gets it. This is the *lost welfare triangle* due to monopoly.

We have seen this before—it is the same triangle that the movie theater lost back in chapter 10 by selling popcorn for $1.00 a bag instead of $0.50 a bag. The theater was using the ticket price to transfer all of its customers' consumer surplus to itself, so any inefficiency, any reduction in total surplus, reduced its profit.

Earlier, I showed how the proof of the efficiency of competitive equilibrium could be generalized to an economy with intermediate goods—typewriters that were the output of one firm and the input of another. Once we introduce monopolies into the picture, the argument no longer works. A firm that buys typewriters measures their cost to it by the price it must pay for them. If the typewriters are produced by a monopoly and sold at a price above marginal cost, that price no longer reflects the real human cost of producing typewriters. The result is a distortion in how goods are produced; firms use a less than efficient quantity of inputs produced by monopolies. If aluminum production is a monopoly and steel production is not, cars will use more steel and less aluminum than would be efficient.

One solution is vertical integration. The aluminum company merges with an auto company. The auto division of the new firm is instructed to decide between aluminum and steel on the basis of what each costs the firm—the price of steel, which the firm buys, but the marginal cost of aluminum, which it produces. The result is a more efficiently designed car and a gain to the stockholders of the joint venture—to be balanced against the cost to the stockholders of any inefficiencies due to the larger size of the firm.

How Not to Run a Railroad

Monopoly may also produce a second and more subtle sort of inefficiency. Consider the following story:

The year is 1870. Somewhere beyond the frontier, there exists a valley that will some day be settled and farmed. Whoever builds the first rail line into it will have a monopoly; there will never be enough business to support a second line. If the rail line is built in 1900, the total monopoly profit that the railroad will eventually collect will be $20 million. If the railroad is built before 1900, it will lose a million dollars a year until 1900, because demand will not yet be adequate to cover costs.

I plan to build the railroad in 1900. I am forestalled by someone who plans to build in 1899; $19 million is better than nothing, which is what he will get if he waits for me to build first. He is forestalled by someone willing to build still earlier. The railroad is built in 1880—and the builder receives nothing above the normal return on his capital for building it.

This phenomenon—the dissipation of above-market returns in the process of competing to get them—is called *rent seeking*. As we will see in later chapters, it appears in a variety of different contexts, including crime and politics. When monopoly profit is dissipated in this fashion, the deadweight cost of monopoly includes not only the welfare triangle in Figure 16–1 but also the monopoly profit—the rectangle minus fixed costs. That is how much worse off consumers and producers are, on net, under single-price monopoly than under a bureaucrat-god. It represents the upper limit of the gains that might be available through replacing monopoly with some more efficient arrangement.

The Second Efficiency Condition. There is one more respect in which monopoly may fail to produce an efficient outcome. Suppose there is no price the firm can charge at which it can cover its costs—profit is negative at any quantity. Nobody will willingly start such a firm. But if investors were compelled by a bureaucrat-god to start the firm and sell its output at marginal cost, the benefit to its customers might be more than the loss to its owners, in which case bringing it into existence would be an economic improvement.

There are two conditions a monopoly must satisfy in order to be efficient. The first is, "Provide the good to anyone to whom it is worth at least its cost of production." The second is, "Produce if and only if, at some quantity, consumer surplus plus profit is positive."

Discriminatory Monopoly: The Solution?

What if, instead of selling all its output at the same price, a monopoly price-discriminates, charging a higher price to consumers willing to pay it? One result is to increase profit; another may be to reduce inefficiency. Perfect price discrimination allows the firm to produce and sell every unit that is valued at more than its cost of production—as in the cookie club example of chapter 10. That not only maximizes profit, it also satisfies the first efficiency condition.

Perfect discriminatory monopoly also satisfies the second efficiency condition. Since every unit is bought at the highest price the consumer is willing to pay for it, all consumer surplus is transferred to the firm. Since the firm receives all of the benefit from its existence, it is worth starting the firm as long as total benefit is more than total cost.

This result—that a price-discriminating monopoly satisfies both efficiency conditions—holds only for perfect discriminatory pricing. Imperfect price discrimination is not only inefficient, it may sometimes be worse than a single-price monopoly. Consider a publisher that sells the same book in England for the equivalent of $10 and in the United States for $15. An American consumer to whom a copy is worth $14 does not get one, an English consumer to whom it is worth $11 does. This is an inefficient allocation—giving the book to the American instead would produce a net benefit of $3.

On the other hand, the ability to sell the book at different prices in different markets may make it in the interest of the publisher to sell more copies, moving quantity closer to its efficient level. And it may make possible products that could not be produced at all by a single-price monopoly—because there is no single price at which a producer can cover its costs. So the efficiency implication of imperfect price discrimination is ambiguous; in some circumstances the result is less efficient than single-price monopoly, in some circumstances more.

It sounds as though perfectly discriminating monopoly, where feasible, is the ideal solution to the problem of natural monopoly; it produces the efficient outcome, although in a way that transfers all surplus to the monopoly. Seen from a point of view sufficiently broad to give the same weight to the interests of stockholders as of customers, the only problem seems to be the difficulty of implementing something close to perfect price discrimination.

There is another problem: rent seeking. Suppose we redo our story of the valley railroad, assuming it is a perfect price discriminator. Perfect price discrimination is now not the best solution but the worst—it transfers all of the benefit to the monopoly, and then burns it all up in the competition to become the monopoly.

WANTED: A BUREAUCRAT-GOD, OR, FIXING A WATCH WITH A HAMMER

A physician invented a cure for which there was no disease. He caught the cure and died.

One reason to look for inefficiency is the hope of curing it—modifying our institutions so as to produce a better outcome. Since we have no bureaucrat-gods available, there may be some outcomes that are inefficient but cannot be improved by any means available to us—but it is still worth looking.

Since competition is efficient, one might think that the solution to the inefficiency of monopoly is to break up the monopoly firm. But if a natural monopoly is broken up into ten smaller firms, average cost will go up—that is why it is a natural monopoly. Since average cost falls as output increases, one of the firms will expand, driving (or buying) out the others. We end up where we started, with a single monopoly firm.

The inefficiency of monopoly is an argument for breaking up artificial monopolies—but I argued, back in chapter 10, that artificial monopolies are for the most part mythical. It is also an argument for breaking up monopolies created by government regulation of naturally competitive industries. But in the case of natural monopoly, competitive equilibrium is simply not an option.

The cure that economics textbooks traditionally offer for the efficiency problems of natural monopoly is government regulation or ownership. One problem with this approach is that it views the owners and managers of a private monopoly as part of the economic system, acting to achieve their own objectives, but sees government officials as bureaucrat-gods standing outside the system. There is no good reason for such an asymmetrical treatment of the two alternatives.

A regulator, or an official running a government monopoly, has objectives of his own—some combination of private benefit to himself and political gains for the administration that appointed him. A sensible policy for the regulator might be (on the historical evidence, often is) to help the monopoly maximize profits in exchange for campaign contributions to the incumbent administration and a well-paid future job for the regulator.

In chapter 19, we will analyze the political market using the same assumptions of rational self-interest that we use for ordinary markets—and discover that public policies designed to maximize the general welfare are not a likely outcome. At this point, however, we will ignore that problem and assume that the regulators in charge of a natural monopoly have only the best of intentions. Their objective is to maximize net benefits by forcing the firm to follow the prescription of the two efficiency conditions: Charge marginal cost, provided that at that price net benefit is positive.

In order to do so, the regulator needs some way of determining what the firm's costs are. One approach is to simply watch, see what it costs to produce each unit of output, and set prices accordingly. But relating costs to output is not a simple matter of observation. To determine marginal cost, for example, we have to know not only the cost of the quantity the firm is producing but also what it would cost to produce other quantities.

A second problem is that the regulator observes what the firm does, not what it could do—and the firm knows the regulator is watching. It may occur to the firm's managers that if they arrange to produce the last few units in as expensive a fashion as possible, perhaps by using a factory that is just a little too small for the amount they plan to produce, the regulators will observe a high marginal cost and permit them to charge a high price.

Suppose, however, that the regulators see through any such deceits, correctly measure marginal cost, and set price equal to it. Marginal cost is usually lower than average cost for a natural monopoly—that is why average cost falls as quantity increases. So if the firm must sell at marginal cost it will eventually go broke—or, if the regulation is anticipated, never come into existence. To prevent that, the regulator must find some way of making up the difference between price and average cost.

One obvious solution is a subsidy paid for by the taxpayers. How does the regulator decide how big the subsidy should be? If he simply sets it equal to the difference between revenue and cost, the management of the firm has no incentive to hold down costs—especially the cost of things that make the life of management easier. Here again, management knows that the regulator is watching—and modifies what it does accordingly.

An alternative is to estimate the cost curves, require the firm to sell at marginal cost, and pay it a subsidy just sufficient to make up its predicted losses. If costs are lower than estimated, the firm makes a profit, if higher than estimated it makes a loss, so management has an incentive to keep costs down.

But how do we make the initial estimates? We could use last year's costs—but if last year's management anticipated our doing so, they had an incentive to run the firm badly then in order to establish a high cost base for future subsidies. Perhaps we could hire our own management team and try to duplicate all of the work that went into the firm's own calculation of how much to produce how and at what cost. That is an expensive solution—and unlike the real managers, we don't get our conclusions continually checked against real-world outcomes.

Even with all the relevant cost information, one more problem remains: the second efficiency condition. There is no point to keeping a monopoly in business if doing so costs the taxpayers more than it is worth. To decide whether the monopoly should exist, we need to know what its output is worth to its customers—the consumer surplus under their demand curve. Unfortunately we can observe only one point on that curve: quantity demanded at the price (equal to marginal cost) that we force the monopoly to sell at. Regulating a monopoly is a straightforward problem in a textbook, where you can read all of the relevant information off diagrams thoughtfully provided by the author, but real-world monopolies do not come with cost curves and demand curves painted on the door.

Selling at marginal cost is the textbook solution to the problem posed by natural monopoly. The solution that utility commissions usually aim at in the real world is price equal to average cost. That is inefficient, since consumers who value the good at more than marginal cost but less than average cost don't get it, but it solves the problem of where to get the money to cover the monopoly's costs—from the customers. It also eliminates the risk of maintaining monopolies that ought not to exist, since such monopolies will find that there is no price at which they can cover their costs.

This approach to controlling natural monopolies is called "rate of return" regulation, since the idea is to set a price that gives the stockholders of the regulated utility a "fair rate of return" on their investment. The cost of inputs other than the stockholder's capital is set at what the regulatory commission thinks it ought to be, based on the experience of past years.

How much do investors have to get to make it worth investing in utilities? The obvious answer is "the market rate of return"—but on what? If regulators measure the investment by how much investors initially put in, investors in new utilities face an unattractive gamble: If they guess wrong the company goes bankrupt and they lose everything; if they guess right they get only the market return.

What about measuring the current value of the investment by the market value of the utility's stock and allowing the utility to set a price that gives a market return on that value? Unfortunately, this ends up as a circular argument. The value of the stock depends on how much money investors think the company will make, which depends on what price they think the regulators will permit it to charge. Whatever the amount the regulators allow the utility to make will be the market return on the value of the stock—once the value of the stock has adjusted to the amount the utility is making.

Regulatory commissions exist in the real world, hold hearings, and publish press releases describing the good they are doing in protecting customers from greedy monopolies. What they really do, however, and what effect they really have, is far from clear. In a famous early article on the economics of regulation, George Stigler and Claire Friedland tried to determine the effect of utility regulation empirically by looking at the returns to utilities in states where regulation came in at different times. As far as they could tell, there was no effect.

Nationalized Monopoly

An alternative to regulating monopolies is to nationalize them. This solves the problem of management lying to the regulators about cost curves; now the regulators are the management. It does not solve the incentive problem; the interests of the managers of a nationalized firm, or of the politicians who appoint them, are not the same as the interests of the population as a whole. Nor does it solve the problem of satisfying the second efficiency condition. Even if the demand for buggy whips disappears, a prudent administrator of a government buggy whip monopoly, in deciding whether to shut down or ask Congress for a bigger subsidy, will remember that his employees are also potential voters and campaign workers.

There is another important respect in which regulation or nationalization may be worse than unregulated monopoly. There are many intermediate points between perfect competition and natural monopoly, and the location of a particular industry along that continuum may change. A firm that finds itself in danger of losing its monopoly may turn to the government that regulates (or owns) it for help.

One example is the regulation of transportation by the Interstate Commerce Commission. In the absence of regulation, the transportation industry would have become competitive when trucking developed as a major competitor to rail transport, since large trucking firms have no important cost advantage over small ones. The ICC regulated—and to a considerable degree cartelized—first the barge industry and then the trucking industry in order to protect its original regulatees, the railroads.

Monopolies for Sale

As we saw a few pages back, a perfectly price-discriminating monopoly satisfies both the first and second efficiency conditions; the only problem is that firms, having transferred the entire surplus to themselves, may compete it all away in the process of getting it. This suggests a possible way of getting an efficient outcome without direct regulation. Suppose we know in 1900 that, starting in 1920, the American aluminum industry will be a natural monopoly. In 1900 the government auctions off the monopoly—the right to produce aluminum after 1920—to the highest bidder. Aspiring monopolists should be willing to bid up to the full present value of the future monopoly profits, so the government will have collected a 100 percent tax on monopoly profits, as estimated by the (prospective) monopolist. This solution depends on our being able to identify prospective natural monopolies in advance. If we guess wrong, we have just turned a competitive industry into a government-enforced monopoly.

Even if we knew enough to limit our auction to industries destined to become natural monopolies, it is not clear we would. The arguments of the last two paragraphs could, after all, provide elegant camouflage for a government that wanted to create monopolies as a source of revenue or in exchange for political support by favored firms and industries. The term "monopoly" originated in just this context—to describe otherwise competitive industries, such as the sale of salt, where one producer had bought from the government the right to exclude all others.

Patents and Efficiency

One form of government-granted monopoly with which most of us are familiar is intellectual property: patents and copyrights. My publisher has a legal monopoly on selling this book; if another firm tries to compete, we call in the lawyers.

Like most monopolies, this one results in an inefficiently low level of output—measured in copies sold. Part of what you paid for the book went to reimburse me for writing it and HarperCollins for editing and typesetting it. Those costs do not depend on how many copies are sold, so they are not part of marginal cost; the efficient price would cover only the cost necessary to print and distribute one more copy. A price higher than that means that some people do not get a copy even though it is worth more to them than it would cost us to produce.

Before concluding that patents and copyrights should be abolished, consider the second efficiency condition. If I could collect nothing for writing this book, it is not likely that I would, at this instant, be sitting in front of a computer screen revising this chapter; there are better ways to spend Christmas Eve. A legal rule that forced writers and inventors to sell their products at marginal cost would give us an efficient number of copies of those books that were produced—but there might not be very many of them.

Intellectual property law is a real-world example of a government selling a monopoly. The price an inventor pays for a temporary monopoly of a new process is that he must first invent the process. The price I am, at this very moment, paying for a monopoly over the production and sale of this book is writing the book.

The Problem

The mistake in most discussions of natural monopoly is the assumption that the problem is monopoly. The problem is a particular kind of production function: one for which minimum average cost occurs at a quantity too high to permit perfect competition. A single-price unregulated monopoly is one (imperfect) solution to the problem posed by such a cost curve. It produces its output at the lowest possible cost but is inefficient in both the quantity it produces (too low) and its decision of whether to produce at all (sometimes it will not when it should). Regulated monopoly is another imperfect solution, one that may do better than unregulated private monopoly with regard to quantity but worse with regard to least-cost production. It is also a solution that may continue, costs and all, even after the problem it is a solution to has disappeared. Government-run monopoly is another imperfect solution with many of the same problems. Perfectly discriminating monopoly, where it is possible, is an elegant solution that avoids the defects of the other alternatives only to introduce a potentially worse defect in the form of rent seeking.

TO THINK ABOUT

Much of the United States became private property through homesteading: Whoever first claimed the land and worked it for a fixed number of years owned it. As the frontier moved west, any particular piece of land was first not worth farming (costs higher than benefits), then just worth farming, then more than worth farming (benefits higher than costs). Under the homesteading law, at what point in this process would settlers start to farm the land? At what point should they have started, from the standpoint of efficiency? Was the Homestead Act the worst single mistake that the U.S. government has ever made?

17

HOW TO GUM UP THE WORKS

In the previous chapter, we considered government actions aimed at reducing the inefficiency due to monopoly. The conclusion was at least mildly pessimistic; while the market outcome is inefficient, correcting the inefficiency is difficult and the attempt can easily do more harm than good. In this chapter we consider government intervention in the market more broadly, without limiting ourselves to either regulation of monopoly or attempts to increase efficiency. We start with a paradoxical result—that the normal effect of price control is to make goods more expensive.

THE PARADOX OF PRICE CONTROL

The price of gasoline has risen to the unheard-of level of a dollar a gallon; the public blames the rise on Middle Eastern sheiks and price-gouging oil companies. Something must be done. The government steps in to protect consumers by making it illegal to sell gasoline at any price above $0.80 a gallon.

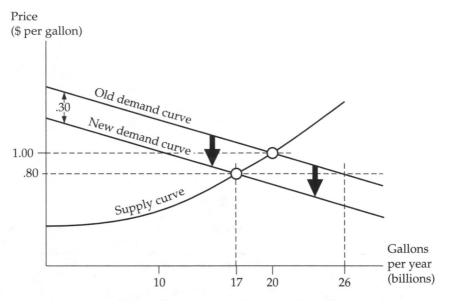

Price
($ per gallon)

Figure 17-1   The effect of price control on gasoline. Price control at $0.80 a gallon produces a shortage; quantity demanded is larger than quantity supplied. Lines grow until their cost shifts demand down far enough to make quantity demanded at the controlled price equal to quantity supplied. Consumers are paying $0.20 a gallon less in money and $0.30 a gallon more in time.

Figure 17–1 shows demand and supply curves for gasoline; they intersect at the market price and quantity: $1 a gallon and twenty billion gallons per year. At $0.80 a gallon, producers only want to pump, refine, and sell seventeen billion gallons per year, but consumers want to buy twenty-six billion. Consumers cannot, for very long, use nine billion gallons more than is being produced; gas stations rapidly run out of gasoline.

One way of making sure you get enough gasoline is by getting up early in the morning and arriving at the station shortly after the tank truck leaves. If everyone tries to do that, the result is a long line. Having to wait in line raises the cost of gasoline to the consumer, adding a *nonpecuniary* cost in time to the cost he is already paying in money.

Another nonpecuniary cost is uncertainty; every time you take a long trip, you risk being stranded in Podunk. Another is frequent visits to the gas station in order to be sure your tank is always full. You may find it necessary to pay bribes to the station owner. During the gasoline shortage created by the price control of the early seventies, one prominent figure bought his own gas station in order to be sure he and his friends would get gas.

If I must pay $0.80 in money plus $0.30 in waiting time and other inconveniences for each gallon of gasoline I buy, I will buy the same amount as if the price were $1.10 a gallon. The additional cost is equivalent to a $0.30 a gallon tax on consumers; like such a tax, it shifts the demand curve down by $0.30, as Figure 17–1 shows.

Waiting in line is a cost to me but not a benefit to the producers of gasoline; they are still receiving only $0.80 a gallon. The demand curve shifts; the supply curve does not. The effect on quantity produced and on the welfare of consumers and producers is the same as if we had simply imposed a $0.30 a gallon tax. The only difference is that nobody gets the tax.

Thirty cents is not a number picked at random. As you can see on the figure, a $0.30 shift in the demand curve is just enough to make quantity demanded equal quantity supplied at the controlled price. If the cost (of lines and other inconveniences) to the consumers was less than $0.30, quantity demanded would still be more than quantity supplied. The attempts of individuals to compete against each other for the limited supply would drive the cost up further: The lines would grow.

The result—that price control results in a cost to the consumer, pecuniary plus nonpecuniary, higher than the uncontrolled price—does not depend on the details of the diagram. Consumers cannot consume more gas than producers produce, so the nonpecuniary cost must be large enough to drive quantity demanded down to quantity supplied. Quantity supplied is lower than without price control, so cost to the consumer must be higher.

Rationing

One way of dealing with this problem is by rationing gasoline. At the controlled price, production is down by 15 percent, so everyone receives ration tickets allowing him to buy 85 percent as much gasoline as he bought last year. Anyone who tries to buy more than his ration is shot. Average cost for buying rationed gas is now only $0.80 a gallon, but marginal cost beyond the rationed amount is very high—your life for the first pint. People keep buying as long as marginal cost is less than marginal value, ending up with as much gas as they have ration tickets for, since at that point marginal cost abruptly increases.

Once we allow the marginal cost of gasoline to the consumer (which determines how much he buys) to differ from the average cost (which determines how much he pays for it), our proof that price control makes consumers worse off is no longer valid. Whether the consumer gains or loses by the combination of price control and rationing depends on whether the gain from getting gasoline for less is more or less than the loss from getting less of it.

In more complicated real-world cases, one should also take account of the cost of running and enforcing a rationing scheme and adjusting it to a changing world. Efficiently allocating gasoline, or anything else, is a complicated problem; price control forces us to substitute an administrative solution for the automatic solution provided by the market.

Gasoline price control—and gasoline shortages—were important issues in the early seventies, thanks to the OPEC cartel and the Nixon administration's response, but they are now only fading memories. Other forms of price control are still with us. One of the most common, rent control, provides an interesting case for discussing the distinction between *allocational* and *distributional* effects.

DISTRIBUTION VERSUS ALLOCATION

Noneconomists tend to think of all issues as distributional: If cars are sold on the market, rich people get them and poor people do not; if we have private schools, rich kids get educated and poor kids don't. Economists tend to be more interested in allocational issues: Consider two people with the same income but different tastes. Let cars and education both be sold. One person buys a car and no education; one buys education and no car. *Allocation* is what goods go where. *Distribution* is who gets how much.

Economists focus on allocational issues not because distribution is unimportant but because we have less to say about it. We can construct allocational changes that benefit (or harm) everyone, so we can evaluate them without worrying about how to balance gains to one person against losses to someone else. Distributional changes are just the opposite. If I lose a dollar and you gain a dollar, there is neither a net gain nor net loss. Efficiency is unaffected, and efficiency is the least unsatisfactory criterion we have for judging what is or is not an improvement.

Consider the common household rule: You made the mess, you clean it up. In any single case, its effects are distributional, since it determines who has to do a particular unpleasant task. Over the long run, however, the distributional effect averages out (unless some members of the household are much messier than others); the main effect is to give people an incentive not to make messes. That is an improvement in the allocation of effort, since it is frequently less work to prevent a mess than to clean it up.

Rent Control

Rents are rising. The city government of Santa Monica decides to protect innocent tenants from greedy landlords by imposing rent control. The obvious effect is distributional: Landlords are worse off and tenants are better off. The less obvious effect is allocational. At the controlled rent, quantity of apartments demanded is higher than quantity supplied. If you are already occupying a rented apartment, you have a good deal; if you are looking for an apartment to rent, you have a problem.

As families change, they move. A young couple has children and moves from a four-room to a six-room apartment; an older couple moves from a six-room to a four-room apartment after the children leave home. But suppose that, under rent control, the older couple has a six-room apartment for $600 a month; controlled four-room apartments rent for $400, but since quantity demanded at the controlled price is larger than quantity supplied, there are no four-room apartments for rent in Santa Monica. Uncontrolled four-room apartments outside of Santa Monica rent for $600. The couple stays put.

The same problem exists for people who want to move from a four-room apartment in one part of town to an apartment the same size but in a different location. As time passes, where people live becomes determined more and more by where they used to live and less and less by where (size and location of apartment) it is now appropriate for them to live. This is an allocational problem: It makes some people worse off without making other people better off.

There is a simple solution: Allow tenants to sublet their apartments—for whatever they can get. There will now be two rents for any apartment: the controlled rent and the rent that a sublessee would pay the original tenant—what the market rent would have been in the absence of rent control. The cost to an elderly couple of remaining in their six-room apartment is now $800—if they moved out, they would not only save $600 in rent, they would also make an additional $200 by continuing to rent for $600 while subletting to someone else for $800. Moving to a four-room apartment (which they sublet from its current tenant for $600) saves them the same amount as it would if there were no rent control.

Rent control plus uncontrolled subletting permits a free market in apartments while giving the original tenant part ownership of the apartment that he occupied when rent control was imposed. The tenants of the six-room apartment are quarter owners; if they choose to sublet for $800, three-fourths goes to the landlord and one fourth to them. This appears to be a way of producing a *distributional* effect (which may be desired for political or other reasons) without *allocational* costs.

One problem is that under such a system, a landlord has little incentive to maintain his property. Before rent control, the rent he could get for his apartment depended on its condition. Now all that matters to him is that the apartment is worth at least the controlled rent. Any deterioration short of that point is at the expense of his initial tenants—either as occupants or as sublessors.

Apartments start to deteriorate; this results in laws (if they do not already exist) specifying how landlords must maintain apartments. A system of uncontrolled rents in which the landlord was led by his own interest to make those repairs and improvements that were worth making has been replaced by a system of rent control in which uniform standards are set and enforced in order to force landlords to do things that it is no longer in their interest to do voluntarily.

Under rent control, part of the value of a new apartment building goes, not to the builder, but to the first set of tenants. That discourages construction. The obvious solution is to exempt new construction from rent control.

But the same forces that made it politically profitable to impose rent control on existing housing this year may make it profitable, five years hence, to impose rent control on buildings built during that interval. Unless the politician can somehow commit both himself and his successors not to do so, potential investors in new construction must allow for that risk. So under rent control, a city's residential housing stock tends to erode. New York City was the only major U.S. city that retained rent control after the end of World War II—and the only one to be plagued by a persistent shortage of residential housing.

Analogous problems arise for other forms of price control. If gasoline is rationed, producers can save money by reducing quality and still sell as much as they want to produce. Law and regulation may be able to prevent some of the more obvious ploys, such as selling three-quart gallons at $0.80 a gallon, but it is hard to measure and control less obvious dimensions of the product, such as the quality of the service and the rest rooms. One cost of price control is a lower quality than customers would choose on an uncontrolled market—just as one cost of rent control is that landlords no longer have an incentive to maintain their buildings.

The equivalent of uncontrolled subletting is a system of marketable ration tickets. The result is an efficient allocation, since if the value of an additional gallon is greater to me than to you, I can buy your ticket. The amount of gas produced is still inefficiently small, since only part of the value of an additional gallon goes to the producer—the rest goes to the owner of the ration ticket for that gallon. The net effect is like a tax on gasoline production, with the revenue allocated to consumers in the form of (valuable) ration tickets.

Why do rationing systems usually forbid the purchase and sale of tickets? Perhaps because marketable tickets make the effect of price control plus rationing more obvious—and harder to defend. It is fairly easy to argue that national hardships should be borne by everyone—that if there is "not enough" gasoline, everyone should be allowed to have as much gas as he "needs" and no more. It is much harder to argue for the peculiar system of taxes and subsidies described in the previous paragraph—which is equivalent to a rationing system with marketable tickets. Yet the shift from strict rationing to rationing with marketable tickets benefits everyone: buyers (who get additional tickets for less than they are worth to them) and sellers (who give up tickets for more than they are worth to them).

Liability Rules

Caveat emptor (Latin for "let the buyer beware") means that the seller or producer of a product is not responsible for defects; *caveat venditor* ("let the seller beware") means that he is. A change in legal rules from *caveat emptor* to *caveat venditor* appears at first glance to be a pure transfer: Consumers gain (and producers lose) whatever producers have to pay the consumers to compensate them for defective products.

This is our old friend naive price theory from chapter 2; it ignores the effect of the legal change on prices. The change raises cost to the producer (when he sells the good, he becomes liable to pay if it is defective) and the value of the good to the consumer. Both the supply and demand curves shift up, so the price must rise.

One's next guess might be that there is no effect at all—on average consumers pay in higher prices what they receive for defective products. This is closer but still not quite right. If the producer is liable for defective products, that is an incentive to avoid defects. If the consumer must bear his own costs, on the other hand, that gives him an incentive to wear safety glasses while using power tools and avoid shaking bottles of warm Coke.

If consumers know the quality of what they are buying, the first incentive is unnecessary. Producers will find it in their interest to make any improvements in quality control that are worth making, since they can more than cover the additional costs with the increased price consumers will be willing to pay for the improved product. But if it is expensive to evaluate products, consumers may choose to buy in partial ignorance, in which case the incentive provided to the producer by *caveat venditor* serves a useful purpose.

This seems to imply that the rule should be *caveat emptor* where the main danger is from careless use by the consumer or where the consumer can readily inform himself of the quality of the good. It seems to imply that the rule should be *caveat venditor* where the consumer cannot readily judge quality and the best way to avoid problems is for the producer to produce better goods.

A still better solution is the combination of either *caveat emptor* or *caveat venditor* with freedom of contract. Suppose the rule is *caveat emptor,* and further suppose that consumers would much prefer to buy under a rule of *caveat venditor,* even at a price that compensated the producers for the cost of that rule. In that case, producers will find that selling their product with a guarantee (at a higher price) is more profitable than selling it without a guarantee. The producer who offers a guarantee is converting the rule for his product into *caveat venditor*—voluntarily making himself liable for product defects.

Suppose instead that the rule is initially *caveat venditor.* The consumer could convert it to *caveat emptor* by signing a waiver agreeing not to sue. One area where such waivers could make a very large difference is medical malpractice. Given the high cost of malpractice insurance, a doctor might offer a much lower price to a patient who agreed to limitations on his ability to sue.

Under present law, such a waiver is unenforceable; the patient can sign it before the operation, then change his mind and sue anyway. That is one example of the movement of our legal system in recent decades away from freedom of contract, a change that some critics regard as a major cause of the sharp increase over the past few decades in the size and frequency of liability suits and the cost of liability insurance. The problem is not so much that the courts have gotten the legal rules wrong as that they have prevented people from correcting the court's mistakes by contracting around them.

How Not to Redistribute Income

I have so far ignored the fact that costs such as waiting in line are different for different people—a busy professional, say, or a student who can study while waiting. Under price control without rationing, consumers on average lose, since nonpecuniary cost must be large enough to reduce demand below its level at the uncontrolled price, but individual consumers to whom the nonpecuniary cost is exceptionally low may gain. Similar results apply to both producers and consumers under other forms of price control and, more generally, other restrictions on freedom of contract.

Most discussions of rent control, liability rules, and similar issues view them as means of redistribution, with price control, rent control, or *caveat venditor* benefiting buyers at the expense of sellers. As we have seen, this is wrong; the principal effect of such policies is to produce a less efficient allocation of resources, a smaller pie to be divided up. Such redistribution as occurs is mostly among consumers and among producers rather than from one group to the other.

Rent control is an exception; it can, and probably often does, produce a substantial transfer from landlords to tenants, at least in the short run. One reason is that the supply of housing is, in the short run, very inelastic; landlords do not start tearing down apartment buildings when rents fall by 10 percent. The short-run effect of rent control on the supply of housing is small compared to the effect of gasoline price control on the supply of gasoline.

The other reason is that rent control comes with a built-in system of rationing: Allocate each apartment to the tenant presently living in it. In the very long run, the case of rent control is the same as the case of price control on gasoline—but the short run is long enough so that many individuals benefit for a period of years and sometimes decades, which may explain why it is more popular than most other forms of price control.

Protecting Consumers from Themselves

Restrictions on price are usually defended as ways of protecting consumers from producers. Restrictions on what you can buy or from whom are defended as ways of protecting the consumer from himself. How many of us, it may reasonably be asked, are competent to judge how good a doctor, or a drug, is?

Such arguments usually ignore the distinction between licensing and certifying, between control of what can be sold and control of how it can be sold. If doctors are licensed, an unlicensed doctor can be jailed for practicing medicine. If doctors are merely certified, an uncertified doctor can still practice—he just can't claim to be certified. The customer might decide that he prefers his own judgment to that of the certifying authority, or that even though he agrees that certified doctors are better, he prefers the uncertified doctor because of his lower charges, greater availability, or ability to speak the customer's language. A similar rule applied to drug regulation would mean that drugs currently illegal, or available only by prescription, could be freely sold, but only with appropriate warnings. In order to argue for licensing over certifying, one must claim that people cannot be trusted to make the right choice even when given the relevant information. One argument on the other side is that, however ill informed I may be, I am one of the few people in the world who can be trusted to make decisions with my interest at heart.

While some regulations, such as compulsory vaccination, may make sense as attempts to force consumers to act in the general interest, many more seem designed to serve very narrow private interests—at the expense of those being "protected." An obvious example is the use of licensing to keep the number of people in a profession down and their salaries up—a reason that, although rarely stated in public argument, seems the most plausible explanation for the severe licensing requirements imposed, in many states, not only upon doctors but upon barbers, egg graders, yacht salesmen, librarians, and a host of other "professionals."

HOW TO CUT TAXES AND RAISE REVENUE

Under a *graduated* income tax, income is divided into brackets, each taxed at a different rate. In a *progressive* system, the higher the bracket, the higher the rate. In a *regressive* system, the higher the bracket, the lower the rate. While "progressive" sounds good and "regressive" bad, the terms are simply descriptions of two patterns of graduation: one in which rates rise (progress) with income and one in which they fall (regress).

The United States at present has a progressive income tax. A number of people have suggested replacing it with a flat tax. I will consider simplified versions of both alternatives. My progressive tax has one bracket from 0 to $10,000 a year, a second from $10,000 a year to $20,000 a year, and a third from $20,000 a year up. You pay nothing on income in the first bracket, 20 percent on income in the second, and 40 percent on income in the third. We will compare it to a flat tax in which everyone pays a fixed percentage of his income.

We can eliminate distributional effects in order to focus on allocational ones by considering a world where everyone has the same income—say $25,000 a year. Under the graduated tax, everyone is paying $4,000 a year—an average rate of 16 percent. What happens if we replace the graduated system with a 16 percent flat tax?

If your answer is "Taxpayers are paying the same amount as before, so the change has no effect," you are not yet thinking like an economist. Once people have adjusted to the new tax system they will be paying more taxes than before—and be better off!

Suppose the wage rate is $10 an hour. If you work one more hour the additional income is in the 40 percent bracket; you get $6 and the IRS gets $4. A rational individual sells his leisure—works—until the marginal value of an additional hour is equal to the price he gets for it. So each taxpayer works up to the point where the marginal disvalue of one more hour of work is $6.

After we switch to a flat tax, the marginal tax rate is 16 percent instead of 40. If you earn an extra $10, you get to keep $8.40 of it. Since, at the amount you are currently working, the marginal disvalue of labor is only $6 an hour, it is worth trading some more leisure for dollars. Everyone increases the number of hours he works until the decrease in his leisure raises its marginal value to $8.40 an hour. Taxpayers are working more hours, receiving more income, paying more in taxes, and better off.

They are making more because they are working more hours. They are paying more in taxes because incomes have risen; 16 percent of the new income is more than the $4,000 produced by the old system. They are better off not simply because they have more money—that must be balanced against the additional hours they are working—but because each person has chosen an outcome, a bundle of a certain amount of income plus a certain amount of leisure, that he prefers to what he had before.

How do I know that? Under the new system, each individual could choose to work the same number of hours as before and pay the same tax—that is how the tax rate was calculated. That he does not choose to do so demonstrates that he now has an alternative he prefers. To put the argument more formally, the old optimal bundle is still in his new opportunity set; the fact that it is no longer optimal means that the new opportunity set contains a bundle he prefers to it. This is the same argument we used back in chapter 3 to explain, why, after I have bought a house, I gain from either an increase or a decrease in housing prices.

If we now lower the tax rate so that everyone pays the same tax as under the graduated system ($4,000 a year), people are even better off. The flat-rate system now produces the same revenue while giving every taxpayer an outcome (a 14 percent flat tax, say) that he prefers to the outcome under a flat rate of 16 percent—which he prefers to the old system. The change is not only an improvement, it is even (under our assumption that everyone is identical) a Pareto improvement. Everyone is better off.

Complications

In proving that, if all taxpayers are identical, a flat-rate tax is unambiguously superior to a progressive tax, I have ignored a number of complications. The most important is the effect on wages of the increased supply of labor due to the change in the tax law. Including that effect would transform some of the gain from producer surplus (going to the sellers of labor) to consumer surplus (going to the buyers); the consumers who are the ultimate purchasers of labor are now getting it at a lower price. If everyone is identical, everyone ends up with an equal share of consumer and producer surplus. The analysis would be more complicated, but the net effect would still be a gain.

The logic of the situation is quite simple. How much of their income people pay in taxes is determined by their average tax rate; how much income they choose to earn is determined by their marginal tax rate. A tax system like ours, which combines high marginal rates with low average rates, is an effective way of reducing national income without collecting very much revenue.

Surprising though it may seem, we have just solved chapter 1's hero problem. When we last saw our hero he was being pursued by forty bad guys and had only ten arrows. The solution that saves him is to shoot the bad guy in front. Then shoot the bad guy in front. Then shoot the bad guy in front. Then the bad guys start competing to see who can run slowest.

The hero saves his life by making *marginal* cost higher than *average* cost. On average, he can kill only a fourth of his pursuers. But on the margin of who runs fastest, he can kill all of them—until he runs out of arrows. No one is willing to face a certainty of death just to give the survivors the pleasure of killing the hero. Once he has made it clear what he is doing, they all decline the honor of running in front.

That is also, as you may remember from chapter 1, how Jarl Sigurd lost the battle of Clontarf: He ran out of men who were willing to carry the banner and accept a certainty of being killed. It is also how you impose a very large penalty for consuming gasoline without actually punishing anyone; if everyone believes he will be shot for exceeding his ration, nobody exceeds it and nobody is ever shot. It is also how you can use a tax system to make us all poorer.

To make the parallelism even closer, consider a graduated tax system with only two brackets. The lower includes 95 percent of income, and is taxed at a rate of 20 percent. The higher includes only 5 percent of income, and is taxed at a rate of 100 percent. Each year we recalculate the brackets. The system is only mildly graduated, since most income is taxed at a uniform rate—but its effect is to reduce taxable income to zero. First you shoot the dollar in front, then you shoot the dollar in front, then . . .

Distribution

In a world of identical individuals, the allocational case against a progressive tax system is overwhelming. The distributional argument for a progressive tax appears only in a world where incomes are unequal and some people wish to make them less so.

One reason to do so is the belief that a dollar provides, on average, more happiness to those who have fewer dollars, so that a transfer from rich to poor may produce a gain in total happiness even if it produces a loss in total value. In a previous chapter I raised, and left unanswered, the question of whether the distribution of income produced by the market is just. If you believe that a more equal distribution would be more just, that is another reason to support a redistribution of income. If one wishes to make the after-tax income distribution more equal than the before-tax distribution, a progressive tax is an obvious—if costly—way to do so.

It is not, however, clear whether the tax system that presently exists in the United States actually does equalize incomes. If you earn your living as an employee of a large organization, public or private, what you report to the IRS is probably very close to what you actually make. If you are self-employed, the opportunities for concealing income, or converting consumption into business expenses for tax purposes, are much greater. For these reasons and others, the actual tax system redistributes in many different directions. There is some tendency for richer people to pay more than poorer, making the income distribution more equal, but also some tendency for people with identical incomes to pay different amounts of tax, making the after-tax distribution less equal. Determining what really happens is difficult. The main source of statistics on incomes and taxes is the IRS, and what one is interested in is, in large part, income that is not reported to the IRS.

Class Warfare as Bad Economics

A fundamental mistake in popular discussions of this issue (and many others) is the assumption that what is good for the rich is *necessarily* bad for the poor, and vice versa. That assumption is an example of the noneconomist's tendency to see all issues as distributional. To take a simple counterexample, consider a rich man who is in a 50 percent bracket, earns $200,000 a year, and (legally or illegally) succeeds in keeping most of it out of reported taxable income—at a cost (to himself) of 45 cents on the dollar. He is behaving rationally—it is worth paying 45 percent to tax lawyers and accountants to avoid paying 50 percent to the IRS. If the tax rate falls to 40 percent, it becomes cheaper to pay taxes than to avoid them; the rich man is better off and the IRS collects more money.

The classic example of this phenomenon is due not to Arthur Laffer—who popularized it under the name of the "Laffer curve"—but to Adam Smith. His example was an import duty so high that all imports were smuggled. If the duty were lowered to the point where it was no longer worth the cost of smuggling, both consumers and tax collectors would be better off.

TO THINK ABOUT

Regulation Q prohibited banks from paying interest on checking accounts. Banks argued that since this lowered the amount they had to pay to get money, it lowered the price at which they could lend it out, hence made mortgages less expensive. Were they right?

18

MARKET FAILURE: WHY WE ARE NOT ALL HAPPY, WEALTHY, WISE, AND MARRIED

The time is rush hour; the scene is Wilshire and Westwood in Los Angeles, said to be the busiest intersection in the world. As the light on Wilshire goes green, ten lanes of traffic surge forward. As it turns yellow, a last few cars try to make it across—and end up caught in the intersection. Gradually the trapped cars make it across, allowing the traffic on Westwood to surge forward—just as the light goes red, trapping a new batch of cars.

If drivers on both streets refrained from entering the intersection until there was room on the far side, the jam would not occur. Traffic would flow faster and they would all get where they are going sooner. Yet each driver is behaving rationally. My aggressive driving on Wilshire benefits me (I may make it across before the light changes, and at worst I will get far enough into the intersection not to be blocked by cars going the other way at the next stage of the jam) and harms drivers on Westwood. Your aggressive driving on Westwood benefits you and harms drivers on Wilshire. The harm is much larger than the benefit, so on net we are all worse off. But I receive all of the benefit and none of the harm from the particular decision that I control. I am correctly choosing the action that best achieves my objectives—but if we all made a mistake and drove less aggressively, we would all be better off.

PLEA BARGAINING: A REAL-WORLD PRISONER'S DILEMMA

The prosecutor calls up the defense lawyer and offers a deal. If the client will plead guilty to second-degree murder, the district attorney will drop the charge of first-degree murder. The accused will lose his chance of acquittal—but he will also lose the risk of going to the chair.

Such plea bargains are widely criticized as a way of letting criminals off lightly. Their actual effect may well be the opposite—to make punishment more, not less, severe.

How can this be? A rational criminal will accept a plea bargain only if doing so makes him better off—produces, on average, a less severe punishment than going to trial. Does it not follow that the existence of plea bargaining makes punishment less severe?

There are a hundred cases per year; the DA has a budget of $100,000. With only $1,000 to spend investigating and prosecuting each case, half the defendants are acquitted. But if he can get ninety defendants to cop pleas, the DA can concentrate his resources on the ten who refuse. He spends $10,000 on each case and gets a conviction rate of 90 percent.

A defendant deciding whether to accept an offer faces a 90 percent chance of conviction if he goes to trial—and makes his decision accordingly. The resulting deal must be more attractive than a 90 percent chance of conviction, but it may well be less attractive than a 50 percent chance of conviction—which is what the defendant would face in a world without plea bargaining. All criminals would be better off if none of them accepted the DA's offer, but each is better off accepting. This is the prisoner's dilemma of chapter 11 in real life.

In both of these cases, rational action by every member of a group makes all members of the group worse off; individual rationality leads to group irrationality. Economists call such situations *market failures* because they explain why real-world markets fail to produce the efficient outcome predicted in the previous chapter. But market failures occur in many contexts other than competitive markets—on battlefields, at intersections, in jails and voting booths. The economic analysis of the varieties of market failure and their causes and cures is relevant to many questions other than how to make competitive markets work—as we shall see.

PUBLIC GOODS

One form of market failure is the *public-good problem*: how to pay for producing a good when the producer cannot control who gets it. An example is a radio broadcast. Anyone with a receiver can listen to it, with or without the broadcaster's permission, so how can the broadcaster arrange to be compensated for producing the broadcast? The fact that the good is public is in part a result of law; we could make it illegal to listen to a broadcast without permission. But it is mostly a fact of nature; even if it were illegal, enforcing the law would probably be prohibitively expensive.

As this example shows, whether a good is public does not depend on whether it is produced by the government. In the United States, radio broadcasts are mostly private; they are still public goods. Mail delivery is a private good even when done by the government; the post office can (and does) refuse to deliver your letter without a stamp.

Private Production of Public Goods

There are a number of ways in which public goods can be privately produced. One is a unanimous contract. The producer gets together all the people who will receive the good if it is produced, tells them how much he expects each to pay toward the cost of producing the good, and announces that unless each agrees to pay his share, the good will not be produced.

Consider the logic of the situation from the standpoint of a single member of the group. He reasons as follows:

If someone else refuses, the deal will fall through and I will not have to pay anything. If everyone else agrees, my refusal saves me the money but costs me the public good. So if the good is worth more to me than my share of the cost of producing it, I ought to agree.

The same argument applies to everyone, so each is willing to pay up to the value to him of the good. If the total value is greater than the total cost of producing the good, so is the amount of money that can be raised. The good gets produced if it is worth producing—the efficient outcome.

Such unanimous contracts are hard to organize for large groups. Some members may refuse to agree in the hope that the entrepreneur will redraw the contract with their names omitted. And the entrepreneur may find it difficult to estimate how much the good is worth to each member of the public. If even one estimate is too high, that individual refuses to sign the contract and the whole deal falls through.

One solution is to find a *privileged minority*: a subgroup of the public that receives enough benefit from the public good so that its members can be persuaded to bear the whole cost, and is small enough so that its members can form their own unanimous contract. When I mow my front lawn, I am acting as a privileged minority of one; the mowed lawn makes the neighborhood more attractive, benefiting everyone, but I receive enough of the benefit to be willing to pay the whole cost.

Unanimous contracts are one solution to the problem of producing a public good. Another is to make the public good temporarily private. Suppose the public good is flood control; building a dam will reduce floods in the valley below, increasing land values. One way to pay for the dam is to buy up as much as possible of the land in the valley, build the dam, then sell the land back at a price reflecting its increased value.

A still more ingenious solution is to combine two public goods and give away the package. The first has a positive cost of production and a positive value to the customer; the second has a negative cost of production and a negative value to the customer. The package has a negative production cost and positive value. This is how radio and television broadcasts are produced; the first good is the program, the second the commercial.

For another real-world example, consider computer programs. Making a copy of Word or Excel for a friend violates Microsoft's copyright, but there is not much Microsoft can do about it. Their copyright is enforceable in practice only against easy targets—distributors openly selling pirated copies and firms large enough to be at risk from an irate employee who happens to have Bill Gates's E-mail address. In order to stay in business, software companies aiming mainly at the individual market must find some way of getting paid for producing a public good.

One solution is to sell a computer and give away the software—

MacWrite with the original Macintosh, for example. The availability of the program makes the computer more valuable, and the increased price you can get for the computer pays the cost of writing the program.

This has become less workable as computers have become increasingly standardized. An alternative is to bundle a program with service: a voice on the other end of a telephone to answer questions about how to make the program work. The seller keeps track of who bought the program and gives help only to registered owners.

As these examples suggest, there are many ways in which public goods are privately produced. Each may succeed under some circumstances in producing some quantity of a public good. None can be relied on to lead to an efficient level of production. The producer collects only a part of the value of what he produces, and so produces it only if part of the value is enough to cover all of the costs. Public goods are produced—but, from the standpoint of efficiency, underproduced.

Many familiar annoyances are public-good problems. One example is the problem of getting anything accomplished in a meeting. Most of us like attention: When we have the floor, we take the opportunity not only to say what we have to say about the issue on hand but also to show how clever, witty, and wise we are. This imposes a cost on other people (unless we really are witty and wise); if there are sixty people in the room, every minute I speak costs a person-hour of listener time. Brevity is a public good—and underproduced.

Public Production of Public Goods

An obvious alternative is to have the government produce the good and pay for it out of taxes. This may or may not be an improvement. The mechanism we rely on to make the government act in our interest—voting—itself involves the private production of a public good. When you spend time and energy deciding which candidate best serves the general interest and voting accordingly, most of the benefit of your expenditure goes to other people. You are producing a public good: a vote for the better candidate. That is a very hard public good to produce privately, since the public is a very large one: the whole population of the country. Hence it is very badly underproduced. The underproduction of that public good means that people do not find it in their interest to spend much effort deciding who is the best candidate—which in turn means that democracy does not work very well, so we cannot rely on the government to act in our interest. Just as with a government agency regulating a natural monopoly, the administrators controlling the public production of a public good may find that their own private interest, or the political interest of the administration that appointed them, leads to policies other than maximizing economic welfare.

Even if the government wishes to produce the efficient amount of a public good, it faces problems similar to the problems of regulators trying to satisfy the second efficiency condition. In order to decide how much to produce of which public goods, the government must know what they are worth to consumers. It cannot learn that by observing demand curves because it cannot control who gets the good. Individuals who want the public good have an incentive to overstate how much they want it, so a public-opinion poll may produce a very poor estimate of demand.

EXTERNALITIES

An *externality* is a net cost or benefit that my action imposes on you. The problem of the long-winded speaker can be described as under-production of the public good of brevity; it can equally well be described as overproduction of a product with negative externalities. Familiar examples are pollution (a negative externality—a cost) and scientific progress as a result of theoretical research (a positive externality—a benefit). When I paint my house or mow my lawn, I confer positive externalities on my neighbors; when you smoke in a restaurant or play loud music at 1:00 A.M., you confer negative externalities on yours.

The problem with externalities is not that they are bad—having to work is bad too, at least when I have a good book to read. The problem with externalities is that since you take only your own costs into account in deciding whether or not to smoke or play the music, you may do so even when the total cost (including the cost to your neighbors) is greater than the total benefit. Similarly, I may fail to mow my lawn this week because the benefit to me is less than the cost, even though the total benefit (including the benefit to my neighbors) is more.

This chapter started with two examples of externality problems. Drivers who block an intersection impose an external cost in lost time on other drivers. Defendants who accept a plea bargain impose a cost on other defendants—by freeing up resources that the DA can use, or threaten to use, against them.

"Externalities" and "public goods" are often different ways of looking at the same problems. A positive externality is a public good; a negative externality is a "negative" public good, and refraining from producing it is a positive public good. In some cases, it may be easier to look at the problem one way, in some cases the other—but it is the same problem.

Efficient Pollution and How to Get It

"Pollution" is not a value-neutral term—as you can easily check by asking friends what the optimal level of pollution is. The natural response is "zero, of course—like the optimal level of murder." If you share that response, you might consider that carbon dioxide is both a pollutant and a by-product of human metabolism. The first step in reducing the level of pollution to zero is to stop breathing—or at least exhaling.

In this case as in many others, the use of a loaded word assumes away all of the interesting questions. Most of the things we want to do involve costs as well as benefits. Calling something "pollution" does not tell us whether it is a cost worth paying. It does not even tell us whether it is a cost or a benefit. Consider "thermal pollution"— hot water from the cooling system of a power plant that raises the temperature of a stream by a few degrees. If you use the stream for swimming and are not a polar bear, thermal pollution is a good.

From the standpoint of economics, what we want is the right amount of pollution. If the damage done by emitting a ton of sulfur oxides into the air is greater than the cost of the cheapest way of pre-venting it—whether smokestack scrubbers, different production methods, or closing down the factory—that pollution is inefficient and should be eliminated. If the damage is less than the cost of pre-vention, the pollution is efficient; we are better off, on net, tolerating it. What we want is efficient pollution and only efficient pollution— however ugly that may sound to the noneconomist.

The obvious approach to getting it is regulation—rules specify-ing what firms are allowed to dump where, how high their smoke-stacks must be, what kinds of fuel they may burn. But in order to do this right, the regulators require a great deal of information, much of which they do not have. They must not only know how much dam-age pollution does but also how much it costs to control it. Polluting firms are unlikely to help with this, since it is in their interest to per-suade the regulators that the cost of reducing pollution is as high as possible—thus persuading them to permit the pollution to continue.

A better solution is to impose the cost on the polluter via an *efflu-ent fee* equal to the cost his pollution imposes on others. If a steel firm is charged $1 for each dollar's worth of pollution it produces, the firm will take that into account in pricing its product—steel will now be more expensive—and deciding how to produce it. If it can elimi-nate a dollar's worth of pollution with less than a dollar's worth of pollution control, it will. The result will be an efficient amount of steel—and an efficient amount of pollution.

This is a better approach than direct regulation, but still not a very good one. The regulator no longer has to measure the cost of controlling pollution—it is now in the interest of the firms to do that—but he must still measure the cost produced by pollution, which can be a hard problem. And even if he can produce the effi-cient outcome, what makes it in his interest to do so?

Private Solutions

One private solution to externality problems is a proprietary com-munity. A developer builds a housing development and requires buy-ers to join the neighborhood association. The neighborhood associa-tion either takes care of lawns, painting, and other things that affect the general appearance of the community or requires the owners to do so. My friend and sometime colleague Gordon Tullock used to live in a private community where, by his account, he was not allowed to change the color of his front door without his neighbors' permission.

This sounds like government regulation masquerading as private contract, but there are two important differences. It is in the interest of the developer to construct the best possible rules in order to maxi-mize the price for which he can sell the houses. And nobody is forced to purchase house and membership from that developer; if the pack-age is not at least as attractive as any alternative, the customer can and will go elsewhere.

Another private solution is a merger. If a factory's water pollu-tion is ruining the nearby resort's business, one solution is for the two firms to join. After the resort buys out the factory or vice versa, the new firm will receive, and try to maximize, the combined income of the two enterprises. If controlling the factory's effluent increases the resort's income by more than it costs the factory, it will pay to control the effluent. The externality is no longer external.

Some externality problems can be dealt with by creating appropriate property rights. Trout streams in Britain, for example, are private property. Each stream is owned by someone—frequently the local fishing club. A polluter dumping effluent into such a stream is guilty of trespass, just as if he dumped it on someone's lawn. If he believes the stream is more valuable as a place to dump his effluent than as a trout stream, he can offer to buy it. If he believes that his effluent will not hurt the trout, he can buy the stream and then—if he is right—rent the fishing rights back to the previous owners.

Unfortunately, in some cases there seems to be no way of defining property rights that does not lead to externalities in one direction or another. If I require your permission to play my stereo when you want to sleep, I can no longer impose an externality on you—but your decision to go to sleep when I want to play my stereo imposes an externality on me. If only two people are involved, they may be able to negotiate an efficient arrangement—but air pollution in Los Angeles affects several million people. Just as in the case of producing a public good, the problems of negotiating a unanimous contract become larger the larger the number of people involved.

One way of looking at this is to view all public-good/externality problems as transaction-cost problems. If bargaining were costless, inefficiencies due to market failure could always be eliminated by bargaining among the affected parties. This argument has a name: the *Coase theorem* (after economist Ronald Coase). Looked at in this way, the interesting question is always, "What are the transaction costs that prevent the efficient outcome from being reached?"

Joint Causation, or Why Not Evacuate Los Angeles?

Part of Coase's contribution to understanding externalities was the observation that, since the problem would vanish if bargaining between the affected parties were costless, it could be analyzed as the result not of externalities but of transaction costs. Another part was the observation that the traditional analysis of externalities contained a fundamental error.

So far I have followed the pre-Coasian analysis in treating an externality as a cost imposed by one person on another. That is not quite right. As Coase pointed out, the typical external cost is jointly produced by the actions of both parties. There would be no pollution problem in Los Angeles if there were no pollution, but there would also be no problem if nobody lived in Los Angeles.

If evacuating Los Angeles does not strike you as a solution to the problem of smog, consider more plausible examples. The military owns bomb ranges: pieces of land used to test bombs, artillery shells, and the like. If you happen to be camping on one, a three-hundred-pound bomb next to your tent can impose serious externalities. It seems more natural to solve the problem by removing the campers than by removing the bombs.

One approach to the problem of airport noise is to reduce the noise: make planes quieter, close the airport when people are asleep, instruct pilots to begin their descent as late as possible. An alternative approach is to soundproof houses under the flight path, keep the land near the airport empty, use it for a water reservoir, or fill it with noisy factories. If we charge the airlines for their noise, as we charged the steel company for its pollution, the airline has an incentive to reduce the noise even if it would be cheaper for the local residents to soundproof their houses or move elsewhere.

The traditional analysis of externalities assumes that we already know which party is the least-cost avoider of the problem—that emission controls for automobiles in southern California cost less than evacuating that end of the state. Where we do not know that, the best solution may be Coase's other idea: negotiations between the parties. Let the legal system clearly define who has the right to do what, then let affected individuals bargain among themselves.

We are left with the problem of how best to define the initial rights. Suppose airlines have an unlimited right to make noise. If the efficient solution is to have nobody living near the airport, we get it with no difficulty. If the solution is noise reduction, on the other hand, we have a problem. The people living near the airport could pay the airlines to keep their noise down. But doing so means producing a public good—silence—for everyone living nearby. The move to the efficient outcome is blocked by the transaction costs that make it difficult to produce a public good for a large public.

Alternatively, suppose each homeowner has an absolute right to be free from airplane noise. Now the public-good problem is replaced by the *holdout problem*. Any one homeowner can try to get the airline to pay him the entire savings from soundproofing the houses instead of the planes by threatening to withhold his consent. The result may well be no deal, and an inefficient outcome.

In this particular case, the best rule may be that homeowners cannot forbid the noise but can collect damages. That allows whichever solution turns out to be most efficient to occur with either no transaction (the airline reduces its noise) or a relatively simple and inexpensive one (the airline pays some homeowners to sound-proof and pays damages to the holdouts). This solution depends, however, on the ability of a court to measure the damage. Where that is difficult or impossible, a different rule might lead to a more efficient outcome.

Voluntary Externalities: Sharecropping . . .

Externalities can be eliminated by contract, as when two firms merge. They can also be created by contract. Consider *sharecropping*.

A sharecropper pays, instead of rent, a fixed percentage of his crop to the owner of the land. It seems an inefficient arrangement. If half my crop goes to my landlord, it pays me to make investments of labor or capital only if the payoff is at least twice the cost. I have, by contract, created an externality of 50 percent.

This raises a puzzle. Sharecropping is a common arrangement, appearing in many different societies at different times in history. If it is so inefficient, why does it exist?

One answer is that it exists because all the alternatives are worse. Converting the sharecropper into an employee increases the problem; instead of collecting half the return from additional inputs of labor he collects none of it. Renting the land at a fixed price gives the farmer the right incentives, but if output varies unpredictably from year to year he may do well in good years and starve to death in bad ones. One way of explaining sharecropping is that it, like insurance, is a (costly) device for spreading risk.

The landlord may be able to reduce the cost by monitoring the farmer—just as he would if the farmer were an employee. If he concludes that the farmer is not working hard enough, the landlord can find another sharecropper next year. Sharecroppers require more monitoring than tenants but less than employees, since they get at least part of the output they produce.

Another explanation for sharecropping is that the landlord is also contributing inputs: experience, administration, perhaps capital. Giving him a fraction of the output reduces the farmer's incentive but increases the landlord's. In this case as in others that we have discussed, the best alternative available still involves accepting some inefficiencies.

Some years back, I was negotiating a textbook contract. One of the questions I raised was whether figures in the book would be in black and white or color; color is more expensive but sells more books. The editor was reluctant to discuss the question; when pushed, she said that they preferred to make such decisions at a later stage in the process—meaning sometime after the contract was signed.

A publisher bears all of the cost of printing a book and shares the revenue with the author. So the publisher's incentive to spend money selling more books—by, for example, printing figures in color—is inefficiently low; like a sharecropper, he bears all of the additional cost and gets only part of the resulting revenue. The author is biased the other way; he gets part of the benefit but pays none of the cost.

That is a good reason for a publisher to stall an author who wants an advance commitment on how the book will be produced. And it is, and was, a good reason for an author who prefers to deal with people he can trust to look for another publisher.

. . . and Cleaning Up

Another case of voluntary externalities is familiar to everyone who has shared household duties. The question is, "Who cleans up after dinner?" The usual answer is "Not the cook."

From the standpoint of externalities, this is the wrong answer. Cooking produces both food and mess. If someone else cleans up the mess, the cook has an inefficiently low incentive to avoid making it—by, for example, wiping spills off the stove before they harden into impermeable grunge.

The reason most of us choose that answer is not fairness—we could always alternate cooking days—but a different dimension of efficiency. Cooks, like other people, have declining marginal utility of leisure. After an hour on your feet making dinner, the last thing you want is to spend another hour cleaning up.

Pecuniary Externalities

Suppose something I do imposes both positive and negative externalities, and they are exactly equal. I will ignore both external costs and external benefits, and, since the net external cost of my action is zero, doing so will produce the efficient result.

One would think it an unlikely coincidence for positive and negative externalities to precisely cancel, but there is an important situation, called a *pecuniary externality,* in which that is exactly what happens. Whenever I decide to produce more or less of some good, to enter or leave some profession, to change my consumption pattern, or in almost any other way to alter my market behavior, one result is to slightly shift some supply or demand curve and so to change some price. When I decide to become the million and first physician, the effect of my decision in driving down the wages of each existing physician is tiny, but to evaluate the effect we must multiply that change by a million physicians, each now earning a tiny bit less.

It appears that there can be no economic action without important externalities. But these are precisely the sort of externalities that can be ignored. When price falls by a penny, what is lost by a seller is gained by a buyer; the loss to the physicians is a gain to their patients. The result is a pecuniary externality. My decision to enter a profession, to buy or to sell goods, may have more than a negligible effect on others through its effect on the price of goods or services they buy or sell, but that effect imposes neither net costs nor net benefits, so ignoring it does not produce an inefficient outcome.

Bad Arguments from Good Economics

The theory of externalities is very useful if you are looking for arguments in favor of government intervention in the marketplace. After all, almost anything we do has effects on other people. If you want to ban or tax something, you look for negative externalities; if you want to subsidize something—your own profession, say—you look for positive externalities.

Two mistakes are common in such arguments. The first is the failure to distinguish benefits from external benefits. A standard example is the argument that the government should subsidize schooling because a better educated population will be more productive. More productive individuals generally get paid more; as we have seen, in a perfectly competitive market the wage equals the worker's marginal product. It is only to the extent that the gain goes to someone other than the individual getting the education that it is an externality.

The second mistake is the failure to include both positive and negative externalities in your calculations. The fact that an action imposes an external cost on someone does not imply that it ought to be taxed or forbidden—perhaps it imposes a larger benefit on someone else.

Consider as one example the usual economic argument for reducing population growth. Supporters of that position add up all of the costs that a parent imposes on other people by having another child; not surprisingly, the result is a negative externality. Voilà, an economic justification for subsidized birth control and a campaign to persuade people to have fewer children.

What are the benefits that this argument leaves out? A larger population means more people among whom to divide the national debt and the cost of national defense, more people to produce public goods associated with new information (the extra child might be destined to find the cure for cancer or invent a better version of solitaire), and more people to pay for goods, such as books, with a large fixed cost. My first piece of economic research involved an attempt to sum costs and benefits in order to estimate the net externality from an additional child; I concluded that not only could I not figure out how big it was, I could not tell if it was positive or negative.

Here is another example. Supporters of laws requiring motorcyclists to wear helmets argue that injuries from accidents impose a negative externality on insurers or state hospitals. As far as insurance is concerned, that implies only that insurers should be free to charge different prices to customers who do or do not agree to wear helmets. As far as the taxpayers are concerned, it is a legitimate argument—provided that the net externality is negative.

Helmets eliminate some serious injuries, but they also convert some accidents from lethal to almost lethal. Intensive care is more expensive than a funeral, so while the change is an improvement from the standpoint of the victim, it is a negative externality from the standpoint of Medicare.

Helmets may also increase the number of accidents. A motorcycle rider balances costs against benefits in deciding how fast and how carefully to ride. The better protected he is, the lower the cost of risk, and thus the more risk he will accept. If part of the cost of accidents is borne by the taxpayers, that produces a negative externality.

If you find the idea that safety devices lead to riskier behavior implausible, you might consider one of Gordon Tullock's proposals: a spike attached to the steering wheel of every car, pointing at the driver. It is hard to believe that that, or the higher-tech version—a hand grenade wired to a collision detector—would not sharply reduce risk taking by drivers. Those interested in empirical evidence should read the classic article by Samuel Peltzman in which he shows that legislation requiring safety devices in cars had almost no effect on the highway death rate. The reduction in deaths per accident was just about balanced by the increase in accidents.

A third example of a one-sided calculation of externalities is the legal doctrine of "fraud on the market." The CEO of a company makes an optimistic speech, predicting increased sales; the company's stock goes up. Sales fail to increase; the stock goes back down again. An enterprising lawyer organizes a class action on behalf of all stockholders who bought while the price was high. He claims that the speech was deceptive, a "fraud on the market," and that his clients are entitled to damages equal to the difference between the price they paid and the price they would have paid if the stock had not gone up as a result of the speech.

One of the many things wrong with this doctrine, from the standpoint of an economist if not a lawyer, is the measure of damages. Even if the speech was deceptive and was responsible for the price rise, its effect should be judged by the net, not the gross, externality. For every buyer who bought at a high price there was a seller who sold at a high price; what the former lost the latter gained. The net damage is zero; the externality is only pecuniary.

Religious Radio: An Application of Public-Good Theory

Whenever I scan the radio dial, I am struck by how many stations are religious. If I go to a newsstand or a bookstore, on the other hand, I see a few religious newspapers, magazines, or books, but they are a much smaller fraction of the total.

There is a simple explanation. Broadcasters, unlike publishers, are producing a public good. Commercials are one solution to the problem of producing a public good; religion is another. Most people who listen to religious broadcasters believe in the religion—including a God who rewards virtue and punishes vice. Donating money to the program is a virtuous act. The preacher may not know which listeners help pay for the show and which do not, but God knows.

Nothing in this analysis depends on the truth of the religion; what matters is that the listeners believe it is true. The result is that religious broadcasters have an advantage over secular broadcasters. Both produce programs that their listeners value, but the religious broadcaster is better able to get the listener to pay for them. The religious publisher has no corresponding advantage over the secular publisher.

INFORMATION AS A PUBLIC GOOD

One cost of buying goods is the cost of acquiring information about what to buy. This may be one reason firms are as large as they are; brand names represent a sort of informational capital. Even if a better deal is available from an unknown producer, the cost of determining that it is a better deal may be greater than the savings. Not only do you know that the brand-name product has been of good quality in the past, you also believe that its producer has an incentive to maintain the quality so as not to destroy the value of his brand name.

Why not simply buy information as we buy other goods? Sometimes we do: *Consumer Reports, Car and Driver, Handgun Tests,* this book. Yet much of the information we use we produce for ourselves. Why?

One problem with producing information for sale is that property rights in it are insecure. If I sell you a car, you can resell it only by giving up its use yourself. If I sell you a fact, you can both use that fact and make it available to your friends and neighbors. This makes it difficult for those who produce facts to sell them for their full value. It is the same problem discussed earlier in the case of computer programs—which can be thought of as a kind of information. Information is in large part a public good; because it is a public good, it is underproduced.

Brand-name retailers such as Sears or Penney's are one private solution to this public-good problem. Sears does not produce what it sells, but it does select it. You buy any particular product only once every year or two, which makes it hard to judge which producer is best. But you buy something from Sears much more often, so you can judge whether Sears gives you good value for your money. Sears sells you information attached to goods. By not telling you who really makes the product, it prevents you from reselling the information—to a friend who would then buy the same brand at a discount store. All you can tell your friend is to buy from Sears.

Adverse Selection

Consider the used-car market. Sellers have a better idea than buyers whether their car is a lemon or a cream puff. If buyers cannot tell which is which, they will pay the same price for good and bad cars—which makes selling a good car an unattractive transaction. Lemons are more likely to sell than cream puffs; buyers adjust their expectations, and offers, accordingly. In the limiting case only lemons are offered for sale—not because the owners of cream puffs do not want to sell them but because they do not want to sell them at lemon prices.

My friend Ami Glaser came up with one solution to this problem. When he found a secondhand car he wanted, he asked the dealer if, for an additional payment, he would provide a one-year warranty. When the dealer refused, Ami went to another dealer. At last he found one willing to sell a suitable car with a warranty. "All right," Ami said, "I'll take the car. I don't want the warranty."

The lemon problem appears in the insurance literature as *adverse selection*. Customers know things about how likely they are to collect on insurance that insurance companies do not—and the more likely they are to collect, the more willing they are to buy the insurance. Companies must allow for that in setting rates—which may price the good risks out of the market.

Insurance companies try to control adverse selection in a variety of ways, including medical checkups for new customers and contract provisions denying payment to people who claim to have no dangerous hobbies and then die when their parachutes fail to open. Another approach is selling group policies. If all employees of a factory are covered by the same insurance, the insurance company is getting a random assortment of good and bad risks. The good risks get a worse deal than the bad, but since they still get insured the rate reflects the risk of insuring an average employee rather than an average bad risk.

Supporters of national health insurance argue that it is a group policy carried to its ultimate extreme—everyone is in the group. It thus eliminates the problem of adverse selection, except for bad risks who immigrate in order to take advantage of the program. That is a good argument, but whether the gain from eliminating adverse selection outweighs other costs of government provision is less clear.

Moral Hazard

Most things we insure against are at least partly under our own control. That is true not only of my health and the chance of my house burning down, but even of "acts of God" such as floods or earthquakes. I cannot control the flood, but I can control the loss—by deciding whether to live in a floodplain or fault zone and how solidly to build my house.

I will take those precautions, and only those precautions, that save me more than they cost me. Once I have bought fire insurance, part of the cost of being careless with matches and part of the benefit of installing a sprinkler system have been transferred to the insurance company. This version of the externality problem is called *moral hazard*.

Insurance companies try to control moral hazard just as they try to control adverse selection. One way is by specifying precautions the insured must take   requiring a factory to install a sprinkler system. Another is *coinsurance*—insuring only part of the value in order to leave the customer with a substantial incentive to avoid fires. If, at the opposite extreme, the insurance company makes the mistake of insuring a building for more than it is worth, the probability of a fire may become very high indeed.

BARTER, MARRIAGE, AND MONEY

The simplest form of trade is barter; I exchange goods I have and you want for goods you have and I want. To do so I must find someone who has what I want and wants what I have. In a complicated society such as ours, this can be difficult. If I want a car, I first look in the classified ads to find someone who is selling the kind of car I want, then call him up and ask him if he wants to learn economics in exchange. This drastically reduces the number of potential trading partners.

The solution is the development of money—some good that almost everyone is willing to accept. It usually starts as something (gold, cloth, cattle—*pecuniary* comes from the Latin word for "cattle") valued for its own sake, and gradually comes to be valued as a medium of exchange. In a money economy, I find one person who wants what I have, sell it to him, and then use the money to buy what I want from someone else.

For an example of the difficulties of barter, it may help to consider the large-scale barter market in which almost all of us participate—the marriage/dating/sex market. If I am going out with or sleeping with or married to you, you are necessarily going out with or sleeping with or married to me. I must find a woman whom I want and who wants me. We observe, in this market, large search costs, long search times, many frustrated and lonely people of both sexes—in other words, a market where traders have a hard time getting together, due largely to the high transaction costs of barter.

Warning

It is easy to misinterpret problems of market failure as unfairness rather than inefficiency. Externalities are seen as wrong because one person is suffering and another gaining, public goods unjust because some get a free ride that others pay for.

That is a mistake. Consider a hundred identical individuals polluting and breathing the same air. There is no unfairness—everyone gains by being able to pollute and loses by being polluted. Yet because each person bears only one-hundredth of the cost of his pollution, each pollutes at far above the efficient level, making all worse off.

The problem with public goods is not that one person pays for what someone else gets but that nobody pays and nobody gets, even though the good is worth more than it would cost to produce. The problem with adverse selection is not that some people buy lemons or write life insurance policies on sky divers. The problem is that cars are not sold, even though they are worth selling, and people do not get insured, even though they are worth insuring. Our favorite barter market leaves lots of us lonely and frustrated.

TO THINK ABOUT

". . . another reason to contribute to our fund-raising campaign is self-interest. The money you give us will improve the quality and reputation of the University, raising the value of your degree. If each alumnus gave $100 . . . " (extract from a fund-raising letter).

For Further Reading

For evidence that making cars safer increases the number of accidents, see Sam Peltzman, "The Effects of Automobile Safety Regulations," *Journal of Political Economy*, pp. 677–725, August 1975.

APPLICATIONS: CONVENTIONAL AND UN

19

LAW AND SAUSAGE: THE POLITICAL MARKETPLACE

"Laws are like sausages. It is better not to see them being made."

—Attributed to Bismarck

The U.S. government does not exist; there is no benevolent elderly gentleman watching over us. What we call "government action" is not the act of a person but the outcome of a political marketplace. In that market as in others, rational individuals act to pursue their own ends—under a set of rules rather different from the rules governing the private market. This chapter is an exploration of that marketplace.

I start with an issue—tariffs—that has long provided a problem for the view of government as a neutral actor, serving the public good as best it can. For more than 150 years, the dominant view among economists has been that most tariffs hurt the nation that imposes them as well as the nations they are imposed against, that most nations, most of the time, would be better off abolishing all tariffs and moving to complete free trade—whether or not other nations reciprocated. Yet throughout that century and a half most of the world, with the notable exceptions of England in the nineteenth century and Hong Kong in the twentieth, has kept its tariffs. When tariff reduction has occurred, it has been by negotiation: We will reduce our tariffs if you will reduce yours. From the economist's point of view, it is rather like my offering to stop hitting myself on the head with a hammer if you agree to stop hitting yourself on the head with a hammer.

The first step is to understand why economists believe that tariffs are a bad idea. The second is to explain why it is nonetheless in the interest of rational legislators to impose them.

HOW TO HIT YOURSELF ON THE HEAD WITH A HAMMER

We saw, back in chapter 6, why arguments such as "The Japanese can produce everything cheaper than we can" or "Tariffs protect American jobs" are wrong, but we have not yet proved that tariffs are bad; there might be other and better arguments. I will now prove, subject to some simplifying assumptions, that *if America as a whole is a price taker in international markets,* then American tariffs, on net, make Americans worse off.

Unfortunately, the proof requires some mathematics. Readers who feel comfortable with high school algebra problems should have no trouble. Readers who develop acute nausea at the sight of an equation can skip down to the verbal proof—but they will be missing something.

Assumptions. Only one good is imported (autos) and one good is exported (wheat). America is a price taker in international markets: Changes in our production of wheat and consumption of autos do not significantly change the rate at which autos exchange for wheat abroad. The wheat and auto industries in the United States are price-taking industries with no substantial net externalities. Transport costs are zero.

The Geometric Proof. Figure 19–1 shows the supply curve for American production of automobiles and the demand curve for American consumption of automobiles, before and after the imposition of a tariff of $\$t$ per automobile. P_A is the market price before the tariff, P'_A after the tariff. Q_A is the quantity of imported cars before the tariff, Q'_A after. Figure 19–2 shows the corresponding curves, prices, and quantities for wheat.

The price at which U.S. quantity supplied equals U.S. quantity demanded is above the world market price, so the United States imports autos. Quantity demanded (by U.S. consumers) is equal to quantity supplied (by the U.S. auto industry) plus imports. The price at which quantity of wheat supplied and quantity demanded in the United States are equal is below the world price of wheat, so the United States exports wheat. Quantity produced (by U.S. farmers) equals quantity demanded (by U.S. consumers) plus exports.

Why does an auto tariff affect the price of wheat? Wheat is what we send foreigners in exchange for the autos they send us. When we impose an auto tariff, fewer dollars go abroad to buy foreign cars. Foreigners have fewer dollars with which to buy American wheat; their demand falls and the price of wheat in America drops.

U_1 in Figure 19–1 is the increase in (American) producer surplus as a result of the tariff; $U_1 + R_1 + S_1 + T_1$ is the reduction in (American) consumer surplus. The shaded area is the net loss (to Americans) of surplus on autos as a result of the tariff. Similarly, in Figure 19–2, U_2 is the gain in (American) consumer surplus as a result of the fall in the price of wheat produced by the tariff on automobiles; $U_2 + R_2 + S_2 + T_2$ is the loss of (American) producer surplus. The shaded area $R_2 + S_2 + T_2$ is the net loss (to Americans) of surplus on wheat as an indirect result of the tariff on autos.

The net loss in surplus must be weighted against the revenue from the tariff. The government collects t dollars on each of Q'_A autos imported each year, so its revenue from the tariff is $t \times Q'_A$. If that is larger than the sum of the two shaded areas, then the tariff makes us, on net, better off—revenue collected is more than surplus lost. If it is smaller, the tariff makes us worse off.

Since America is a price taker in international markets, the tariff does not affect the relative prices of autos and wheat outside the United States. Before the tariff, the price ratio is P_A/P_W. After the tariff, the price of wheat abroad (in dollars) is P'_W, the price of autos abroad is P'_A-t, so the price ratio is $(P'_A-t)/P'_W$.

Why is the world price of autos P'_A-t? P'_A is the price of autos in

Price of autos

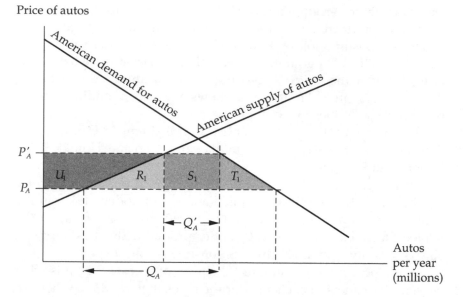

Figure 19-1   The effect on the domestic auto market of a tariff on autos. Imports of autos, equal to the difference between domestic demand and domestic supply, fall from Q_A to Q'_A. The U.S. price rises from P_A to P'_A.

Price per bushel

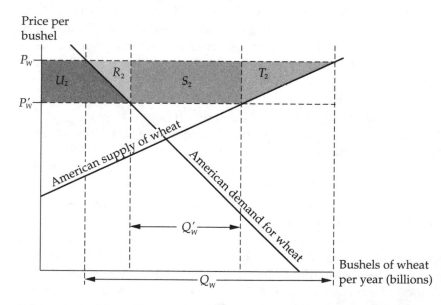

Figure 19-2   The effect on the domestic wheat market of a tariff on autos. Exports of wheat fall from Q_W to Q'_W; the U.S. price falls from P_W to P'_W.

the United States. In order to get foreign autos into the United States, you must pay their world price plus the tariff t; the price in the United States is P'_A, so the world price must be P'_A-t.

Since the price ratio outside the United States is the same before and after the tariff, it follows that:

$$\frac{P_A}{P_W} = \frac{P'_A-t}{P_W} \qquad \text{(Equation 1)}$$

Autos are, by assumption, our only import and wheat our only export, so the total number of dollars foreigners get for the cars they sell to us must equal the number of dollars they spend for the wheat they buy from us. Using prices and quantities after the tariff is imposed, this gives us:

$$P'_W \times Q'_W = \text{\$ spent on wheat by foreigners} = \\ \text{\$ received for cars by foreigners} = (P'_A-t)Q'_A. \qquad \text{(Equation 2)}$$

(We spend P'_A on each car, but since t goes to the government to pay the tariff, only P'_A-t goes to foreigners.)

Finally, from Figures 19–1 and 19–2, we have:

$$S_1 + S_2 = (P'_A - P_A)Q'_A + (P_W - P'_W)Q'_W \qquad \text{(Equation 3)}$$

Equations 1 and 2 imply that:

$$Q'_W = Q'_A \frac{P'_A-t}{P'_W} = Q'_A \frac{P_A}{P_W}$$

Substituting this into Equation 3 gives us:

$$S_1 + S_2 = Q'_A(P'_A - P_A) + Q'_A \frac{P_A}{P_W} (P_W - P'_W) =$$

$$Q'_A\{P'_A - P_A + \frac{P_A}{P_W}(P_W - P'_W)\} = Q'_A\left\{P'_A - P_A + P'_A - P'_W \frac{P_A}{P_W}\right\}$$

Using Equation 1 to replace $\frac{P_A}{P_W}$ with $\frac{P'_A-t}{P'_W}$, we get:

$$S_1 + S_2 = Q'_A\left\{P'_A - P'_W \frac{P'_A-t}{P'_W}\right\} = \qquad \text{(Equation 4)}$$

$$Q'_A(P'_A - P'_A + t) = Q'_A \times t$$

$S_1 + S_2$ is only part of the lost surplus due to the tariff; $Q'_A \times t$ is all of the revenue. The tariff costs us more than it brings in; on net it makes us worse off—by $R_1 + T_1 + R_2 + T_2$. And that is without taking account of the additional costs it imposes on our trading partners abroad.

The Verbal Proof. I have now proved my result—that if the United States is a price taker in international markets and American firms are price takers in domestic markets, American tariffs on net injure Americans—mathematically. Next I will prove it again in another language: English.

From the standpoint of the United States, foreign trade is a technology for turning wheat into autos at the rate P_A/P_W. We proved in chapter 16 that a competitive industry is efficient. Hence the result of the competitive industry for turning wheat into autos is efficient. A tariff alters that result, taxing the conversion of wheat into autos and so reducing the quantity of wheat used and autos produced. That change could be made by a bureaucrat-god. A bureaucrat-god cannot improve an outcome that is already efficient—that is the definition of "efficient." So a tariff cannot be an economic improvement.

Capital in Action. We have spent the previous eighteen chapters accumulating intellectual capital, learning a complicated set of ideas, some of which must, at times, have seemed entirely useless. Using that capital, we have now, with a few pages of high school mathematics plus a paragraph of reasoning, proved one of the more important practical results of economic theory—twice.

Each proof, each language, has advantages and disadvantages. The advantage of the verbal proof is that it helps us intuit why tariffs are undesirable—provided we have previously learned to intuit why a competitive industry is efficient. Trade is simply a technology for converting exports into imports; a competitive industry uses that technology up to the point where the benefit of one more unit of imports is balanced by the cost of producing the exports that must be exchanged for it. A tariff adds an additional cost of production; the industry reduces its output, depriving some consumers of imported goods that they valued at more than their cost but less than their cost plus the tariff. The tariff is a tax on a particular way of producing things; the net loss is the resulting excess burden, just as with any other tax.

The mathematical proof depends on assuming that the United States is a price taker in international markets; that is how we got Equation 1. In the verbal proof, I only said that the export and import industries were price takers within the United States (and therefore efficient). That is not at all the same thing. If U.S. agriculture consists of a million small farms that together produce 90 percent of the world's wheat, each farmer is a price taker but the United States as a whole is not.

The verbal proof does depend on the United States being a price taker. If the United States is not a price taker, then the quantity of wheat exported (and autos imported) affects the price ratio abroad—the rate at which we can convert wheat into autos. From the standpoint of Americans, that is an externality; when I buy autos abroad, I drive up their price (and drive down the price of the wheat I use to pay for them), making it more expensive for you to buy autos abroad. Externalities lead to inefficient outcomes. So if the United States is a price searcher, the initial situation (without a tariff) is not efficient, and it is possible that a tariff may improve it.

From the standpoint of the world as a whole, the effect on price is a pecuniary externality. If my purchases of automobiles drive up the world price, that is a loss to other buyers but a gain to sellers. But if the buyers are Americans, the sellers are foreigners, and we consider only the interests of Americans, there is a net externality— we count the loss and ignore the gain. So if the United States is a price searcher in international markets, the outcome without tariffs is efficient if all interests are considered but inefficient if only American interests are.

The Exceptions: "Good" Tariffs

Like most economic arguments, this one depends on assumptions that may not always be true. What happens if we drop some of them?

America as a Monopolist. Suppose the United States as a whole has something close to a monopoly on producing wheat or a monopsony on buying automobiles; changes in the amount we sell or buy have a large effect on the world price. A tariff on automobiles reduces U.S. demand, driving down the world price. An export tax on wheat reduces U.S. output, driving up the world price. So if we are price searchers in international markets, a tariff or export tax may produce net benefits for us.

The result is a gain analogous to the gain to firms from forming a cartel. When we drive the international price of autos down (by imposing a tariff that decreases our consumption) or the international price of wheat up (by imposing an export tax on wheat), we benefit, since we are sellers of wheat and buyers of autos. Our trading partners lose, since they are buyers of wheat and sellers of autos. Just as in the monopolies discussed earlier, the result is a net loss but a gain for the monopolist. Demand and supply curves are more elastic in the long run than in the short, so the gains, like other monopoly profits, are likely to fall over time. There are many places where grain can be grown.

Protecting Infant Industries. Suppose the United States has no tin industry. A company that tries to start a tin foundry in the United States will have a hard time of it—American workers do not know how to work with tin, American railroads have no experience shipping tin and no special freight cars designed to carry it, and American coal mines have no experience producing the particular kinds of coal needed to refine tin from tin ore. (Warning: The technology of this example is wholly imaginary.) Until those problems are solved, American tin will be more costly than imported tin. If only the tin industry could get established it would be profitable, but nobody wants to be first.

One solution is for tin companies to accept losses in the first few years, treating them as an investment to be paid back out of later profits. If they are not willing to do that, perhaps the profits are not large enough, or certain enough, to make the losses worth taking. To avoid this argument, assume that the development occurs within the industry but outside the firm. No firm can do it by itself, but if they all do it together, workers will become skilled in working tin, subsidiary industries will grow up to support tin manufacture, and so on.

Since the initial firms do not include external benefits in their calculations of profit and loss, they may never start production unless subsidized by a temporary tariff that raises the cost of imported tin. This is the argument for an infant-industry tariff. We have dropped the assumption that firms in the industry have no important externalities. In this case, unlike the previous one, a tariff may be desirable even if we take into account the interests of everyone concerned. If the United States has the potential to produce tin less expensively than it can be imported, the gains to U.S. producers and their customers will outweigh the losses to foreign producers.

Should Versus Will. Such exceptions to the general case against tariffs exist in economic theory, but they do not explain why tariffs exist. The tariffs we observe in the real world are rarely those that can be defended as economically desirable. It is not infant industries that get protection but senile industries—American auto, shoe, and steel producers.

To understand why, we need an economic theory of politics, a theory not of what laws *should* exist but of what laws *will* exist. It is called *public-choice theory*.

PUBLIC CHOICE: THE ECONOMICS OF POLITICS

The version of democracy we learn in school is a simple one. Politicians want votes. Voters want the government to do good things. So politicians, in order to get elected and reelected, run the government in the general interest. That is the underlying pattern, and everything else—most of what governments actually do—is experimental error.

Part of what is wrong with this theory is that, while it assumes that politicians are rational, it assumes that voters are not. Figuring out what policies are in the general interest and which politicians one should therefore support is not costless; few politicians campaign with the slogan "I am the bad guy." A rational individual, whether voter or consumer, acquires information only if the benefit of having it is worth the cost of getting it. If the information is not worth the price, he remains rationally ignorant.

Suppose the value to you of having the right person elected president is $100,000—a high figure for most of us. Further suppose the chance that your vote will change the outcome of the election is one in a million—again a high estimate. Your expected return from voting is then ten cents. That does not justify spending much more than a minute figuring out which candidate to vote for.

We have explained why most voters are ignorant, but we are left with another puzzle—why do they vote at all? I start with a brief detour.

The Market for Partisanship

Major sports teams, in the United States and elsewhere, are almost always associated with a city or university. The pattern is so familiar that it rarely occurs to us to wonder about it. Yet the same pattern is rarely seen in other industries—not even other parts of the entertainment industry.

The explanation is that part of what sports teams are selling is partisanship. Fans come not merely to watch a game but to cheer for their side. A fan who believes that his cheering helps his side play better can even feel that he is part of the game—even if only a very small part. Identifying with a city or a university is a cheap way of obtaining a pool of partisans.

Every four years, a game is played out on nationwide television, with the fate of the world at stake. On election night, they add up the score—one team wins, one loses. You can not only cheer, you can even play. The admission price—an hour of your time. As a way of influencing the fate of the world, it is a poor deal—an hour of time for one chance in a million of affecting the outcome. But as a way of adding excitement to election night, it is cheap at the price.

In order to improve the state of the world, you must not only vote, but vote for the right candidate—which requires additional hours spent considering candidates and issues. Sports fans do not have to know which team is more deserving of their support. Neither do political fans. Quite a large fraction of voters cannot name their own congressman, and only a small minority can give an accurate account of the policy positions of the candidates.

A common response to this argument is, "You are saying that we should all be politically ignorant, but if we are, democracy won't work." That is correct; true beliefs need not always have desirable consequences. Some people acquire political information for fun, or to win arguments at cocktail parties; some even read books on economics—if they are sufficiently entertaining. For such people, the information necessary to informed voting is costless—they get it as a by-product of other activities. Others acquire their information as a by-product of reading a newspaper for entertainment. The outcome of democratic elections is driven by free information—and reflects the quality of what you get at that price.

If the civics-class model of democracy fails because of rational ignorance, we should look for another model. Like our model of ordinary markets, it should start with rational individuals, each finding the best way of achieving his goals, and reason from there to predictions and explanations of what we actually observe.

The Market for Legislation

Consider the market for legislation. Individuals offer payments to politicians for supporting or opposing legislation. The payments may take the form of promises to vote for the politician, of cash payments to be used to finance future election campaigns, or of (concealed) contributions to the politician's income. The politician is seeking to maximize his own utility, subject to the constraint that he can sell legislation for only as long as he can keep getting elected.

Is It Efficient? Consider a simple transaction on this market. A legislator proposes a bill that imposes costs of $10 each on a thousand individuals (total cost, $10,000) and grants benefits of $500 each to ten individuals (total benefit, $5,000). What will be bid for and against the law?

The total cost to the losers is $10,000, but the amount they will offer a politician to oppose the law is much less. An individual who contributes to a campaign fund to defeat the bill is providing a public good for all thousand members of the group. The arguments used in chapter 18 to show that public goods are underproduced apply here. The larger the public, the lower the fraction of the value of the good that can be raised to pay for it.

The benefit provided to the winners is also a public good, but it goes to a much smaller public—ten individuals instead of a thousand. A smaller public can more easily organize to fund a public good. Even though the benefit to the small group is smaller than the cost to the large one, the amount the small group is able to offer politicians to support the bill will be more than the amount the large group can offer to oppose it.

That conclusion is strengthened by a second consideration—information costs. For the individual who suspects that the bill may injure him by $10, it is not worth trying very hard to check out that suspicion. His possible loss is small, and so is the chance that he will be willing to do anything likely to alter the outcome. The member of the *dispersed interest* chooses (rationally) to be worse informed than the member of the *concentrated interest*.

Think of "concentrated" and "dispersed" as shorthand for the whole set of characteristics that determine how easily a group can fund a public good; the number of individuals in the group is only one such characteristic. Consider, for example, a tariff on automobiles. It benefits hundreds of thousands of people—stockholders in auto companies, autoworkers, property owners in Detroit. But GM, Ford, Chrysler, the UAW, and the city of Detroit are organizations that already exist to serve the interests of large parts of that large group of people. For many purposes, one can consider all of the stockholders and most of the workers as "being" five individuals—a group small enough to organize effectively. The beneficiaries of auto tariffs are a much more concentrated interest than a mere count of their numbers would suggest.

The public-good problem leads to inefficiency in private markets because some public goods that are worth more than it would cost to produce them fail to get produced. It leads to inefficiency in public markets because both costs and benefits are only fractionally represented in the bidding for legislation. If potential gainers and losers raise different fractions of their gains and losses to bid for and against the laws, as will usually be the case, laws that impose net costs may pass and laws that impose net benefits may fail.

Predictions. What predictions can we make on the basis of this simple model of individuals and interest groups bidding for legislation? One is that legislation will tend to benefit concentrated interest groups at the expense of dispersed interest groups. One good example is how governments treat farmers. In rich countries such as the United States, France, and Japan, where farmers are a small fraction of the population, farm policy is designed to raise the price farmers get for their crops. In poor countries, such as many in Africa and Asia, farmers are a large part of the population and farm policy is designed to lower food prices, buying the political support of urban workers and the urban elite at the cost of the dispersed masses of impoverished farmers.

A second confirmation is the history of tariffs and tariff negotiations. A tariff benefits a concentrated interest (producers of a good that faces competition from imports) at the cost of a dispersed interest (buyers of that good and producers of export goods). Total costs, as we have seen, are usually larger than total benefits—but they are less heavily weighted on the political marketplace.

From the standpoint of national welfare, tariff negotiations make

no sense, since both nations would be better off starting the negotiation by abolishing their tariffs. But from the standpoint of the political welfare of those doing the negotiation, they make a great deal of
sense. American politicians are willing to give up a valuable source
of political support only if their opposite numbers in Japan agree to
provide something in exchange.

A second prediction is that although the political market often
generates inefficient outcomes, it has some tendency to prefer efficient ones. The lower the cost to the victims of a transfer, the less they
will spend to oppose it; the higher the benefit to the gainers, the
more they will spend to support it. So a politician who is going to
transfer from a dispersed interest to a concentrated one has an incentive to do so in the most efficient possible way.

If this is right, why do we observe inefficient transfers such as tariffs? Why not simply tax the proposed victims and turn the receipts
over to the proposed beneficiaries, thus reducing transfer costs to the
unavoidable minimum: the administrative cost of collecting the tax
and paying out the benefits, and the associated excess burden?

One answer is that there is a third prediction implicit in our
model. Politicians prefer transfers for which the information cost of
figuring out what is happening is as high as possible for the victims
and as low as possible for the beneficiaries; if the cost is the same for
both victims and beneficiaries, high information costs are preferred
to low ones, since the beneficiaries are a concentrated interest, and a
more concentrated interest is better able to pay for information.

The preference for high information costs helps to explain the
existence of inefficient forms of transfer; the sponsors of legislation
designed to benefit some people at the expense of others prefer to
disguise it as something else. A bill to tax consumers and give the
money to GM, Ford, Chrysler, and the UAW will encounter more
opposition than an auto tariff designed to do the same thing—
because the auto tariff can be defended as a way of "protecting us
from the Japanese."

We now have three predictions about the outcome of political
markets: They favor concentrated interests, they prefer more efficient
to less efficient transfers, and they prefer transfers disguised as something else. How do these fit what we observe?

Tariffs in the Real World. Real-world tariffs tend to go, not to infant
industries, but to senile ones. The American steel industry is a pow-

erful concentrated interest; potential infant industries that do not now exist but could be created by an appropriate tariff are not. So it is the old industries that get the protection.

This explains why infant industries do not get tariffs, but not which industries do get them. If tariffs tend to go to declining industries, a satisfactory theory should explain why. The discussion of sunk costs in chapter 13, combined with the prediction that politicians prefer transfers that give the highest possible ratio of benefit to cost, all other things being equal, does so.

Suppose a tariff is imposed on imports that compete with a competitive industry. Before the tariff, price was equal to average cost, so economic profit was zero. The tariff reduces the supply of imports, so prices and the industry's output rise. But once enough new firms have entered the industry to reestablish equilibrium, average cost is again equal to price—profit is again zero.

If some inputs used by the industry are in fixed supply, such as certain types of land, their value will be bid up; their owners may be willing to offer part of the increase to get the tariff passed and maintained. If the inputs instead have a highly elastic supply curve, or if their ownership is divided among many individuals (a dispersed interest), only transitional profits are available to reward supporters of the tariff.

In a declining industry, there is an important resource in fixed supply: factories that produce enough revenue to be worth keeping but not enough to be worth building. The ownership of that resource is as concentrated as the industry is. The tariff increases demand for domestically produced goods by raising the cost of the competing imported goods and so increases the present value of the factories. Much of what the consumers lose in higher prices the producers receive in increased wealth.

The cost of the tariff is still larger than the benefit—but the cost is spread among many consumers and the benefit is concentrated on a few producers. Since the benefit to the industry is much larger in the case of a declining industry than in the case of a growing one, declining industries will offer more for tariffs, which explains why they are more successful in getting them. The result is a pattern of tariffs almost exactly opposite to the pattern that might be justified as efficient.

The same analysis explains why agriculture is particularly likely to be taxed if dispersed and subsidized if concentrated. The relevant fixed resource is land. Because its supply is relatively inelastic, it is possible to transfer income to or from landowners with less excess burden than if the transfer was to or from owners of an input in more elastic supply. That makes it attractive both as a beneficiary and as a victim of transfers.

RENT SEEKING AND THE COST OF GOVERNMENT: HOW NOT TO GIVE THINGS AWAY

A government is giving out favors—pieces of paper giving the recipient permission to do something. A thousand are to be given out. Each is worth $1 million to potential recipients.

At a price of zero, there will be no shortage of claimants. Some way must be found to choose among them. The permits are to go to firms that will use them "in the public interest." The society is a democratic one; government officials try to give the permits to the firms that the voting public prefers.

If your firm wants a permit and does not expect to get it, it may be worth spending money improving your public image—perhaps by advertisements telling the general public how important your product is to the national welfare, how many jobs depend on you, and how crucial it is that you get the permit.

How much will you be willing to spend? If it makes the difference between success and failure, anything up to the value of the permit. When other firms observe that your $100,000 ad campaign is going to result in your getting one of the permits and their not getting one, they start their own ad campaigns—budgeted at $200,000. You reevaluate the situation and increase your budget. They do the same.

As long as it takes less than $1 million of advertising to get a government favor worth $1 million, there will always be more firms willing to enter the game. By doing so, they either raise the amount that must be spent or lower the probability of success. Equilibrium is reached when each firm, on average, spends as much to get the permit as the permit is worth.

From one standpoint, the result is unsurprising; in equilibrium, marginal cost (as usual) equals marginal value. From another, it is very surprising indeed. The government is giving out, for free, a billion dollars' worth of special favors, and the recipients are ending up with nothing—the full value of the favors is used up in getting them. I like to call this Friedman's Second Law: "The government cannot give anything away."

The term "rent seeking" was introduced to economics in an article by Anne Krueger. The examples she considered were countries with exchange controls that maintained the official value of the country's currency above its market value. An import permit allowed an importer to exchange local currency for dollars at the artificially high official rate, import foreign goods, and sell them at a large profit. She concluded that a conservative estimate of the market value of the permits and other favors given out by the governments of Turkey and India, and hence the amount wasted on rent-seeking activity, was about 7 percent of national income for India and 15 percent for Turkey.

Rent seeking is not limited to poor countries with exchange controls. If special interests buy legislation from politicians, that increases the value of being a successful politician, which in turn increases the amount spent on getting and keeping political office. This brings us to an interesting puzzle.

The Cost of Elections

It is common, especially around election time, to read articles lamenting how much is spent on campaigning. What surprises me is how little is spent on political campaigns, considering the stakes. In a presidential year, total expenditure by both parties on the presidential race and all congressional races is less than a billion dollars. The prize is control of the federal government for several years, during which that government will spend several trillion dollars—thousands of times the amount of campaign expenditures.

One explanation for the disproportion between the prize and what is spent to get it is the public-good problem faced by even a relatively concentrated interest group. If a group can only raise, for political contributions, 10 percent of the value to its members of what it is buying, then the ability to deliver a dollar's worth of benefits is worth only $0.10 to the politician delivering it. A second explanation is the inefficiency of even relatively efficient transfers; a government expenditure of $10 million on behalf of some interest group may provide only $1 million worth of benefits. Combining the two effects reduces $10 million in expenditure to $100,000 in campaign contributions.

A final explanation is that much of the cost of buying a political office never appears in records of campaign expenditure, not even the politician's private records. It consists of promises of a share of the loot—or, to use less loaded language, political commitments given to individuals and groups in exchange for their support.

TO THINK ABOUT

A tariff and an export tax have the same effect; they tax the same transaction (trading wheat for autos) at different points. Yet we observe that tariffs are common, export taxes rare. Why?

For Further Reading

The article that first used the term "rent seeking" is Anne Krueger, "The Political Economy of the Rent-Seeking Society," *American Economic Review*, vol. 64 (June 1974), pp. 291–303, but the idea appeared earlier in Gordon Tullock, "The Welfare Costs of Tariffs, Monopolies and Theft," *Western Economic Journal*, vol. 5 (June 1967), pp. 224–232, and David Friedman, *The Machinery of Freedom: Guide to a Radical Capitalism* (New York: Harper & Row, 1971; Arlington House, 1978; Open Court, 1989), chapter 38.

Gary Becker, "A Theory of Competition Among Pressure Groups for Political Influence," *Quarterly Journal of Economics*, vol. 98 (1983), pp. 371–400, is an important source for the model of the political market described in this chapter. Other classics of public-choice theory include: James Buchanan and Gordon Tullock, *The Calculus of Consent* (Ann Arbor, MI: University of Michigan Press, 1962), and Mancur Olson, *The Logic of Collective Action* (Cambridge, MA: Harvard University Press, 1965).

20

RATIONAL CRIMINALS AND INTENTIONAL ACCIDENTS: THE ECONOMICS OF LAW AND LAWBREAKING

PART 1: THE ECONOMICS OF CRIME

Many years ago, I was living in a part of Manhattan near Columbia University. When I found it necessary to go out at night, I carried with me a four-foot walking stick. My friend Ernest Van den Haag argued that I was making a dangerous mistake; potential muggers would see my behavior as a challenge and swarm all over me. I responded that muggers, like other rational businessmen, would prefer to obtain their income at the lowest possible cost. By carrying a stick, I was not only raising the cost I could inflict on them if I chose to resist, I was also announcing my intention of resisting. They would rationally choose easier prey.

I never did get mugged, which is some evidence for my view. More comes from observing who does get mugged. If muggers are out to prove their machismo, they ought to pick on football players; there is not much glory in mugging little old ladies. If muggers are rational businessmen seeking revenue at the lowest possible cost, on the other hand, mugging little old ladies makes a lot of sense. Little old ladies—and other relatively defenseless people—get mugged. Football players do not. It is said that someone once asked Willie Sutton why he robbed banks. "That's where the money is" was his reply.

The economic approach to crime starts from one simple assumption: Criminals are rational. A burglar burgles for the same reason I teach economics—because he finds it a more attractive profession than any other. The obvious conclusion is that the way to reduce burglary—whether as a legislator or a homeowner—is by raising the costs of the burglar's profession or reducing its benefits.

The analysis that helped me decide what to take with me on my evening strolls around Manhattan's Upper West Side can also be applied to a point that comes up in arguments over gun control. Opponents argue that gun control, by disarming potential victims, makes it more difficult for them to protect themselves. Supporters reply that since criminals are more experienced in violence than victims, the odds in an armed confrontation are with the criminal. This is probably true, but it is almost entirely irrelevant to the argument.

Suppose one little old lady in ten carries a gun. Suppose that one in ten of those, if attacked by a mugger, succeeds in killing the mugger instead of being killed by him—or shooting herself in the foot. On average, the mugger is much more likely to win the encounter than the little old lady. But—also on average—every hundred muggings produce one dead mugger. At those odds, mugging is an unprofitable business—not many little old ladies carry enough money to justify one chance in a hundred of being killed getting it. The number of muggers declines drastically, not because they have all been killed but because they have, rationally, sought safer professions.

When, as children, we learn about different sorts of animals, we imagine them in a strict hierarchy, with the stronger and more ferocious preying on everything below them. That is not how it works. A lion could, no doubt, be fairly confident of defeating a leopard, or a wolf of killing a fox. But a lion that made a habit of preying on leopards would not survive very long; a small chance of being killed and a substantial risk of being injured is too high a price for one dinner. That is why lions hunt zebras instead.

In analyzing conflict, whether between two animals, criminal and victim, competing firms, or warring nations, our natural tendency is to imagine an all-out battle in which all that matters is victory or defeat. That is rarely if ever the case. In the conflict between the mugger and the little old lady, the mugger, on average, wins. But the cost of the conflict—one chance in a hundred of being killed—is high enough so that the mugger prefers to avoid it. In this case as in many others, the problem faced by the potential victim is not how to defeat the aggressor but only how to make aggression unprofitable.

Economics Joke #2: Two men encountered a hungry bear. One turned to run. "It's hopeless," the other told him, "you can't outrun a bear." "No," he replied. "But I might be able to outrun you."

Economics of the Spaceways

My favorite illustration of this point is a science fiction story by Poul Anderson. The setting is a far future with interstellar travel. There is a potentially profitable trade route connecting two groups of stars. Unfortunately the route runs through the territory of a nasty little interstellar empire. The nasty little empire (Borthu) has a policy of seizing passing starships, confiscating their cargo, and brainwashing their crews; the crew is then added to Borthu's fleet, which is critically short of trained manpower.

Borthu is a nasty *little* empire; the trading corporations could, if they chose, get together, build warships, and defeat it. But doing so would cost more than the trade route is worth. They could arm their trading ships—but the cost of building and manning an armed ship would more than wipe out the profit the ship would generate. They can win—but, being rational profit maximizers, they won't.

The problem is solved by Nicholas Van Rijn, the head of one of the trading corporations—after he has first persuaded his competitors to offer a fraction of their profits on the route to whoever solves the problem. The solution is to arm one ship in four. Warships carry larger crews than merchant ships. Three times out of four, the empire attacks a trading ship, capturing it and its four-man crew. One time out of four, the trading ship is armed; the empire loses a warship and its twenty-man crew. Every four attacks cost the empire, on net, eight crewmen. Piracy is no longer profitable, so it stops.

The logic of the problem, and the solution, is nicely summed up in Van Rijn's reply to one of his colleagues, who suggests that they should fight even if it costs more than the trade is worth to them.

> Revenge and destruction are un-Christian thoughts. Also, they will not pay very well, since it is hard to sell anything to a corpse. The problem is to find some means within our resources to make it *unprofitable* for Borthu to raid us. Not being stupid heads, they will then stop raiding and we can maybe later do business.

> —"Margin of Profit," in *Un-man and Other Novellas* by Poul Anderson

Superthief

I once came across a discussion of the economics of crime and crime prevention written from the inside—in several senses. The title was *Secrets of a Superthief* (by Jack Maclean). The author was a skilled burglar specializing in high-income neighborhoods. As he tells it, he ran a class act—when a house contained nothing he thought worth stealing, he would pile up the rejected booty on the kitchen table and steal the control panel from the burglar alarm. Except in such cases, he usually reset burglar alarms on his way out, to make sure no less discriminating thief broke in and messed up the house.

Eventually Superthief made a professional error and found himself taking an unplanned vacation, courtesy of the state of Florida. Being an energetic fellow, he spent his time behind bars polling fellow inmates on their techniques and opinions and writing a book on how not to get burgled. One of Superthief's principal insights is the same as Van Rijn's—the essential objective in any conflict is neither to defeat your enemy nor to make it impossible for him to defeat you but merely to make it no longer in his interest to do whatever it is that you object to.

Superthief argues that making it impossible for a burglar to get into your house is not an option; few doors will stand up to a determined burglar properly equipped. The function of strong doors and locks is not to make burglary impossible but to make it more expensive, by increasing the skill and equipment needed by the burglar as well as the chance that he will be detected before finishing the job.

A less expensive approach is to use what Superthief calls "mind games." Figure 20–1 shows my version of one of his suggested tricks—in the form of a note I used to keep taped to my back door. Both Mrs. Jones and Rommel are wholly imaginary. A potential burglar may suspect that, but he has no way of being sure. Exterminators are common enough in that part of the country, the reference to the back rooms is vague enough to make it uncertain just where he can go without breathing insecticide, and Rommel, presumably a German shepherd or Doberman (can you imagine a poodle named Rommel?), is in the room that, according to Superthief, burglars consider most worth robbing. Superthief's version referred to pet rattlesnakes loose in the house—a better story than mine but less likely to be believed. Superthief gives many other examples of simple and inexpensive mind games—such as leaving a large dog-feeding dish or a jumbo-sized rubber bone lying around the backyard.

The second note shows another of my precautions. One room in my house had its own lock. A rational thief will assume I am a rational victim and deduce, correctly, that if I have a lock on that door it is because I have things worth stealing behind it. My solution was the second sign shown in Figure 20–1. It was intended to suggest an alternative explanation—dangerous chemicals in the room and a curious child in the house. The solution is original with me, but I believe Superthief would approve.

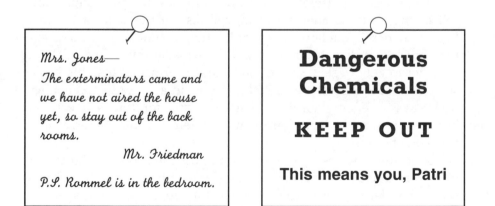

Figure 20-1 Low-cost burglar repellents. Fictitious notes to a fictitious cleaning lady and a real son.

Illegal Markets

> "[On earth they] even have laws for private matters such as contracts. Really. If a man's word isn't any good, who would contract with him? Doesn't he have reputation?"
>
> —Manny in *The Moon Is a Harsh Mistress* by
> Robert Heinlein

We are used to thinking of markets as public, socially accepted institutions such as the stock market, the wheat market, or a supermarket. But the concept is broader than that. There are markets for political influence in Russia—and in Washington. There are markets for illegal drugs and stolen goods. There are markets for sex, both legal (see chapter 21) and illegal.

Economics applies to illegal markets as well as to legal ones. When one input to production is eliminated, substitutes become more valuable. Since participants in illegal markets cannot enforce their contracts in court, substitutes such as reputation become more important. The traditional definition of an honest politician is one who stays bought.

Handling information is costly in illegal markets; facts about your employees that you want in order to decide on your future dealings with them are also useful to a prosecutor deciding on his future dealings with you. This is one of the reasons I suspect that accounts of the Mafia as a sort of General Motors of Crime are mythical: Large firms require a lot of information flowing up and down the hierarchy. It seems more likely that most crimes are committed by individuals or small firms, with organized crime not a giant corporation but something more like a chamber of commerce or better business bureau for the criminal market.

Such an interpretation flies in the face of what we are usually told in newspapers and congressional hearings. Before you reject it on that basis, consider the incentives that generate that information. Newspapers want to sell copies and politicians want to get reelected; downplaying organized crime is a poor way of doing either. Their sources of information are law enforcement officials, who want to prove that they need more money and power to fight organized crime, and criminals testifying in exchange for immunity—with an obvious incentive to say whatever their captors wish to hear. It is interesting, in reading such accounts, to compare descriptions of the power and importance of the Mafia with descriptions of how the witnesses actually ran their criminal enterprises—as independent entrepreneurs, not employees of a criminal superfirm.

Academic studies of the criminal market involve difficulties not present in most other fields of research, but nonetheless some have been done, and they provide some scholarly evidence for my conclusions. A study of illegal gambling in New York, based on records produced by police wiretapping, found that bookies were small independent operators. Not only did they not have much ability to use violence against competitors, they even had difficulty enforcing profit-sharing agreements with the subcontractors who brought in their customers.

Inside accounts, or purported inside accounts, provide a more entertaining source of information on organized crime. *The Last Testament of Lucky Luciano* contains a revealing incident. After a gangland war over who was to be *Capo di Tutti Capi*—boss of the Mafia— the winner called together gangland leaders from all over the country. He announced that

> everything would now be combined into a single organization under one rule—his. . . . The key was discipline, Maranzano emphasized repeatedly, rigid discipline, with Maranzano himself the supreme arbiter of all disputes, as he would be supreme in everything. That discipline . . . would be strictly enforced.

In less than five months he was dead.

My own conjecture is that what the Mafia really is, at least in part, is a substitute for the court system; its function is to legitimize the use of force within the criminal community. Suppose you are engaged in some criminal enterprise and one of your associates pockets your share of the take. Your obvious response is to have him killed—murder is one of the products sold on the market you are operating in. The problem with that is that if your partner gets killed and it becomes known that you are responsible, other participants in the illegal marketplace will become reluctant to do business with you.

The solution is to go to some organization with a reputation, within the criminal market, for fairness. You present the evidence of your partner's guilt, invite him to defend himself, and then ask the court to rule that he is the guilty party. If it does so—and he refuses to pay you appropriate damages—you hire someone to kill him; since everyone now knows that he was in the wrong, the only people afraid to do business with you will be those planning to swindle you.

Drugs, Law Enforcement, and Violence

It is widely believed that illegal drugs are responsible for much of the violence in U.S. cities. This raises an interesting question: Does stricter enforcement of drug laws increase or decrease violence?

Increased enforcement raises the street price of drugs. If users commit crimes to pay for drugs, and if the demand for drugs is inelastic, as the usual portrayal of addicts suggests, the result should be increased expenditure on drugs funded by increased amounts of drug-related crime. Whether or not demand is inelastic at current prices, it seems clear that complete legalization of drugs would greatly decrease such crime. Almost all of the current price of illegal drugs is due to the fact that they are illegal. A heroin addict who kept his expenditure on heroin constant while prices fell twenty- or thirty-fold would not last long.

A second explanation for violence is that it is a form of rent seeking. On this account, criminal firms have local monopolies, which they must defend against the competition of rival firms. The greater the monopoly profit, the more will be spent trying to capture or defend turf. Increased enforcement effort increases the cost of doing business, decreasing monopoly profit, so increased enforcement should result in less violence.

A third possibility is that violence is simply a consequence of insecure property rights. Drug sellers have lots of portable wealth in the form of money and drugs, and do not have the option of calling the police if someone steals it. The result is violence by drug dealers defending their property and by other people trying to steal it. That fits the account in *The Cocaine Kids*, written by a sociologist with contacts in that market. A similar pattern appears in descriptions of the Prohibition era, with bootleggers hijacking trucks full of booze belonging to their competitors.

The amount of such violence should be roughly proportional to the amount of wealth to be stolen or defended, which depends on the total value of drugs sold. If demand is inelastic, the increased price due to increased enforcement effort will produce a less than proportional decrease in quantity demanded, so total revenue will rise, resulting in increased violence. If demand is elastic, increased enforcement should lead to less revenue and less violence.

We have three different explanations for drug-related violence. One implies that marginal increases in enforcement will decrease violence, two that they will increase violence if demand is inelastic, decrease it if demand is elastic. All imply that legalizing drugs would eliminate drug-related crime.

PART 2: THE COST OF CRIME

What Is Wrong with Robbery Anyway?

We take it for granted that certain activities, such as robbery, theft, and murder, are bad things that ought to be prevented. From the standpoint of economic efficiency, it is not immediately obvious why. Theft appears to be merely a transfer; I lose $100 and the thief gains $100. From the standpoint of efficiency, that looks like a wash—costs measured in dollars just balance benefits in dollars. If so, what is wrong with theft?

If that were all that happened, theft would indeed be neutral from the standpoint of efficiency. It is not. Theft is not costless; the thief must spend money, time, and effort buying tools, casing the house, breaking in, and so forth. How much time and effort? To answer that question, we do not have to find actual thieves and interrogate them. Economic theory tells us what the cost will be—at least for the marginal thief. In equilibrium, on the thieves' market as on other competitive markets, marginal cost equals average cost equals price.The analysis goes as follows:

Suppose that anyone who wished to become a thief could steal $100 at a net cost, including operating expenses, value of time, and risk of being caught, of only $50. Revenue is greater than cost, so economic profit is positive; firms enter the industry. If stealing pays better than alternative occupations, people will leave those occupations to become thieves.

As more people become thieves, the marginal return from theft falls. Many of the most valuable and easily stolen objects have already been stolen. Every diamond necklace has three jewel thieves pursuing it. A thief breaks into a house only to discover that Superthief has stolen all the valuable jewelry—and reset the alarm. Just as in other industries, increased output drives down the return, although not for quite the same reason. The "price" that a thief gets for his work, the amount he can steal for each hour of his own time that he spends stealing, falls.

How far does it fall? As long as stealing pays better than alternative occupations, people will leave those occupations to become thieves. Equilibrium is reached when, for the marginal thief, his new profession is only infinitesimally better than his old—and for the next person who considers becoming a thief and decides not to, it is infinitesimally worse. In equilibrium, the marginal thief is giving up a job that paid him, say, $6 an hour in order to make, net of expenses of his new profession such as lawyer's fees and occasional unpaid vacations, $6.01 an hour.

So in equilibrium, theft is not a transfer but a net cost. The marginal thief who steals $100 spends about $100 in time and money to do so. His costs and his return almost exactly cancel, leaving the cost to the victim as a net loss.

What about a thief who is unusually talented at stealing or unusually incompetent at alternative professions, making theft a particularly attractive profession for him? When he steals $100, he does so at a cost of only $50, leaving him $50 ahead. Since the victim ends up $100 behind, the result is still a net loss, although not by as much as in the case of the marginal thief.

If all thieves are marginal thieves—if, in other words, there is not much variation among potential thieves in their comparative advantage for thievery—the net cost of theft, including costs and benefits to both thieves and victims, is about equal to the amount stolen. If thieves vary widely, the net cost is still positive, but less than the amount stolen.

So far we have ignored the costs of defense against theft. These include both private costs—locks, burglar alarms, security guards, and the like—and the public costs of police, courts, and prisons. My guess is that such costs are much larger than the net gains of theft to the inframarginal thieves, making the total cost of theft more, not less, than the value of all goods stolen.

Theft is inefficient for the same reason as other forms of rent seeking. Both thieves and victims are competing for possession of the same objects—all of which initially belong to the victims. Expenditures by a thief result either in his getting the loot instead of some other thief or in his getting the loot instead of its owner keeping it. Defensive expenditures by the victims are rent seeking as well—the function of a burglar alarm is to make sure that the property remains in the hands of its original owner.

If property rights are insecure, some individuals have an incentive to spend resources trying to get property transferred to them, while some have an incentive to spend resources keeping property from being transferred away from them. That is true whether the transfer is private or public. Not earning taxable income or not buying taxed goods are (costly) ways of defending yourself against taxation, just as installing a burglar alarm is a (costly) way of protecting against theft. Making campaign donations to a candidate who promises to provide special benefits to you and your friends is an expenditure on transferring property in your direction almost precisely analogous to a burglar's expenditure on tools.

PART 3: EFFICIENT CRIMES AND THE EFFICIENT LEVEL OF CRIME

I have spent twenty hours searching art galleries to find a painting I particularly like and then bought it for $100. A thief who steals it injures me by considerably more than $100. The thief himself will be lucky to get $50 for it; even if he finds the right gallery and the right buyer—one who does not recognize the painting and does recognize its quality—he will get what the gallery pays for paintings, not what it charges for them.

In such a situation, the value to the thief of what he steals is much less than its value to the victim. That is why in many societies, including our own, there are well-established procedures by which thieves sell things back to their owners. Kidnappers provide an extreme example. They steal something—a person—whose only value to them is what they can get by selling it back to (representatives of) its "owner." Such institutions make theft more efficient but also more profitable, and thus more common.

This divergence between value to victim and value to thief suggests another way of looking at the inefficiency of theft. If you have something that is worth more to me than to you, I have no need to steal it; I can buy it from you. Goods that a thief is willing to steal but would not be willing to buy must be worth more to their present owner than to the potential thief. So the additional transfers that become possible as a result of theft are inefficient ones—transfers of a good to someone who values it less than its present owner.

There are exceptions—"efficient crimes." You are lost in the woods and starving. You come upon an empty, locked cabin. You break in, feed yourself, and use the telephone to summon help. The value to you of using the cabin was greater than the cost you imposed on its owner; you will be glad to replace both his food and his lock. Your "crime" transferred a resource—temporary control of the cabin—to someone to whom it was worth more than its value to the initial owner. You could only do it by a crime, not by purchase, because the owner was not there to sell it to you.

A less exotic example is speeding when you are in a hurry; there are times when getting somewhere quickly is sufficiently important to justify doing so at eighty miles per hour. One way the law might deal with such situations would be to make it illegal to drive faster than seventy miles per hour except when there is an important reason to do so. That is how we handle the problem of the lost hunter—he is excused from criminal liability under the doctrine of necessity. But treating the speeder in the same way requires information about how good his reason for speeding was, which the law is unlikely to have.

An alternative is to impose a penalty large enough so that only those who really have a good reason to drive faster will find it worth breaking the law and paying the penalty. Seen in this way, a speeding law is a Pigouvian tax, like the emission fee discussed in chapter 18. If air polluters must pay an emission fee equal to the damage done by the pollution, they will pollute—and pay—only when the value of what is being produced is greater than the cost, including the cost of the pollution. If speeding imposes costs on other drivers, we can use traffic tickets to force motorists to take account of those costs in deciding how fast to drive.

This suggests a simple rule for setting punishments: "The amount of the punishment should equal the damage done by the crime." That way, only efficient crimes will be committed—crimes for which the value to the criminal is greater than the amount of damage done.

Criminals are not always caught; a potential offender with one chance in ten of being caught and convicted will discount the punishment accordingly. In order to assure that only efficient crimes occur, the punishment must be scaled up enough to compensate—multiplied by ten if the criminal is risk neutral.

This raises an interesting problem. The same deterrence might be provided by a certainty of a $1,000 fine, a 50 percent probability of a $2,000 fine, a 10 percent chance of a $10,000 fine, or one chance in a hundred of being hanged. How should we decide which to use?

The problem is one we solved back in chapter 9: choosing the mix of inputs to produce an output. The output is deterrence, the inputs are probability and punishment. The solution is to generate a total cost curve for deterrence by finding, for each level of deterrence, the least costly punishment/probability pair that produces it.

The cost of catching criminals is higher the more you are trying to catch, so enforcement cost rises with probability. On the other hand, fines are a more efficient punishment than execution or imprisonment, since someone gets what the criminal loses, and it is easier to collect small fines than large ones. So punishment cost tends to increase with the size of punishment. Somewhere between one extreme (catching 100 percent of the criminals and making them give back what they stole) and the other (catching only one criminal and boiling him in oil), there is an optimal combination.

We now have a simple rule for deterring all inefficient offenses: Impose an expected punishment equal to the damage done, using the least costly combination of probability and punishment that does so. But deterring all inefficient crimes may not be the efficient thing to do. A crime that produces a net cost of $10 is inefficient, but it is not worth deterring it if doing so requires $100 in additional enforcement and punishment costs. The efficient level of crime, taking account of enforcement costs, may leave some inefficient crimes undeterred— because it is not worth the cost of deterring them. Less obviously, the efficient level might deter some efficient crimes—because by deterring them we save ourselves the cost of punishing them.

Why Not Hang Them All: The Efficiency of Inefficient Punishment

Our discussion of punishment costs raises an interesting puzzle: Why does our legal system make so much use of imprisonment when more efficient punishments are available? Suppose a convicted criminal is indifferent between a certainty of ten years in jail and one chance in six of execution. Instead of giving him a ten-year sentence, we roll a die: 1–5 we turn him loose, 6 we hang him. The criminal is, on average, no worse off than before, deterrence is unaffected, and we save a lot of money on prisons. We can save still more by throwing away the die, cutting the police budget, catching a sixth as many offenders as before, and hanging all of them.

Execution is more efficient than imprisonment, but a fine is better still. Why not have a system of punishment designed to squeeze as much money out of convicted criminals as possible, then provide any additional punishment in less efficient ways? We could, for example, offer criminals the option of buying shorter sentences or lower probabilities of execution. And if we are going to imprison people, why not get something out of them by using them as some form of slave labor? If we must execute criminals, why not let their bodies forfeit to the state to help ease the shortage of organs for organ transplants? If one has no scruples about how criminals are treated, there are quite a lot of ways of decreasing the net cost of punishment.

The problem with an efficient punishment is that somebody collects it. Suppose we had a legal system that did a very good job of squeezing money out of convicted criminals, say by auctioning them off as slaves for a price of a few hundred thousand dollars each—not an unreasonable price for a slave in a modern society. It would then be in the interest of whomever was running the law enforcement system to convict lots of people—whether or not they were guilty. The result would be a society where large amounts were spent by people either trying to appropriate other people's human capital by convicting them of something or trying to keep their own human capital from being appropriated—rent seeking with large stakes and large costs.

This is not a wholly imaginary problem. One way of looking at current problems with punitive damages, product-design liability, class actions, fraud-on-the-market claims, and the like is as just such a rent-seeking struggle. Plaintiffs sue not to improve products but to transfer money from producers to themselves, and producers defend themselves by not producing products that some jury somewhere might think were defective—with the result that the United States no longer produces small airplanes and has a hard time finding a firm willing to manufacture vaccines. Similar problems arise with civil forfeiture, under which police departments can seize property on the claim that it has been used in connection with illegal activities—not necessarily by the owner. There have been allegations of serious corruption in connection with civil forfeiture, including one case in which law enforcement officials apparently killed a landowner while trespassing on his property looking for marijuana plants—after first checking on the (multimillion-dollar) value of the land. The economic analysis of crime must take into account the rational self-interested behavior of everyone involved—including the police.

PART 4: PRIVATE OR PUBLIC ENFORCEMENT OF LAW?

If someone breaks your arm, you call the police, but if he breaks a window or a contract, you call a lawyer. In the one case, law is enforced by the government and its agents, in the other by the victim and his agents. In our system, the division between public and private enforcement roughly corresponds to the division between criminal and civil law. The form is in many ways different, but the substance is similar. In both cases it is alleged that someone has done something he should not have, and in both something unpleasant happens to the convicted defendant—whether we call it a punishment or a damage payment.

Both forms of enforcement have advantages and disadvantages. One problem with private enforcement is that there is little incentive to sue someone who has no money to pay damages. One problem with public enforcement is illustrated by the following immoral tale.

You are a police officer. You have got the goods on me: sufficient evidence for a conviction. The resulting punishment would be equivalent, to me, to a $20,000 fine. Perhaps the punishment is a $20,000 fine; perhaps it is a period of imprisonment that I would pay $20,000 to avoid. For the purposes of the story, we will assume the former.

Arresting me will improve your professional reputation, slightly increasing your chances of future promotion. That is worth $1,000 to you in increased future income. Seen from the viewpoint of *Dragnet,* the rest of the story is clear; you arrest me and I am convicted. Seen from the viewpoint of this book, the result is equally clear. You have something—the collected evidence against me—that is worth $1,000 to you and $20,000 to me. Somewhere between $1,000 and $20,000, there ought to exist a transaction in our mutual benefit. I pay you $5,000, and you burn the evidence.

This is a satisfactory outcome for us but not a very effective way of enforcing the law. In this respect, the public enforcement system is not *incentive compatible.* The system requires you to do something—arrest me—in order for it to work, and the system makes it in your interest to do something else. The system, of course, can and will try to control the problem—for example, by punishing police officers who are caught accepting bribes. But the fact that it must devote some of its limited resources to catching police officers instead of catching criminals is itself a defect.

Another way to solve the problem is to pay you, not a wage, but the value of the fines collected from the criminals you convict. Now burning the evidence costs you $20,000, so that is the lowest bribe you will accept. Since $20,000 is also the cost to me of being convicted, there is little point in my offering you that much to let me off—save perhaps as a way of saving the time and expense of standing trial. If I do bribe you, no damage has been done; I have still paid $20,000 and you have still received it. We have merely eliminated the middleman.

This may sound like an odd and corrupt system, but it is how civil law is presently enforced. What we call bribery in criminal law is called an out-of-court settlement in civil law. The only addition to my scheme needed in order to make it correspond to ordinary civil law is to make the claim against the criminal the property of his victim; the police officer—now a private entrepreneur rather than a government employee—buys the claim from the victim before hunting down the criminal.

Elements of such a system existed in the United States in the last century, reflected in the "Wanted Dead or Alive: $200 Reward" posters familiar in films and books. The policemen of that system were called bounty hunters. Other elements existed in England in the eighteenth century, when prosecution of crimes was almost entirely private, usually by the victim. A complete system of private enforcement existed in Iceland in the early Middle Ages. Not only was killing treated as a civil offense, but the enforcement of court verdicts, including the job of hunting down convicted defendants who refused to pay and were consequently declared outlaws, was left to the plaintiffs and their friends. Odd as it may seem, the system appears to have worked fairly well; the society of which it was a part was one of the most interesting and in some ways one of the most attractive then existing. It was the source of the original *sagas*—historical novels and histories written in the thirteenth and fourteenth centuries and in many cases still in print today in English translations.

Economics Joke #3: Incentive Incompatibility.

José robbed a bank and fled south across the Rio Grande, with the Texas Rangers in hot pursuit. They caught up with him in a small Mexican town; since José knew no English and none of them spoke Spanish, they found a local resident willing to act as translator, and began their questioning.

"Where did you hide the money?"

"The gringos want to know where you hid the money."

"Tell the gringos I will never tell them."

"José says he will never tell you."

The rangers all cock their pistols and point them at José.

"Tell him that if he does not tell us where he hid the money, we will shoot him."

"The gringos say that if you do not tell them, they will shoot you."

José begins to shake with fear.

"Tell the gringos that I hid the money by the bridge over the river."

"José says that he is not afraid to die."

PART 5: ACCIDENT LAW

The economic analysis of accidents starts with the observation that they are not entirely accidental. I do not choose to run my automobile into a pedestrian, but I do choose what kind of car I drive, how often and at what speed I drive it, and how often to have my brakes checked. How can I be induced to make the right choices—when some of the costs are borne by other people?

The simplest approach is direct regulation—of how cars must be built, how many miles people may drive and at what speed, how often their brakes must be checked. This solution runs into problems that we have already discussed in other contexts. To write efficient rules, the legislature requires detailed information about individual tastes and abilities that it has no way of getting. Much of the behavior you wish to regulate is unobservable—how does the policeman know how much attention I was paying to the road and how much to the radio?

And even if the legislature could calculate and enforce optimal behavior, why would they want to? Why not use the power to do something more useful—such as writing regulations that disadvantage foreign cars, in exchange for political support from domestic automakers?

A better solution is to charge by results: If I cause an accident I must pay the cost. Externalities are internalized; I have an incentive to engage in an efficient level of accident prevention on every margin. If I pay too much attention to the radio, or the conversation with my passenger, I pay for any resulting accidents. The court does not know I am driving carelessly—but I do. We have switched from safety regulation to civil liability for damages.

This produces new problems. Driving becomes a lottery with large negative prizes. The risk averse have an incentive to insure themselves—and, by doing so, reduce their incentive to take precautions. Many drivers will be judgment-proof, unable to pay the cost of a major accident. That can be solved by requiring drivers to be insured, but again with negative effects on incentives.

There is another and deeper problem. Accidents depend on your decisions as well as mine, on how carefully you cross the street as well as how fast I drive. Ideally both of us should take all cost-justified precautions. But if I must make good your damages, you have no incentive to take precautions.

One response is a negligence rule: Damages are owed by the party that failed to take appropriate precautions. But here again we run into information problems; many of the precautions, and many of the costs and benefits, are unobservable. How can the court know whether the value to me of taking that particular trip was greater than the cost, in risk of accident, that it imposed on other drivers?

A different approach is to make each party fully liable for the entire cost of the accident—not to the other party but to the state. If each party must separately pay the full cost, each has the efficient incentive to avoid the accident. The damage award has been converted into a fine.

This solution brings new problems. If both parties face fines for their role in the accident, that is a good reason not to report it. By converting damages into fines we have gone from a private to a public system of law and must provide some public mechanism to report damages and institute cases.

Bureaucrat-god judges, like bureaucrat-god regulators and bureaucrat-god legislators, are in short supply. We are left with a choice among imperfect solutions, private and public, criminal and civil. In law as in many other areas, economics does a great deal to clarify the problem but does not, by itself, generate any simple answer. Not only are the theoretical problems sometimes hard ones, but a solution requires us to combine theory with facts: real-world tastes and production functions. We cannot decide how to divide the job among the courts, private bargaining, enforcement by victims, enforcement by police, enforcement by some police of restrictions on other police, enforcement by the rational self-interest of victims and offenders, direct regulation, and other alternatives without knowing a good deal about the technology of fact-finding by courts, bargaining by individuals, and other complicated facts about the real world.

TO THINK ABOUT

Two Bedouins got into an argument over which one had the slower camel and agreed to a ten-dinar bet on whose camel would take longer getting to the next oasis. An hour later they were still sitting on their camels side-by-side in the desert, neither willing to move a step for fear of losing the bet.

A wise man came by and asked them why they were sitting still on the camels in the hot sun. They got down and explained the problem. The wise man whispered two words to them. The men leaped on the camels and rode off for the oasis as fast as they could go.

What were the two words?

For Further Reading

My analysis of private enforcement is in "Efficient Institutions for the Private Enforcement of Law," *Journal of Legal Studies* (June 1984). My book *The Machinery of Freedom* contains a discussion of how a fully private system of courts, police, and laws might work and a description of the Icelandic system. A more detailed account of optimal punishment is in my "Should the Characteristics of Victims and Criminals Count? *Payne v. Tennessee* and Two Views of Efficient Punishment," *Boston College Law Review,* 34 no. 4 (July 1993), pp. 731–69. My essay "Economic Analysis of Law" in *The New Palgrave: A Dictionary of Economic Theory and Doctrine*, John Eatwell, Murray Milgate, and Peter Newman, eds. (Macmillan, 1987), gives a general overview of the subject and further references.

The Last Testament of Lucky Luciano, by Martin A. Gosch and Richard Hammer (Boston: Little, Brown: 1974), claims to be based on information given to Gosch by Luciano. *The Cocaine Kids: The Inside Story of a Teenage Drug Ring*, by Terry Williams (Addison-Wesley 1989), provides a more recent view of an illegal market.

"Fact, Fancy, and Organized Crime," by Peter Reuter and Jonathan B. Rubinstein, *The Public Interest,* 53 (Fall 1978), pp. 45–67, provides evidence and arguments that support my view of organized crime, including the results of the study of bookmaking mentioned in this chapter.

21

THE ECONOMICS OF LOVE
AND MARRIAGE

WHAT AND WHY IS MARRIAGE?

(Miss Manners) also asks that you not bore her with explaining the comparative quality of marital and nonmarital relationships, especially when using the term "honesty" or asking the nonsensical question of what difference a piece of paper makes. Miss Manners has a safe-deposit box full of papers that make a difference.
> —*Miss Manners' Guide to Excruciatingly Correct Behavior* by Judith Martin

Some things are too close to see. Viewed from a sufficient distance—Mars, say—human institutions are distinctly odd, and marriage one of the odder ones. Most of us take it for granted that we will do our shopping, even for a single sort of good, in many stores. But most of us also take it for granted that the ideal life involves entering into a mutual bilateral monopoly for the barter of a considerable range of goods and services—and sticking with it till death do us part.

There are, of course, gains from division of labor—but forming a two-person firm is not the only way of getting them. Most of us take advantage of the comparative advantage of the butcher, the baker, and the brewer, but we do not have to marry them to get our dinner. The wife in a traditional marriage may have a comparative advantage over the husband in cooking and the husband a comparative advantage over the wife in carpentry. But outside of the household, there are better cooks and better carpenters than either of them. Why does the couple rely on household production for so much of what it consumes—most meals, most domestic cleaning, much child care and education?

One reason is transaction costs. To build a house, you hire a carpenter. If you are fixing a few loose shingles, the time and trouble of finding a good carpenter, negotiating mutually satisfactory terms, and making sure he does the job may more than wipe out the carpenter's comparative advantage. The carpenter is better at fixing shingles than I am, but I am the one who gets wet if the roof leaks, so I have an incentive to do a good job even if nobody is watching me. And I have no incentive to waste time and energy haggling with myself over the price.

A second reason may be specialization. The cook at the restaurant my wife and I would go to if we spent less time cooking and more time earning money to pay for restaurants may be better at cooking than we are. But the restaurant cook is worse than we are at cooking *for us*. The same may be true for other services.

Why the assumption of permanence—why don't we simply plan to share bed and board for a while, then move on when one of us discovers a better opportunity? Why, in other words, is marriage a long-term contract? To answer that, we go back to our earlier analysis of why long-term contracts exist.

We choose our mates on a large and competitive market, however much we may protest that there could never have been anyone else. But once married, we acquire what in other contexts is known as *firm-specific capital*. Changing partners involves large costs. Our specialized knowledge of how to live with each other becomes worthless. One, at least, must leave a familiar and accustomed home. Our circle of friends will probably be divided between us. Worst of all, the new mate, whatever his or her advantages, is not the other parent of my children.

Firm-specific capital creates a bargaining range. Each party is tempted, in trying to get things his or her way, to take advantage of the fact that the other is better off, over a considerable range of demands, giving in than leaving. It seems as though the ideal solution to such bargaining problems would be a long-term contract that completely specified the obligations of both parties. Before the contract is signed, there is no marriage, no bilateral monopoly, and not much of a bargaining range. After the contract is signed, there is nothing left to bargain about.

To some extent, traditional marriage is such a contract. It is, in principle, possible for a husband or wife to claim that the other is not living up to his or her responsibility—for a wife to sue a husband for failing to support her, for example. The problem is that one cannot write and enforce a contract detailed enough to cover all relevant terms. Just as under price control, an individual legally obliged to provide a product at a specified price can evade the obligation by lowering quality. So far as I know, nobody has ever successfully sued his or her spouse for cooking—or making love—badly. A considerable amount of bargaining room remains, and is used, in a traditional marriage.

Love and Marriage. So far I have said nothing about love, which is widely believed to have some connection with marriage. It may seem odd to ask why we marry someone we love, instead of marrying someone whose tastes agree with and whose skills complement our own and then conducting our respective love lives on the side, but it is a legitimate question.

One answer is that love is associated with sex, for reasons that can be explained (by *sociobiology*—economics applied to genes instead of people) but will not be here, and sex with having children. Parents much prefer rearing their own children to rearing other people's, and much of child rearing is most conveniently done in the home of the rearer. So it is convenient for a child's parents to be married—to each other.

A second answer is that love reduces, although it does not eliminate, the conflicts of interest that lead to costly bargaining. If I love my wife, we have a common interest in making her happy. If she also loves me, we have a common interest in making me happy. Unless our love is so precisely calculated that our objectives are identical, there is still room for conflict, in either direction; if we love each other too much, my attempts to benefit her at my expense will clash with her attempts to benefit me at her expense.

The Decline of American Marriage. Now that we have a sketch of an economic theory of marriage, we might as well do something with it. One obvious application is to explain the decline of marriage in the United States (and similar societies) over the course of this century. Why has marriage become less common and why has the effective term of the contract become so much shorter?

The simple answer is that the amount of time spent in household production has declined drastically, and with it the amount of firm-specific capital acquired by the partners, especially the wife. Earlier I remarked that it was not necessary, in order to get dinner, to marry one's butcher, baker, and brewer. In fact a few hundred years ago, it was not uncommon for a man to be married to his baker and brewer and a woman to her butcher—all three professions were to a considerable extent carried out within the household, especially in rural areas.

One factor reducing the amount of household production has been increased specialization. Bacon, clothing, jams, and many other items are now usually mass-produced. Clothes and dishes are still washed at home, but a good deal of the work is done by the washing machines.

An even bigger factor has been the enormous drop in infant mortality. It used to be necessary for a woman to produce children practically nonstop in order to be fairly sure of having two or three survive to adulthood, with the result that bearing and rearing children was virtually a full-time job. In a modern society, a couple that wants two children produces two children.

The result of these changes has been, for much although not all of the population, to make "housewife" a part-time profession. With fewer children and less spouse-specific capital, the costs of divorce are much lower than they were a few generations ago.

Divorce is not all costs. There are benefits too; otherwise nobody would ever get divorced. If the benefits remain unchanged and the costs are reduced, the number of cases in which at least one partner finds that benefits are greater than costs will increase. It has.

Diamond Chains

Most of us take for granted the practice of giving diamond engagement rings. It is actually quite a recent custom; prior to the

1930s, such a gift was uncommon. Statistics on diamond sales are not very good until recent years, but it looks as though the use of engagement rings increased sharply during the thirties and forties, peaked in the fifties, and has declined somewhat since. Why?

There is a simple explanation, proposed by economist Margaret Brinig. Prior to 1935, forty-seven of the forty-eight states permitted actions for breach of promise to marry—civil actions in which a woman who had been jilted by her fiancé could sue for damages. While damages could be based on a variety of injuries, the important one was loss of virginity, which in the marriage market as it then existed substantially decreased a woman's opportunities for marriage. While men were reluctant to marry a woman who had slept with someone else, sex between engaged couples was common. The breach of contract suit served to discourage the traditional male strategy, immortalized in song and story, of seduce and abandon.

Between 1935 and 1945, the action for breach of promise was abolished in states containing about half the U.S. population; it is now almost unknown. Brinig argues that the custom of presenting a valuable engagement ring, which the woman was entitled to keep if the man broke off the engagement, arose as a substitute—a performance bond for a promise that had become legally unenforceable. She supports that conjecture with a careful statistical analysis of the available data relating diamond imports, income, marriage rates, and legal changes. More recently, as changing sexual mores have eliminated the problem to which both breach of promise actions and diamond rings were a solution, the use of diamond engagement rings has gone back down.

Deregulating the Spice Market

In our society, only *monogamous* marriages are permitted—one husband, one wife. In various other societies, *polygynous* marriages (one husband, two or more wives) and *polyandrous* marriages (one wife, two or more husbands) have also been legal. What would the effect of legalizing polygyny or polyandry be on the welfare of men? On the welfare of women? On the net welfare of all concerned?

In many societies, marriage is accompanied by payments—bride price paid by the groom or his family to the family of the bride, dowry provided by the bride's family to the new couple, and so on. While explicit payments of this sort are not part of our marriage institutions (unless you count the wedding and the wedding gifts), people who get married do so with some general understanding of the terms they are committing themselves to: how free a hand each will have with the common funds, what duties each is expected to perform, and so on. The terms of this understanding correspond to an implicit price, paid by the partners to each other.

Suppose a plague kills off many young women of marriageable age. One result will be to shift the terms of marriage in favor of women—to increase the cost of a wife. This is particularly likely if the threat of divorce is available to enforce the terms of the contract; if the man who promised before the wedding to do everything his wife wanted proves less accommodating afterward, some other man will be willing to take his place.

Think of the price of a spouse as defined relative to some arbitrary "standard" contract. Any actual marriage contract can be viewed as the standard one plus or minus a certain number of dollars paid by the husband to the wife; plus represents a contract more favorable to the wife than the standard, minus represents one less favorable. Supply and demand work just as on any other market. The quantity supplied of wives—the number of women willing to marry—will be higher, and the quantity demanded lower, the higher the price. The model is symmetrical; we can as easily speak of the quantity demanded and quantity supplied of husbands. As on any barter market, each participant is both buyer and seller.

Omissions. Some people are worth marrying more than others; the definition of the standard contract should include quality of spouse. To get your offer up to zero—the equivalent of the standard contract—you must balance the benefit to you of an unusually desirable wife by offering her more favorable terms in other dimensions. Perhaps you agree to wash all of the dishes.

Seen from this standpoint, attractiveness is a kind of wealth. A man or a woman with good looks or a pleasant disposition is wealthier, has a greater command over the desirable things of life, than someone without, just as someone who has inherited a million dollars is wealthier than someone who has not.

We are still leaving out another important feature of marriage: not everyone has the same tastes. The woman I recognized as a one in ten thousand catch was not even being pursued by anyone else, with the result that I married her on quite reasonable terms; I did not even have to agree to wash all of the dishes. Some of the women that my friends married, on the other hand, were of no interest to me at all. Yet my friends obviously preferred them, not only to remaining bachelors but to trying to lure my intended away from me. Equilibrium on the marriage market is in part a problem of supply and demand, but in part also a problem of sorting different people according to differing tastes and attributes. That is a complication that I will ignore here, but would want to include in a more extensive analysis.

What would be the effect of legalizing polygyny? One way to answer that question is a formal analysis, using supply/demand diagrams like those we used to analyze the effect of a tariff. Mathematically inclined readers may want to work that problem through for themselves. I will limit myself here to presenting it in verbal form.

Price is defined relative to a standard contract, which has monogamy as one of its features. A bigamist who matches a monogamist's offer is promising more favorable terms in other respects to balance the cost of sharing a husband. Since a bigamous marriage offer at any price is by definition equivalent (from the standpoint of potential wives) to a monogamous offer at the same price, the number of women willing to accept it will be the same. The legalization of polygyny has no effect on the supply curve for wives.

Legalizing polygyny allows some men who before wanted one wife to try to marry two instead—provided that they are willing to offer terms at which potential wives are willing to accept half a husband apiece. So the demand curve for wives shifts out. The supply curve stays the same, the demand curve shifts out, so the price must go up. Women are better off.

Most men end up with only one wife and are worse off, since they must offer her more favorable terms than before. The effect on a husband with two wives is ambiguous; he prefers two wives to one, but he might prefer one wife at the old price to two at the new price.

The net result is a gain. To see this, imagine that we make the change in two steps. The first consists of changing to the new price, while keeping the allocation of husbands and wives (to each other) fixed. That is a pure transfer; wives gain what husbands lose. The next step is to allow husbands and wives to adjust to the new price. Men who do not change the number of wives they have are unaffected; men who reduce the number of wives they have from one to zero in response to the higher price or increase the number above one to take advantage of the legalization of polygyny, and women who at the old price did not choose to marry but at the new price do, are better off. A pure transfer plus an improvement adds up to an improvement.

The analysis of the effects of legalizing polyandry is identical, with the roles of women and men reversed. Since some women now buy two (or more) husbands, the demand curve for husbands shifts out. At the old price for husbands, quantity demanded is greater than quantity supplied, so the price rises. Women marrying only one husband must compete against the polyandrous women to get him, hence must offer better terms than before. Men are better off, monogamous women are worse off, and polyandrous women may be better or worse off. The net effect is an economic improvement.

To many readers, the conclusion may seem extraordinary—how can women be made better off by polygyny and men by polyandry? That reaction reflects what I described in chapter 2 as naive price theory: the theory that prices do not change. If polygyny were introduced and nothing else changed, women would be worse off—except for those who prefer to share the burden of a husband. But when polygyny is introduced, something does change; the demand curve for wives shifts up, and so does the price implicit in the marriage contract. Wives who end up with one husband get him on more favorable terms—he must bid more for a wife because of the competition of his polygynous rivals. Those who accept polygynous marriages do so because the price they are offered is sufficient to at least balance, for them, the disadvantage of sharing a husband.

The result would seem less paradoxical if we substituted cars and car buyers for wives and husbands (or husbands and wives). Suppose there were a law forbidding anyone to own more than one car. The abolition of that law would increase the demand for cars. Sellers of cars would be better off. Buyers who did not take advantage of the new opportunity would be worse off, since they would have to pay a higher price. Buyers who bought more than one car would be better off than if they bought only one car at the new price (otherwise that is what they would have done) but not necessarily better off than if they bought one car at the old price, an option no longer open to them.

When I talk about women being better off "after" polygyny becomes legal, it sounds as though I am describing a future in which, after polygyny becomes legal, some men divorce one wife to marry two others, and some women insist on renegotiating their marriage contracts. But that is misleading; here, as in similar discussions elsewhere, "before" and "after" are stages in the analysis, not the world being analyzed. I am comparing two alternative futures, one with polygyny (or polyandry) and one without. The man who would have married one wife if polygyny had remained illegal either marries one wife on different terms if polygyny is legal, marries two (or more) wives, or is priced out of the market and remains a bachelor.

Money, Beauty, and Folk Songs

The Brown Girl she has house and lands, fair Ellender she has none.

> —No. 73 of *The English and Scottish Popular Ballads* collected by Francis James Child

A young man in a folk song must choose between two women, one beautiful and one rich. Almost invariably he chooses the rich one. The result is tragedy; at least two and often all three of the parties end up dead. The lesson is clear: Marry the beautiful woman.

It is clear in such songs that marrying a woman for her money is bad, but marrying her for her beauty is not. It is less clear why. True, the Brown Girl (dark complexioned, hence less attractive than "Fair" Ellender) has done nothing to deserve her wealth; one could argue that she therefore does not deserve to get Lord Thomas. But no more does Fair Ellender deserve her beauty. All either of them has done is to pick the right parents, the one for wealth and the other for looks. Why then is it good and noble for Lord Thomas to reject wealth for beauty and base and wicked for him to reject beauty for wealth?

One answer may be that the plot depends on something that I earlier assumed away. In the world of folk songs—and in many, perhaps most, human societies—the bride and groom are not the only ones whose interests are involved in their marriage, nor are they the only ones with some control over it. If Lord Thomas marries Fair Ellender, he will be the only one to benefit by her beauty; if he marries the Brown Girl, his parents may reasonably hope to get their hands on some of her wealth. Perhaps they are counting on it to support them in their old age. It is Lord Thomas's mother who persuades him to marry the Brown Girl.

If that is what is going on, it is clear enough which side of the generation gap the singer—or at least his intended audience—is on.

THE ECONOMICS OF ALTRUISM

I have claimed several times that economics assumes objectives, but that they need not be selfish ones; I am about to prove it. Consider two people, an altruist Anne and a beneficiary Bill, perhaps parent and child. The altruist cares about the welfare of the beneficiary. So does the beneficiary. If you find the assymetry implausible, ask any parent.

Anne has a limited amount of money which she divides between two goods: her consumption and Bill's. By transferring income to Bill, she decreases the amount of one good and increases the amount of the other, just like the consumer moving down a budget line back in chapter 3.

Suppose Anne's income is $75 dollars a week and Bill's is $25. If she gives him nothing, that is what each consumes. If she gives him everything, she will consume nothing and he will consume a hundred dollars a week. Between those extremes there is a range of alternatives, different divisions of their combined income corresponding to different amounts she could give him.

The situation is shown in Figure 21–1. Anne's optimal point, where her budget line is tangent to her indifference curve, is Y. She gives Bill $15, leaving herself with $60 and him with $40.

Suppose her income increases to $90 and his decreases to $10. Her alternatives are shown on her new budget line. They include all of the points on the old budget line, plus some new ones. The new points are all dominated by Y, since they are below its indifference curve. She increases her transfer by $10. Consumption is back at Y.

Y is, from Anne's viewpoint, the ideal way of dividing a hundred dollars between herself and Bill. As long as their combined income is a hundred dollars, and as long as Anne starts with at least sixty, she has the option of moving to Y—and will. It follows that, from the standpoint of both Anne and Bill, all such combinations of income— a hundred and zero, ninety and ten, sixty and forty—are equivalent. They all result in the same consumption pattern for both altruist and beneficiary.

There is nothing special about a hundred dollars; the argument applies to any income. As long as the altruist starts with enough to get to her preferred division, it is only the total, not the initial division, that matters.

Since it is the combined income of the two that determines how much the beneficiary ends up with, a rational beneficiary will find it in his interest to pay as much attention to maintaining the income of the altruist as to maintaining his own. In this respect, the beneficiary

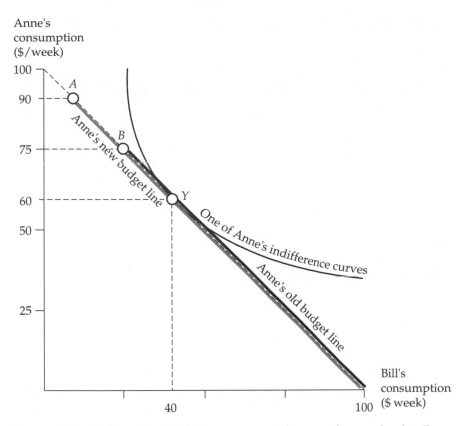

Figure 21-1 Budget line/indifference curve diagram for an altruist. By choosing how much of her income to give to the beneficiary, the altruist is choosing a point on the budget line L.

acts rather as though he too were an altruist—even though he is indifferent to the altruist's welfare.

The argument can be generalized by defining an altruist as someone who has the utility of someone else as one of the variables on which his utility depends. The generalization of the result is that it is in the interest of the beneficiary to take any action that produces an economic improvement for the two-person society of altruist and beneficiary. Any such change will make the beneficiary better off, once we include in our calculations the effect of the change on the amount that the altruist chooses to transfer. I have demonstrated this result graphically in a simple two-dimensional case where all changes are in money; the proof in the more general case (where the loss might be a broken arm, a broken window, or even a broken heart) is similar but more complicated. As in the simpler case, the result is limited to situations where the altruist is rich enough to be able to get to her preferred division.

It is easy to misread this as a threat game: if the beneficiary hurts the altruist, the altruist punishes him by reducing the transfer, so the beneficiary finds it in his interest not to offend his patron. That is not what is happening. Nothing in the argument depends on the altruist knowing that the beneficiary is responsible for the change. Exactly the same thing will happen in the case of a change produced by some third party, or by nature. If the change is a net improvement, both beneficiary and altruist end up better off after the change—and the resulting change in the amount the altruist chooses to transfer. If it is a net loss, both end up worse off.

The Rotten Kid Theorem

Consider a situation with one altruist ("parent") and two beneficiaries ("kids"). One of them is a rotten kid who would enjoy kicking his little sister. The analysis I have just described implies that if the dollar value to the rotten kid of kicking his sister (the number of dollars worth of consumption he would, if necessary, give up in order to do so) is less than the dollar cost to the sister of being kicked, the rotten kid is better off not kicking her. After the parent has adjusted his expenditure on the kids in response to the increased utility of the kid and the decreased utility of the kicked sister, the rotten kid will have lost more than he has gained. Here again, the argument does not depend on the parent observing the kick but only on his observing how happy the two kids are.

This result—that a rotten kid, properly allowing for the effects of parental altruism, will find it in his self-interest to kick his sister only if it is efficient to do so—is known as the *Rotten Kid Theorem*. Because of the altruist's peculiar utility function—which contains the beneficiaries' utilities among its arguments—both altruist and beneficiaries find it in their private interest to maximize efficiency, to make decisions according to whether the net effect on altruist and beneficiaries is or is not an economic improvement.

Altruism and Evolution

Gary Becker, the economist whose ideas I have been describing, has offered them as a solution to one of the puzzles of sociobiology:

the existence of altruism. If, as the theory of evolution seems to imply, we have been selected by evolution for our ability to serve our own reproductive interest (roughly speaking, to act in such a way as to have as many descendants as possible), those who sacrifice their interest for the interest of others should have been selected out. Yet altruism seems to occur among a variety of species, possibly including our own.

One explanation is that altruism toward kin (most obviously toward my children, but the argument applies to other relatives as well) is not really altruism from the point of view of evolution; I am serving my reproductive interest by keeping my children alive, since they carry my genes. This still leaves altruism toward non-kin as a puzzle to be explained. Becker's argument is that altruism generates cooperative behavior via the mechanism described above and so benefits the altruist as well as the recipient, giving each recipient an incentive to behave efficiently vis-à-vis the entire group. A group containing an altruist will be more successful than one that does not, will have more surviving descendants, and its genes, including the genes for altruism, will become increasingly common.

Although the altruist is promoting the reproductive success of his group over other groups, he is sacrificing his own reproductive success relative to other members of his group by transferring resources from himself to them. If Becker's analysis is correct, genes for altruism should be becoming less frequent over time within groups containing one or more altruists, but the genes of such groups should be becoming more frequent over time; only if the second process at least balances the first will altruism survive.

Fair Ellender and the Rotten Kid

In the first part of this chapter, I asked why marrying for beauty is better than marrying for money. We now have a possible answer. It is widely believed that beauty is, and wealth is not, one of the things that makes men fall in love with women. Our analysis of altruism suggests that people will work together more easily if one of them is an altruist with regard to the other, since it is then in the interest of both altruist and beneficiary to maximize their joint welfare. Lord Thomas is in love with Fair Ellender and is not in love with the Brown Girl, as he informs her immediately after the wedding—with the result that the Brown Girl stabs Fair Ellender, Lord Thomas kills the Brown Girl, and Lord Thomas then commits suicide, thus ending the song and presumably teaching his parents a lesson. If we are willing to identify "being in love" with altruism, perhaps the moral of the song is correct. If you marry the beautiful woman, you get not only beauty but also the advantage of being part of an efficient household—coordinated by your own altruism.

Of course, it only works in one direction; we have no reason to believe that Fair Ellender's beauty makes her any more likely to act altruistically toward Lord Thomas. But that is not an important objection to the argument; we know, from the Rotten Kid Theorem, that one altruist in a family is enough.

A more serious objection is that it is not clear how close the relationship is between "being in love" and altruism; Fair Ellender's response to being jilted by the man she was "in love" with was to dress up in her finest ("every village she came through, they thought she was some queen") and go spoil her ex-boyfriend's wedding. "Being in love" seems to describe a mix of emotions, some far from altruistic. To what extent elements in the mix associated with physical beauty involve altruism, and, if they do, whether they are likely to survive the first six months of marriage, is an open question.

Gift vs. Money

Why do people ever give gifts in any form other than money? If each individual knows his own interest, surely he is better off getting money and buying what he wants instead of getting what the donor decides to buy for him.

There are two obvious reasons to give gifts instead of cash. The first is that the donor has some objective other than the recipient's welfare. I may give you a scholarship not because I like you but because I want there to be more educated people in the society or more smart high school students going to my alma mater.

A second reason for restricted gifts is paternalism. If you believe that you know better than the recipient what is good for him, you will naturally want to control how he spends your money. The obvious example is the case of parents dealing with children.

It is not entirely obvious that paternalism is a sensible policy even applied to children. When I was quite small, my family traveled by train from Chicago to Portland, Oregon, to visit grandparents. The trip took three days and two nights. My father offered me and my sister the choice of either having sleeping berths or sitting up and being given the money that the berths would cost. We took the money.

This brings us back to the question of why we give gifts instead of cash—to our friends and even our parents on Christmas, birthdays, and the like. Even if paternalism is appropriate toward one's children, it hardly seems an appropriate attitude toward one's parents. A possible answer is that, in this particular small matter, we do think we know their interest better than they do—we are giving a book we have read and are sure they will like. I doubt that this is a sufficient explanation; we frequently give people gifts we have no special reason to think they will like.

I suspect that the correct answer is somehow connected with the hostility to money, especially in personal interactions, which seems typical of our society. Consider, for example, the number of men who would think it entirely proper to take a woman to an expensive restaurant in the hope of return benefits later in the evening, but would never dream of offering her money for the same objective.

Such an explanation leads to a further problem—explaining why our society is hostile to the use of money, especially in personal relations. As an economist, I would like to find an economic explanation even for "anti-economic" behavior. I'm still working on it.

Suspension of Disbelief

Some of you may wonder whether I expect you to take this chapter seriously. Do I really believe that love and marriage can be analyzed with the abstract logic of economics? Do I really believe that a seven-year-old boy, deciding whether or not to kick his little sister, works out a cost-benefit calculation based on economic theory that is fully understood by almost no one without a Ph.D. in economics?

The answer is "yes, but." I believe the analysis of this chapter is useful in understanding love, marriage, and children as they exist in the real world. I do not believe that the analysis is *sufficient* to understand them, without also knowing a good deal about what it is like to be human, to love, to be a child, to be a parent. Nor do I believe that if theory clashes with what we observe in the real world, it is the real world that must back down; I am not willing to say, in the words of a famous German philosopher confronted with unwelcome evidence, "So much the worse for the facts."

Economics is a way of understanding the real world. To find out whether you have succeeded you see how well the predictions of the theory fit what you actually observe. It is most unlikely that they will fit perfectly, but an imperfect theory may still be better than no theory at all.

All that being said, it is also true that for some of us the creation of economic theory, especially economic theory of things that everyone else regards as outside of economics, is an entertaining game and even, perhaps, a form of art. As long as that is all it is, the theory is properly judged by artistic criteria: elegance and consistency. It is only when we stop sketching out theories for fun and start testing them against the real world that economics becomes a science as well as an art and its analysis useful as well as entertaining.

TO THINK ABOUT

Suppose my sister and I correctly perceived our own interest when we chose money over berths for our train trip. Why might letting us make the choice nonetheless have led to an inefficient outcome? (It helps, for this one, to be a parent).

For Further Reading

For a more advanced discussion of the economics of marriage (and other things), I recommend Gary Becker, *A Treatise on the Family* (Cambridge: Harvard University Press, 1981).

FINAL WORDS

Before ending this book, I owe you a brief warning about my professional biases. The view of economics I have presented, economics as a powerful tool for understanding a wide range of behavior, is not unique to me, but neither is it universal among my colleagues. If you pick an economist at random and ask him to define economics, the answer is quite likely to be either "the science of allocating limited resources to diverse ends" or "what economists do."

The broader perspective presented in this book is not yet universally accepted, but it has proved immensely productive. A list of its champions would include James Buchanan, Gary Becker, Ronald Coase, Robert Foley, Douglas North, and George Stigler—all Nobel Prize winners in economics—as well as a considerable number of similarly talented scholars who have not yet attracted the attention of the Swedish Academy.

One reason for the successes of economic imperialism is that interesting ideas attract interesting people. Another is that we are working territory untouched by economists at least since the days of Adam Smith and Jeremy Bentham, and virgin lands often prove fertile. There is a world of puzzles out there awaiting our tools. The land rush has just begun.

TO THINK ABOUT

Give a consistent and plausible-sounding economic explanation of something that you are sure cannot be explained economically. Reread it. Are you still sure your explanation is wrong?

For Further Reading

My first economics article was "An Economic Theory of the Size and Shape of Nations," *Journal of Political Economy*, Vol. 85, No. 1 (February, 1977), pp. 59–77.

Students who would like to learn economics from its inventors should read Adam Smith, *An Inquiry into the Nature and Causes of the Wealth of Nations* (New York: Oxford University Press, 1976); David Ricardo, *The Principles of Political Economy and Taxation* (Totowa, N.J.: Biblio Distribution Centre, 1977); and Alfred Marshall, *The Principles of Economics* (8th ed., London: Macmillan, 1920).

The three books are very different. Smith's is the most far ranging and entertaining, Ricardo's the most difficult. Marshall's *Principles* is where modern economics was first put together; it is the only one of the three that could, for a sufficiently courageous reader, substitute with some advantage for a modern economics text.

INDEX

Page numbers in italics refer to figures.

accident law, 314–316
adverse selection, 275–277
advertising, truth in, 25–26
aggregate demand curves, 59
aggregate supply curves, 59–60, *60*, 62
aggressive personality, 150–152
Agriculture Department, U.S., 182–183
airlines, 164
  noise pollution and, 269–270
  youth fares of, 134, 140
allocation
  defined, 248
  distribution vs., 248–258
  efficient, 176–177, 227–228, 229, 234
altruism, 326–332, *327*
American Revolution, 8
Anderson, Poul, 300–301
antitrust actions, 162, 163
Apple, 158
arbitrage, 75–76, 219
At the Hand of Man (Bonner), 175
average cost, 118–121, *118, 121*, 125, 127, 128, 228, 247
  monopoly and, 142, 238, 239–240, 244
average value, 46

backward-bending supply curves for labor, 61–64, *62*
Baird, Douglas G., 166
balance of trade, 70–73, 179
banks, central, 185
barter, 277–278
Becker, Gary, xi, 297, 328–329, 332
Bonner, Raymond, 175
book industry, 131–133, 140, 237, 270–271
Brinig, Margaret, 321
Buchanan, James, 297
budget lines, 28, *29*, 30, 63
  of antitrust, 326, *327*
  prices and, 32–37, *35*
  subsidies and, 37, *38*
bureaucrat-gods, efficiency and, 220–221, 227–229, 232–233, 237

capital, 113, 114, 125, 197, 201–202, 204–207, 209–210, 230
  firm-specific, 318–319, 320
  human, 205–206, 207
  inflow of, 72–73, 179
  interest on, 197, 198–199, 204
capital goods, 55, 115, 126, 205
cars, 6, 16, 18, 44, 156
  crime and, 309, 314–316
  efficiency and, 221–222, 230
  industry supply curve and, 122, *123*, 124, 125–126
  input market and, 116, 117
  safety of, 273–274, 278
  tariffs and, 221–222, 282–288, *284*, 292
  trade and, 69–70
  traffic jams and, 260–261, 265
  used, 275–276
cartels, 140, 160–161, 163–164, 165
certification vs. licensing, 254
Child, Francis James, 325
China, materials supply in, 18
choice, 25–42, 220
  necessity vs., 17–18
  opportunity sets and, 41–42
  public, 289–295, 297
  time and, 48–49
  uncertainty and, 185–193
  value and, 14–16
Civil Aeronautics Board (CAB), 140, 164
Coase, Ronald, 268, 269
Coase theorem, 268
Cocaine Kids, The (Williams), 305, 316
coinsurance, 277
commitment, strategy of, 148–150, 160
comparative advantage, 69–73
computers, 69–70, 134, 158–159, 263–264
consumers, consumption, 16–19, 21, 25–53, 63
  of gasoline, 17–18, 90–91
  law of declining marginal value in, 28, 30, 43, 66, 116
  postponed, 198
  preferences of, 100–104, *103*, 106

consumers, consumption *(cont.)*
  price indices and, 33–34
  protection of, 251–254
  see also budget lines; demand, marginal
    value and; demand curves; indifference
    curves
consumer surplus, 46–53, *50,* 87–88, *88,* 105,
  107, 138, 139, 218, 220
  marginal value and, 46–48, *46, 47*
  monopoly and, *234,* 235, 237
contracts, 112–113, 127, 262–263, 268, 270
  marriage, 319, 322, 323
  present value of, 168–170, *169*
cookie industry, price discrimination in,
  135–139, *136, 137, 139*
cooking, 56, *56,* 67–68, 122, 271
Copernican revolution, 65, 66
copyright, 140, 243, 263
Cornplanter Oil, 142–143
corporations, *see* firms
cost, *see* price, price theory; *specific types of cost*
cost curves, 118–122, *118,* 124, 126, 240
  total, 115, 118, *118,* 127, 228, 310
crime, 298–316
  accident law and, 314–316
  cost of, 306–308
  economics of, 298–306
  efficiency and, 308–311
  public vs. private law enforcement and,
    311–314
currency
  exchange rates for, 71–72, 185
  stability of, 185

Dawkins, Richard, 13
demand, marginal value and, 44–45
demand curves, 45, 79–98, *80,* 101–102, *103,*
  220, 240
  aggregate, 59
  for cookies, 135, 136, *136, 137, 139*
  elasticity of, 82–83, 87, 88, *89,* 288
  for gasoline, 246, *246, 247*
  of Giffen good, 61
  marginal value curve linked with, 45, 106,
    107
  for potatoes, 50–51, *50*
  for rental housing, 92–95, *93*
  shifts in, 81–82, *82,* 97–98, 105
  straight–line, 132, *132*
depletable resources, 171–177, 179
diamond-water paradox, 45
diminishing returns, law of, 116, 197–198,
  199
discount rate, internal, 176, 178
diseconomies of scale, 119–120, 162
dish washing, 56, *56, 58,* 59, 67–68
Disneyland, 42, 48, 144–145, 146
distribution, 248–258
Doctor Strangelove (movie), 149–150
"Does Altruism Produce Efficient
  Outcomes?" (Friedman), 226
doomsday machine, 149–150, 160
drugs, 305–306

economic errors, 18–20
economic imperialism, 209–210
economic improvement, efficiency and,
  218–225, 227–228
"Economics of Exhaustible Resources, The"
  (Hotelling), 179
"Economics of War, The" (Friedman), 13
economic value, 16–17
economies of scale, 119–120, 162
education, 210–211, 272
"Effects of Automobile Safety Regulations,
  The" (Peltzman), 278
efficiency, 217–244, 248, 265, 291–292
  in allocation, 176–177, 227–228, 229, 234
  bureaucrat-gods and, 220–221, 227–229,
    232–233, 237
  characteristics of, 217
  crime and, 308–311
  decentralized planning and, 227–233
  economic improvement and, 218–225,
    227–228
  externalities and, 266–267
  as least bad solution, 224–225
  monopoly and, 233–244
  Pareto improvement and, 221–223
  patents and copyrights and, 243
efficient markets hypothesis, 11–12
effluents fees, 267
eggs, marginal value of, 46–47, *46*
elasticity
  of demand, 82–83, *82–91, 89,* 288
  of supply, 82–83, 87, 90, 288
elections, cost of, 296–297
Engels, Donald W., 13
England, 63, 91, 156, 282
English and Scottish Popular Ballads, The
  (Child, collector), 325
equilibrium, 12, 198
  competitive, 128, 229–232, 235, 238
  general, 27, 104–105
  hawk-dove, 151, 152
  Nash, 156, 158, 165
  in oligopoly, 165
  partial, 104–105, 106
  price, *80,* 81, 96, 101–102, *103,*
    124–125
  varieties of, 81
  wages and, 210, 212
equimarginal principle (P=MV), 64,
  115
evolutionary biology, 12–13, 151
  altruism and, 328–329
excess burden, 88–91, *89, 90,* 203, 204
exchange rates, 71–72, 185
expected return, 187
exploitation, production and, 128–129
externalities, 265–274, 287
  bad arguments and, 272–274
  joint causation and, 268–270
  pecuniary, 271–272, 287
  pollution and, 266–270
  private solutions to, 267–268
  voluntary, 270–271

famines, 183–184
firms, 21, 55, 111–145
    cost curves and, *see* cost curves
    defined, 113
    and economies vs. diseconomies of scale,
        119–120, 162
    efficiency and, 227–244
    input market and, 115–117, 127
    joint stock corporations, 113–114, 125
    marginal, 126
    monopolies and, 130–145
    and myth of corporate tax, 127
    present-value calculations of, 170–172
    price discrimination and, 133–140, 145,
        237–238
    as price takers vs. price searchers, 130
    profit-making of, 116, 120–122, *121*,
        125–128, 131–132, *132*, 135–140, *136*,
        162, 165, *234*, 235
    residual claimant and, 13
    sunk costs and, 181–182
    supply curve of, 121–128, *121, 123*
    theory of, 114–115
Fisher, Sir R. A., 12
fixed costs, 131, 135, 234
food prices
    grocery store problem and, 25–26, 28–33
    price supports and, 182–183
Frank, Robert, xi, 166
"fraud on the market" doctrine, 274
Friedland, Claire, 241
Friedman, Milton, 194
Friedman's Law for Finding Men's
    Washrooms, 6

gambling, rational, 186–192
game theory, games, 147–166
    bilateral monopoly and, 148–156, 161
    monopolistic competition and, 157–159,
        157
    Nash equilibrium and, 156, 158
    oligopoly and, 157, 159–165
    prisoner's dilemma and, 152–154, *153*
    two-player fixed–sum, 155–156
gasoline, 17–18, 90–91, 245–248
    price controls and, 245–247, *246*, 248
    rationing of, 247–248, 250–251
Gates, Bill, 210, 263
general equilibrium theory, 27, 104–105
General Motors (GM), 117, 119
George, Henry, 213
Gertner, Robert H., 166
Giffen good, 61–62
gifts vs. money, 330–331
Glaser, Ami, 276
goods
    allocation of, 227–228, 234
    capital, 55, 115, 126, 205
    continuous, 47–48, *47*
    Giffen, 61–62
    inferior, 61
    lumpy, 46–47, *46*
    public, 262–265, 274–277, 291–292

Goodwin, Archie, 176
government regulation, 160, 162–165,
    245–259
    distribution vs. allocation and, 248–258
    monopoly and, 140, 239–241, 244
    price controls and, 60, 97, 245–251, *246*, 253
    public goods and, 264–265
    rationing and, 247–248, 250–251, 253
grocery stores, 9–10
    prices in, 25–26, 28–33

hawk-dove equilibrium, 151, 152
Heinlein, Robert, 303
Hicks-Kaldor improvement (potential Pareto
    improvement), 222, 226
holdout problem, 269
Hong Kong, 97, 282
Hotelling, Harold, 179
housing, 91, 134–135
    price of, 33–36, *35*
    rental, 19, 91–95, 93
Hunt brothers, 185

IBM, 158–159
immigrants, 206–209
income, 16, 21, 33, 42, 61, 63, 100–102, *103*,
    106–107, 112–113, 127
    distribution of, 195–199, 253
income effect, 61, 62, 63
indifference curves, 28–34, *29*, 36, 37, 48, 63,
    100
    of altruist, 326, *327*
inflation, 33–34, 168
information, 192–193
    as public good, 275–277
insurance, 190–191, 252–253, 276–277
interest rates, interest, 167–168, 170–171, 172,
    177–179, 259
    on capital, 197, 198–199, 204
    nominal vs. real, 168
Interstate Commerce Commission (ICC), 160,
    164, 242
investment, 177–179, 203–206
    in education, 210–211
    foreign, 209–210

Japan, 66, 69–72, 74, 179
job offers, comparing, 168–170, *169*
job search, 192–193
joint stock corporations, 113–114, 125
Justice Department, U.S., 162, 163, 165

Kahn, Herman, 149–150
Kipling, Rudyard, 183
Krueger, Anne, 296, 297

labor, 21, 55, 66, 115–117, 126, 197, 199,
    201–202, 229–230
    immigration restrictions and, 207–209
    marginal disvalue of, 56–57, *58*, 64, 118,
        122, 230
    marginal product of, 197–198
    supply curve for, 57, 61–64

Laffer, Arthur, 258
land, 55, 90, 115, 126, 174–175, 199–204, 207,
     230, 294–295
    rent of, 197, 203–204
    restrictions on use of, 210
lane-changing strategy, 10–11, 12
Laspeyres price index, 33, 34
Last Testament of Lucky Luciano, The (Gosch
     and Hammer), 304, 316
law enforcement, 305–306, 311–314
lawn mowing, 56–59, *56, 58,* 62, 122
legislation, market for, 291–295
leisure, 56, 59, 61–64, 197, 230, 231
    marginal value curve for, 63–64
liability rules, 251–253
licensing, 164–165, 254
lost welfare triangle, 235
lottery-insurance paradox, 190–192, 194
love, 319–320, 331–332
Luce, R. Duncan, 166

McGee, John S., 143, 164
Maclean, Jack, 301–302
Mafia, 303–305
marginal cost, 98, 118–119, *118,* 121, *121,* 125,
     131, 132, 162, 198, 247–248
    monopoly and, *234,* 235, 239–241, 243
marginal cost curves, 121, *121,* 127, 135, *136,*
     137, 139
marginal disvalue curve for labor, 57, *58*
marginal disvalue of labor, 56–57, *58,* 64, 118,
     122, 230
marginal firm, 126
marginal product, 115, 116, 197–198, 199
marginal revenue, 131
marginal revenue curves, 132, *132,* 135, *136*
marginal revenue product (MRP), 116, 197,
     198, 230
marginal utility, declining, 186–188
marginal value, 42–45, *43,* 98, 197, 198
    declining, 28, 30, 43, 66, 116
    demand and, 44–45
marginal value curves, 45, *46,* 63, *80,* 81,
     106
    consumer surplus and, 46–48, *46, 47,* 51
    for leisure, 63–64
"Margin of Profit" (Anderson), 301
market failure, 260–278
    externalities and, 265–274
    plea bargaining and, 261–262
    public goods and, 262–265, 274–277
markets, illegal, 303–305
marriage, 148, 152, 277–278, 317–325, 331–332
    for beauty vs. money, 325, 329–330
    decline of, 320
    deregulation of, 321–325
    love and, 319–320, 331–332
Marshall, Alfred, 49, 98, 219–226
Martin, Judith, 317
Marx, Karl, 27
medical care, 15, 17
mergers, 162, 163, 267, 270
Microsoft, 159, 263

*Miss Manners' Guide to Excruciatingly Correct
     Behavior* (Martin), 317
money, 14, 32, 38, 49, 106–107, 219, 277
    beauty vs., 325, 329–330
    gifts vs., 330–331
    transfer of, 231–232
monopolistic competition, 157–159, *157*
monopoly, 130–145
    artificial, 141–143, 238
    bilateral, 73–74, 112, 148–156, 161, 318
    defined, 140–141
    discriminatory, 237–238
    Disneyland as, 144–145, 146
    efficiency and, 233–244
    nationalized, 241–242
    natural, 141, 238–244
    sale of, 242–243
    single-price, 234–236, *234,* 244
Monopoly (game), 83
Moon Is a Harsh Mistress, The (Heinlein), 303
moral hazard, 276–277
Morgenstern, Oskar, 166, 193–194

Nash equilibrium, 156, 158, 165
Newton, Sir Isaac, 65
Njal Saga, 8
nuclear weapons, 149–150

Oi, Walter, 146
oil, 177
    as depletable resource, 172–174
oil prices, 163–164, 171–174, 177
    increase in, 17–18, 90–91, 171–174
    insecure property rights and, 172, 174
oligopoly, 157, 159–165
Olson, Mancur, 297
OPEC oil cartel, 161, 173
opportunity cost, 32, 57, 59, 125
opportunity sets, 41–42, 51, 53
oranges, marginal value of, 42–43, *43,* 44
Orwell, George, 141

Paasche price index, 34
Pareto, Vilfredo, 221–223
Pareto improvements, 221–223
    potential (Hicks-Kaldor improvement),
     222, 226
parks, design of, 5–6
partial equilibrium theory, 104–105, 106
partisanship, 290–291
patents, 243
pecuniary externalities, 271–272, 287
Peltzman, Samuel, 273–274, 278
Picker, Randal C., 166
planning, decentralized, 227–233
plea bargaining, 261–262, 265
politics, 6, 239, 281–297
    public-choice theory and, 289–295, 297
    rent seeking and cost of government and,
     295–297
    tariffs and, 281–289, *284,* 292–295
pollution, 266–270, 278, 309
polyandry, 321, 324–325

polygyny, 321, 323–325
popcorn, price of, 51–53, *52*, 107–108, 139–140, 145
population growth, 273
potato subsidies, 36–39, *38*, 50–51, *50*
"Predatory Price Cutting" (McGee), 143, 164
present value, 168–172, *169*
price, price theory, 18–108
    budget line and, 32–37, *35*
    cartels and, 161
    consistent, 75–77
    cutting of, 142–143
    equilibrium, *80*, 81, 96, 101–102, *103*, 124–125
    firms and, 120–126, *121*, *123*, 127–128, 131, 181–182
    grocery story, 25–26, 28–33
    of housing, 33–36, *35*
    monopoly and, 234–240
    naive, 20–21, 251
    of popcorn, 51–53, *52*, 107–108, 139–140, 145
    in simple economy, 78–99
    speculation and, 183–185
    stabilization of, 184
    two-part, 138
    worth of, 45–48
price controls, 60, 97, 245–251, *246*, 253
price discrimination, 133–140, 145, 237–238
    perfect, 137, 237, 238, 242, 244
price indices, 33–34, 107
price searchers, 130, 140, 287, 288
price supports, 182–183
price takers, 130, 228, 229, 231, 282–287
Principles of Economics (Marshall), 225
Principles of Political Economy, The (Ricardo), 27, 66
prisoner's dilemma, 152–154, *153*
privileged minority, 263
probability distribution, 186
producer surplus, 55, 57, *58*, 59–60, *60*, 87, 88, *88*, 105, 218, 283
    industry supply curve and, 122, *123*, 124, 126
production, factors of, 200–210
    application of, 207–210
    see also capital; labor; land
production, producers, 21, 39, 199
    aggregate supply curve and, 59–60, *60*, 62
    backward-bending supply curve for labor and, 61–64, *62*
    cost of, 23, 70–71, 173, 174, 182–183, 229–231, 286
    efficiency and, 228–231, 234
    exploitation and, 128–129
    joint, 112–113
    law of diminishing returns in, 116, 197–198, 199
    with multiple inputs, 55, 114–129
    of public goods, 262–265
    in single–input world, 54–64
    trade with, 67–68
production function, 100–102, *103*

firm and, 115–118, 126, 127
profit maximization, 5, 51–53, *52*, 107, 113
    of firm, 116, 120–122, *121*, 125–128, 131–132, *132*, 135–140, *136*, 162, 165, *234*, 235
Progress and Poverty (George), 213
property rights, 172, 174, 175, 268, 305, 308
proprietary communities, 267
Ptolemy, 65, 66
public-choice theory, 289–295, 297
public goods, 262–265, 291–292
    information as, 275–277
    religious radio as, 274
punishment, 309–311, 316

quantity, efficiency and, 227–229, 234–235
quasi-rent, 204, 211

Raiffa, Howard, 166
"rate of return" regulation, 241
rationality
    assumption of, xi, 3–13, 106, 107
    defined, 3, 7
    examples of, 5–13
    lottery-insurance paradox and, 190–192
    uncertainty and, 185–193
rationing, 247–248, 250–251, 253
raw materials, 55, 115, 126
recycling paper, 174–175
regression fallacy, 196
religious radio, 274
rent, 197, 203–204, 270
rental housing, 19, 91–95, *93*
rent control, 217, 249–251, 253
rent seeking, 236, 238, 295–297
residual claimant, 113
resources, depletable, 171–177, 179
revealed preference, principle of, 16–17, 107, 220
revenue, 88–91, *89*, *90*, 112–113, 131, 240
    of firm, 116, 120, 124–125
    marginal, *see* marginal revenue; marginal revenue curves
    tax cuts and raising of, 254–258
    total, 120, 124–125
Ricardo, David, 27, 66
risk averters, 187–191, *188*, *189*
risk preferrers, 187–191, *188*, *189*
robbery, 306–308
Rockefeller, John D., 141–143, 164
Rotten Kid theorem, xi, 328

Saudi Arabia, 161, 172
Savage, Leonard J., 194
saving, 177–178
Schelling, Thomas, 166
search cost, 192, 277
search unemployment, 192–193
Secrets of a Superthief (Maclean), 301–302
Selfish Gene, The (Dawkins), 13
sex ratios, 12–13
sharecropping, 270
shortages, 96–97

silent student problem, 9
Smith, Adam, 63, 113–114, 213, 258
smoking, 15, 16, 90
Soviet Union, U.S. relations with, 148–150
speculation, 183–185
Standard Oil Trust, 141–143
steel, 116
    price of, 116, 122, *123*, 124, 126
Stigler, George, 241
stock, stock market, 5, 11, 12, 113–114, 125
strategic behavior, 147–166
    see also game theory, games
strikes, 74
subsidies, 36–39, *38*, 50–51, *50*, 92, *93*, 240, 272
substitution effect, 61, 62, 63
sunk costs, 180–182, 210
supply curve for labor, 57
    backward-bending, 61–64, *62*
supply curves, 57–64, 79–98, *80*, 101–102, *103*, 203
    aggregate, 59–60, *60*, 62
    elasticity of, 82–83, 87, 88, 288
    firm and industry, 121–128, *121*, *123*
    for gasoline, 246, *246*, 247
    for lawns, 57, *58*
    for rental housing, 92–95, *93*
    shifts in, 81–82, *82*, 97–98, 105
    upward-sloped, 125–127
surplus, 66, 97
    see also consumer surplus; producer surplus

tariffs, 60, 63, 66, 69–72, 208, 217, 281–289, *284*, 292–295
    "good," 287–289
    Pareto improvements and, 221–222
taxes, 60, 83–91, *84*, *85*, 99, 104, 172, 254–258, 264, 286–287
    corporate, myth of, 127
    excess burden of, 91, 204
    on land, 203, 204
    on landlords, 91, 92, *93*
    opportunity sets and, 42
    progressive, 254–258
    real cost of, 48, 87–91, *88*, *89*, 90
    regressive, 254–255
    subsidies and, 37–39, *38*, 50–51, *50*
    trade and, 66, 69
textbooks, reselling of, 19–20
theaters
    children's prices at, 133–134
    popcorn prices at, 51–53, *52*, 107–108, 139–140, 145
theory
    incorrect, 21
    living, 39–40
    price, *see* price, price theory

Theory of Games and Economic Behavior (von Neumann and Morgenstern), 166, 193–194
time, economics and, 48–49, 167–179, 232
Tolkien, J. R. R., 184
total cost, 120, 124–125
total cost curves, 115, 118, *118*, 127, 228, 310
total revenue, 120, 124–125
trade, 21, 65–77, 106, 111, 277–278
    assumptions about, 66
    bilateral monopoly and, 73–74
    comparative advantage and, 69–73
    competitiveness and, 66, 68, 70–71
    deficit in, 66, 72–73, 179
    with production, 67–68
    surplus in, 66
transaction costs, 74, 76–77, 113, 268, 277, 318
Tullock, Gordon, 267, 273, 297

uncertainty, 180–194, 232–233, 246
    rational choice and, 185–193
    speculation and, 183–185
    sunk costs and, 180–182
unemployment, search, 192–193
unions, 66, 74
United Arab Emirates, 161
utility, 186–190, 193, 218–219
"Utility Analysis of Choices Involving Risk, The" (Friedman and Savage), 194

value, 14–17, 23, 107, 197, 218, 229–231
    average, 46
    choice and, 14–16
    defined, 31–32
    economic, 16–17
    indifference curves and, 31–33
    marginal, *see* marginal value; marginal value curves
Van den Haag, Ernest, 298
violence, drugs and, 305–306
virtue, economics of, 151–156, 166
voluntary associations, 152
von Neumann, John, 148, 155–156, 166, 187, 193–194
voting, 6, 114, 264, 289

wages, 11, 21, 56–57, *58*, 61, 63, 116–117, 197, 198, 230, 231, 272
    determination of, 210–213
    present value of, 168–170, *169*
Walras, Leon, 27
warfare, 7–8, 13, 74, 153–154
water, demand for, 45, 83
Wealth of Nations, The (Smith), 63, 213
wheat, tariffs and, 282–288, *284*
Wigner, Eugene, 147
Williams, Terry, 303, 316